REBEL STOREHOUSE

REBEL

STOREHOUSE

Florida in the Confederate Economy

Robert A. Taylor

THE UNIVERSITY OF ALABAMA PRESS
TUSCALOOSA & LONDON

F 19.

33 0. 9 7 5 9

T d y

Copyright © 1995

The University of Alabama Press

Tuscaloosa, Alabama 35487-0380

All rights reserved

Manufactured in the United States of America

∞

The paper on which this book is printed meets the minimum requirements of American National Standard for Information Science-Permanence of Paper for Printed Library Materials, ANSI Z39.48-1984.

Library of Congress Cataloging-in-Publication Data

Taylor, Robert A., 1958–

 Rebel storehouse : Florida in the Confederate economy / Robert A. Taylor.

  p. cm.

 Includes bibliographical references (p.) and index.

 ISBN 0-8173-0776-1 (alk. paper)

 1. Florida—Economic conditions. 2. Agriculture—Economic aspects—Florida—History—19th century. 3. Florida—History—1821-1865. 4. Confederate States of America—Economic conditions. I. Title. *5, Florida. Agriculture. Economic*

HC107.F6T39 1995 *aspects - History - 19th Century*

330.9759'05—dc20   94-28532

British Library Cataloguing-in-Publication Data available

To
George R.
and
Genevieve Taylor

Contents

Illustrations

Preface

The pioneer historian of the Old South, Ulrich B. Phillips, wrote in his classic study *Life and Labor in the Old South* (1929) that Florida "formed in the main a southward extension of the United States rather than an integral part of the South." Scholars following Phillips continued to treat Florida's relationship with the Old South region and its Confederate offspring as ambiguous and almost immaterial. Some have gone so far as to neglect the state entirely, whereas others label Florida relatively unimportant in the overall history of the Civil War era. After completing a review of the state's cattle trade during those years, I realized that such conclusions were at best premature, for no one had examined the peninsula's economic contributions to the Confederate States in any real depth.

This volume is an attempt to explore one aspect of Florida's role in the Civil War. I hope it will spur others to reconsider such essential though unglamorous subjects as Confederate logistics and transportation and the efficiency of the Confederate bureaucracy. Like others drawn to refight the great rebellion, I am intrigued by the question of why the South lost its bid for independence. Whether it was poor leadership at the highest levels, lack of will, refusal of white women to continue unending sacrifice, or the collapse of the home front in general, the reason or reasons for Confederate failure will not be completely divined until all features of the Confederate experience off the battlefield come to light. This work does not claim to be a comprehensive history of Florida during the war (though one is truly needed), but perhaps it will heighten interest in the topic if nothing more.

A large debt of appreciation is owed to numerous librarians and archivists who aided me in the research and made this monograph possible. In Florida I would like to thank the staffs of the P. K. Yonge Library of Florida History, University of Florida at Gainesville; the Florida Historical Society in Tampa; and the Florida State Archives in Tallahassee, especially David M. Coles. The following institutions provided invaluable assistance: the Georgia Department of Archives and History; the James W. Woodruff, Jr., Confederate Naval Museum, Columbus, Georgia; the Special Collections Division, University of Georgia Libraries in Athens; the South Caroliniana Library of the University of South Carolina at Columbia; the Manuscript Division, William R. Perkins Library of Duke University at Durham; and the Southern Historical Collection of the University of North Carolina–Chapel Hill.

Many individuals provided help, guidance, and encouragement over the years it took to complete this project. Dr. John Hebron Moore of Florida State University, who directed it as a dissertation, offered tireless enthusiasm and a willingness to let me explore such uncharted waters as these. Dr. Philip D. Morgan, also of Florida State, took time away from his own research to carefully read the manuscript and offered important criticisms. Two members of the history department of the University of South Florida also merit gratitude for their major contributions. The idea for this study began there as a paper written for a seminar on Florida history conducted by Dr. Gary R. Mormino, who continued to support it along the tortured path to doctoral dissertation. Professor John M. Belohlavek gave more to me than he ever knew by his example as a historian, teacher, and friend.

Thanks must also go to Dean of Graduate Studies Russell H. Johnsen and the Florida State University for the Dissertation Fellowship that freed me for a year of full-time research and writing. Lastly, I must voice my appreciation to my parents, who aided my work in a thousand ways. Their faith never flagged, even during the difficult times. This is for them.

Fort Pierce, Florida   Robert A. Taylor

1 Florida's Economy in the 1850s

"The Peninsula of Florida," proclaimed a correspondent of the respected journal *Southern Cultivator* in 1860, "as a whole may be regarded as a poor country. . . . Ninetenths of the peninsula is worthless for agricultural purposes."[1] This negative opinion of Florida's agricultural potential was not shared, however, by a majority of the general public of the United States at the time. During the 1850s the cultivation of cotton and sugar, basic economic activities of the antebellum South, had flourished in the southernmost member of the Union. Consequently, before the end of the decade it had acquired a reputation akin to that of Eden; an inexhaustible garden seemingly self-maintained. Thus, in order to understand Florida's pre–Civil War economy and how it interacted with those of neighboring states, one must begin with its basis, agriculture.

Antebellum farmers commonly evaluated the agricultural potential of soil by scooping up a handful and testing it by taste and touch. Visitors and newcomers to Florida using this method found there a wide variety of soils suitable for many different crops. In rich lands of middle Florida, for example, the ground was "a dark color, composed of sand, clay, lime, and iron, and having an unctuous feel as though it contained fatty material."[2] Even the pine prairies in the southern half of the state contained some rich hammock lands whose chocolate brown color translated into rows of sugar cane, cotton, or corn. Reports that there were such fruitful acres in Florida were welcome news to Southerners well aware of the limits to the westward expansion of the cotton-growing industry.[3]

Equally welcome was the low price of these prime Florida lands. At the beginning of the decade of the 1850s Florida offered the least expensive land of any state in the lower South. Furthermore, a lessening of the danger of Indian attacks increased interest in the state among agriculturalists who were pondering whether to relocate southward. The editor of *De Bow's Review* stated, "It is quite certain that as soon as the character of these lands becomes generally known, they will sell at a price corresponding to their intrinsic value, which has already been shown, as greater than that of other lands in the United States."[4] Outputs of some Florida farms supported that assertion. Bartolo Masters of Saint Augustine, for example, reputedly made from one acre of sugar cane 450 gallons of syrup, 4 barrels of sugar, and 3,000 canes. His net profit was $333, to which was added the proceeds of 150 bushels of corn and 200 bushels of sweet potatoes from an undisclosed number of additional acres. This and other accounts of successes suggested to would-be farmers that Florida was the "best poor man's country in the world," capable of abundant crop yields. Not surprisingly, Masters used the proceeds from his bountiful harvest to purchase a slave to share his toil in the fields.[5]

A majority of white Floridians in the 1850s had small or medium-sized farms; they either possessed a few slaves or aspired to become slaveholders. Family-sized agricultural units at that time could be profitable, given hard work and a little luck. In 1860 the census reported that there were more than 6,500 "farms" in Florida, an increase of almost 2,300 since 1850. A look at the state's premier agricultural county, Leon, reveals that the farmer and not the planter dominated the Florida frontier numerically: There were 83 agricultural units consisting of more than five hundred acres in 1860, but farms of between twenty and five hundred acres numbered 283. Throughout Florida, farmers predominated during the decade. Thus, it is obvious that yeoman farmers were able to carve satisfactory places for themselves in Florida's economy in the best traditions of Jeffersonian America and the Old South. "Nature has been lavish of her bounties," commented one Floridian; "we need only the sweat of man's brow to yield rich fruit to reward his industry."[6]

Despite their numerical superiority in Florida, as in other Southern states, the farmers looked for leadership to members of the planter class. Slave-worked plantations of hundreds of acres, similar to those in other states of the cotton kingdom, shared the Florida landscape with smaller farms. A majority of these plantations were founded during the agricultural depression of the 1840s, but by the last decade of the pre–Civil War era Florida planters enjoyed prosperity generated by sales of cotton, sugar, and tobacco. Although planter status symbolized success in the antebellum South, farmers in the 1850s shared to a lesser degree the affluence created by the production of staple cash crops. In several counties in north central Florida—Leon, Jefferson, Gadsden, Marion, Jackson, and Madison—the agricultural accomplishments of both farmers and planters were most evident.[7]

The middle region of north Florida, much more than the eastern or western parts of the state, had plantations typical of the prewar South. Half of the slave population of the state labored in Jackson, Gadsden, Leon, Jefferson, and Alachua counties by 1860. Roughly thirty thousand African Americans lived and worked in farming operations of various sizes in these counties. As a result the number of agriculturalists owning more than fifteen slaves rose from 217 in 1850 to 1,177 in 1860. The state's total number of improved acres was 765,213, 447,561 of them located in these fecund counties in 1860. Middle Florida also clearly led the other sections of the peninsula in improved land value, claiming $111,622 out of the total of $116,435 for all of Florida. These statistics show that planters were intermingled with small and medium-sized freeholders and that both classes were important to Florida's agriculture-based economy.[8]

Despite the financial gains that they shared with other planters of the lower South in the 1850s, Florida growers as a group were not agricultural innovators. An editor of the Tallahassee *Floridian and Journal* complained that planters "remained strangely apathetic upon the subject of the foundation of Agricultural Societies for the development of our resources."[9] They knew very little about plows, plowing, or fertilizing under Florida conditions, he maintained, and they had much to learn. Solon Robinson, a noted Northern agricultural writer, surveyed Florida lands early in the decade and recorded sorrowfully what "the present generation of land destroyers" was doing to the countryside. By 1860 many state newspaper editors and correspondents were arguing that a pressing need for agricultural reform truly existed. Editorials and letters in the Tallahassee *Floridian and Journal* urged farmers to utilize such improved techniques as deep-soil plowing and to "complain less of the irregularity of the seasons." Many reports that planters were actually quitting the state after wearing out their lands in only a few years demonstrate that the warnings of reformers like Robinson were rarely being heeded.[10]

The boom of the 1850s was built on cotton. Florida, after becoming a state in 1845, had quickly joined the other fiefdoms of the cotton kingdom, which stretched from the Carolinas to Texas. The editor of the *American Agriculturalist* declared that the southernmost state offered greater advantages for the prospective cotton grower than any other area east of the Mississippi. Improved lands there sold for as little as five to ten dollars per acre in 1851 and could be paid for with a single good crop. Long-staple cotton and the Florida climate appeared made for each other, and planters desiring to cultivate it quickly sought out available tracts of suitable land. An enthusiastic writer in *De Bow's Review* went as far as to state in 1851, "There is in no part of the world a country of such extent so well adapted, both in climate and soil to the production of this staple as East Florida."[11] Despite such glowing descriptions, an advantage for the would-be Florida sea-island cotton planter was declining competition, for the original sea islands of South Carolina and Georgia by the 1850s were showing signs of wear.

By decade's end, Florida had surpassed the states to the north in the production of sea-island cotton. More than sixty-five thousand bales of cotton were harvested in Florida in 1860, much of it probably the sea-island or upland variety. Reports of a single acre yielding three hundred pounds of long-staple fiber and slave workers picking at least $250 worth per hand and sometimes doubling that amount under favorable conditions filtered throughout the entire South. Some writers went so far as to claim that Florida's soils presented a serious challenge to the best cotton

Cotton cultivation in Florida. (Photograph courtesy of Florida State Archives)

lands of the Old Southwest. Florida's cotton, both sea island and its short-staple cousin, found its way to markets in all trading centers. Nevertheless, despite these proven advantages, the lack of an improved transportation system prevented Florida from becoming one of the nation's most valuable cotton-raising regions.[12]

Cotton plantations in Florida were not immune to the unpredictability of the farmer's best friend and occasional foe, the weather. Rains of the heaviest kind often damaged or even devastated entire crops. In the fall of 1858, for example, a hurricane swept through the countryside destroying fences, gin houses, corn cribs, and stables. During the period of torrential rainfall cotton rotted in the fields while that portion of the crop already picked moldered in the cotton houses. In the aftermath of the storm slaves were kept busy stirring the cotton in the storage sheds, but to no avail. A planter in Waccahootee despaired that the few unspoiled bolls left in his fields by the storm served as food for an infestation of bollworms and caterpillars. Another Jefferson County resident lost eleven of his mules when a barn housing them collapsed under the battering of gale-force winds.[13]

Notwithstanding the hazards of wind and weather, Florida cotton growers joined ranks with others across the South in seeking to protect their economic interests. At a meeting in Tallahassee in 1851 a convention of planters passed a resolution calling for an organization of multistate associations that would own warehouses in major Southern port cities and handle the marketing of the yearly cotton crop. Their plan's underlying purpose was to eliminate the Northern middlemen and thus maximize profits for the actual producers. Delegates argued in favor of this "Florida Plan" at the planter and commercial conventions held throughout the South during the 1850s. Such efforts strengthened feelings of solidarity and emphasized common interests among Florida's growers and those in the other cotton states. If such a thing as a basic Southern ideology existed, these men certainly stood as ready subscribers.[14]

Close after cotton came sugar. Sugar had been cultivated as early as the 1760s in the northwestern corner of colonial Florida, and by the 1850s it had spread south of Tampa Bay to the banks of the Manatee River. The productivity of Florida soils and their easy adaptability to sugar agriculture inspired journalists to describe eastern Florida especially as sugar country. They reported that lands there produced three hogsheads of sugar to the acre with less labor than elsewhere in the Southern states. Sugar cane stalks yielding three to four gallons of juice were common. In one case, an Orange County planter, with the work of fifteen slaves, made sixty-five hogsheads of sugar along with close to four thousand gallons of molasses. While these were without doubt exceptional cases, and many sugar growers were far less successful, such exaggerated accounts of large crops of sugar added to Florida's growing reputation as an agricultural power in the region.[15]

"Sugar should be preferred to all crops in East Florida" wrote the editor of the Saint Augustine _Ancient City_ in 1850; he believed it to be more profitable than cotton or tobacco. Some long-staple cotton planters switched temporarily to sugar cane during slumps in cotton prices in the 1840s. This sweet staple, however, never replaced cotton as Florida's main commercial crop during the 1850s. Sugar production in Florida consistently lagged behind that of Louisiana and Texas for the entire decade.[16] Nevertheless, for a time it appeared that cane fields in south Florida might give the plantations of the Creoles a real contest. In Florida the growing season lasted some four to six weeks longer than that in Louisiana, and the danger to sugar cane from frost was negligible. While Louisianians were compelled to begin grinding cane in October, before it reached full maturity, Floridians could feed cane to the presses from November until the middle of February, with increased juice yields as the result.[17]

Planters like Robert Gamble prospered from the thousands of pounds of sugar and thousands of pounds of molasses he shipped down the Manatee to market in New Orleans in the mid-1850s.[18] Although sugar cane thrived on the rich hammock lands in the South, growers were restrained from expanding their operations by a shortage of capital and inadequate transportation. As a consequence sugar in Florida failed to become an equal to cotton as a state agricultural industry. In 1853 and 1854 very large crops in Louisiana combined with imports of cheap Cuban sugar lowered prices to the level where Floridians could no longer compete. One by one sugar plantations converted to other crops or ceased operations entirely. By 1856 prices had revived somewhat, but too late to help numbers of struggling sugar growers. Rising cotton prices lured many Florida sugar producers back to cotton although sugar continued to be cultivated around the state. "The high price of sugar of late should stimulate our planters," said a correspondent of the Jacksonville _Florida News_ in 1857. With the prospect of being able to use newly constructed railroad lines to haul the raw sugar and molasses to the Atlantic coast cities or to New Orleans more inexpensively than before, some observers predicted that the Louisiana sugar growers might relocate to south Florida to take advantage of the abundant harvests. Such forecasts did not become fact, however, and the Florida sugar industry remained in the doldrums for the rest of the antebellum years.[19]

Tobacco, as well as sugar, was a favorite of both planters and farmers interested in sowing proven cash crops. During his 1851 visit to north Florida, Solon Robinson described tobacco grown from Cuban seeds then in use there. He was told that this variety enjoyed a high reputation among cigar makers for use as wrappers. Moreover, the flavor of Florida-grown leaf compared favorably with that produced on the island of Cuba when planted on old, well-manured land. The tobacco industry centered in Gadsden County and suffered its share of financial hardships, but a majority of planters at least broke even, and some made large profits from tobacco cultivation. Beginning in 1854, tobacco yields in that county went from 600,000 pounds per year to an estimated 1.2 million by 1860. Higher prices spurred by foreign buyers fueled for a time what appeared to be a growing industry of great promise and importance to the state's future.[20]

The most reliable grain crop raised in antebellum Florida was corn. This common grain was the staple of farmers large and small and was grown extensively throughout the cotton kingdom. Besides serving as fodder for livestock, corn was an important food source for white Southerners and a key component of the basic ration for their slaves. Since wheat had to be imported and was costly, neither blacks nor whites often saw bread made from anything but corn meal. Most maize produced in Florida and its neighbor states was consumed on the farm or plantation, and its role as the major food crop was never questioned. In fact, by 1859 more corn ripened in Southern fields than in those in the North. Florida's contribution, however, from 1,966,809 bushels in 1850 to 2,824,391 bushels in 1860, was the smallest among all the Southern states. Of course the state's relatively small population helps to explain Florida's corn shortcomings in comparison to the rest of the South.[21]

Just how much corn Florida agriculturalists could grow per acre is not easy to determine from printed sources. *De Bow's Review* reported in 1851 that thirty to forty bushels per acre were being produced on good-quality land in the interior. Many crops of corn of this size were allegedly produced in Alachua County by local farmers with a single hoeing, thinning, and plowing. Six years later a Jacksonville publication predicted harvests of no more than fifteen bushels to the acre. Finally, at the end of the decade a correspondent with *De Bow's Review* attempted to halt inflated expectations with solid evidence. "As good a crop, grown on as good lands as I have seen in Florida," he wrote, "did not average more than 25 bushels to the acre. Ten or fifteen bushels to the acre may be considered a fair general average."[22]

The 1860 census showed Leon, Jefferson, and Jackson counties to be the leaders in corn production in the state with a combined total of over one million bushels a year. So abundant was corn during the antebellum period that it was rarely imported by Florida from other states. However, spot shortages caused by droughts or waves of intense heat sometimes led to hunger among the lower classes even on the fertile peninsula. In one instance, crops in the northern tier of counties wilted from lack of rain and extremely high temperatures in 1860; in some areas entire cornfields appeared burnt as if by brush fires. What little grain remained was so damaged that gathering it seemed almost a waste of energy. Meanwhile, from Georgia, a Macon paper reported that a good harvest was expected generally throughout Florida with moderate-sized surpluses.[23]

Other cereal crops raised in Florida included wheat, oats, rye, and barley, but none ever came close to matching the total yields of South Carolina, Georgia, or Alabama. Some planters experimented with rice cultivation, but production had declined by 1860, primarily because of the labor-intensive nature of the shallow-rooted rice plants. Others tried growing hemp, with the same lack of success as with the rice operations. Arrowroot, a source of starch, was gathered in south Florida along the Miami River, and workers earned as much as three dollars per day extracting it from the earth. Even the few Seminoles left in the vicinity tried their hands at the task. Small quantities of sweet potatoes, indigo, cochineal, silk, and olives rounded out a fairly diversified list of products.[24]

A reader of the *Southern Cultivator* in 1860 complained to its editor that he searched past issues in vain for reports of fruits grown in his native state of Florida. Feeling slighted, the subscriber believed that Florida "should stand preeminent for its fine fruits, and where all the choice fruits can be produced in the highest excellence. The Orange, the Lemon, the Pomegranate, the grape, and all the fruits of the Southern States here attaining a sugary richness and high flavor not equalled in any other section."[25] Although the growth of citrus fruits on the peninsula dated from the earliest Spanish settlement, it was during the brief British occupation that it first developed on a commercial basis. Orange groves, particularly around Saint Augustine, produced both fruit and profit until a devastating 1835 freeze damaged many trees. Coupled with an insect infestation three years later, it dealt a serious blow to the orange orchards.[26]

Saint Augustine was left alone to recover after the great freeze. Stagnation still plagued the old town in the 1850s, when orange growing resumed on a commercial scale. Locals hoped prosperity would return and that fruit would earn Florida a reputation as the Italy of North America. New groves sprang up on the banks of the Indian River and along the shores of the Manatee, as well as in Hillsborough and Dade counties. Boosters sang the praises of raising citrus for those Florida settlers of limited means. "The culture is well adapted to persons of small capital," said one, "whose health requires a residence in Florida." Land suitable for planting food crops lay at the ready, and both farmers and planters could rest assured that growing oranges would in no way interfere with other crops. By the late 1850s the industry showed definite signs of recovery, and growers looked to the future with increasing enthusiasm.[27]

Citrus fruit joined other Florida staples as exports to other Southern states during the decade. Limes, for example, sold in Savannah and Charleston for as high as twenty dollars a barrel. Southerners learned to look southward to the land of flowers for a variety of edibles for their tables. That frontier region, in the minds of many, contained such agricultural riches that neighboring states needed not worry about shortages because Florida's luxuriant harvests were certain. As streams of foodstuffs flowed northward in a seemingly natural progression, so people in the lower South grew accustomed to depending on Floridians for commodities common or unusual.[28]

Another product of the Florida peninsula was beef cattle. During the 1840s and 1850s Florida came to embody two traditions of the Old South: the planter watching his slaves toil in the fields from the back of a horse, and the wandering herdsman picking his way through the scrub pines along with his beef cattle. The role of cattle raising in the South can be traced back to the first days of exploration and settlement. Cattle herds roaming at large through the forests of colonies like South Carolina helped provide sustenance during the "starving time" sometimes faced by colonists there and at other European beachheads on the Atlantic coast. Livestock raised for meat and hides played an important part in the development of what became the Old South, as recent scholarship has suggested. Yet beef was not a mainstay of the diet of Southerners. Instead, salted pork and pork products like bacon dominated the eating habits of planters, farmers, and slaves right up to the outbreak of the Civil War. Salted beef pleased few palates, so beef was consumed usually as freshly slaughtered meat.[29]

A large cattle industry grew up in the Southern colonial backcountry, but the herders and their beeves were forced to move westward by decreased forage and advancing farmers. By the 1850s the herds had been pushed into Texas and the wilds of the Florida peninsula.

Lack of demand only partially explains the slow development of the Southern cattle industry. Several other obstacles hampered the introduction of cattle breeding during the antebellum years. In general beef was not needed for the slave population, since black Southerners consumed about as little of it as did their masters. Therefore, only a slight impetus for a commercial livestock market existed in the lower South other than in a few urban centers. Competition from proven cash crops like cotton or tobacco also contributed to beef's secondary status. A lack of improved pasture lands and a dearth of quality fodder worked against growth in cattle production and general improvements in the animals raised. In spite of this, most farmers, large and small, kept a few head wandering about for their hides and sometimes meat. "Cattle," one man recorded, "are plenty and just as mean as could be deserved. They are worthless to the cotton planter, causing him to build a great deal of fence and affording no profit."[30]

Florida proved to be a clear extension of the South's cattle economy. Floridians boasted that their state became the birthplace of the American beef cattle industry when Ponce de Leon introduced a few cows during his expedition of 1520. Later Franciscan missions and early rancheros maintained cattle herds, and many of these animals fell into Native Americans' hands. These people, Miccosukees, and later the Seminoles, were the first truly successful herders on the peninsula. During the British era white residents carried on a lively trade in beef with such tribes near the towns of Saint Augustine, Pensacola, and others, continuing through the late 1780s.[31]

For years after Florida became American territory in 1821, relatively few settlers dared push southward into its wilderness because of the hostility of the Indians. Thus the ongoing conflict with the Seminoles retarded the region's economic development by frightening off potential settlers and investors. After the Second Seminole War ended in 1842, however, hardy cattlemen from the Carolinas and Georgia began herding deep inside the future state, grazing their animals as far south as the Kissimmee and Peace River valleys. These drovers personified the traditions of cattlemen throughout the frontier South, keeping beeves for their own use and for selling in seaport markets. Because they did little to improve the quality of the bovines they controlled, the grass-fed cattle never received high praise from agriculturalists. Florida beeves weighed about seven hundred pounds on average, and each yielded about three hundred pounds of meat. By modern tastes such flesh would be judged tough, and it closely resembled venison in flavor.[32]

The number of cattle in Florida showed a marked rise between the end of the Second Seminole War and the firing on Fort Sumter. Estimates grew from 118,000 in 1840 to 287,725 in 1860, figures that excluded oxen and dairy cows. Settlers in the state were earning profits not only from the meat garnered but also from leather and candles made from cowhides and tallow. In the meantime a general decline in beef production in the deep South created an increased demand for Florida beef, making the sale of herds driven all the way from south Florida to cities like Savannah and Charleston attractive to their owners.[33]

By the end of the 1850s the heart of cattle raising in prewar Florida centered in the lower portion of the state. There, thousands of square miles of unimproved pine flatlands readily served as open ranges for grazing. "As a grazing country it is unequaled," reported one traveler. "The grass grows most luxuriantly; on the prairies, magnificently, all seasons of the year the cattle are amply supplied and fat."[34] The major areas were the Myakka, Caloosahatchee, and the lower Peace River valleys, along with the Kissimmee River region. Hillsborough County, especially east and south of Tampa Bay, had a ratio of thirteen cows to every resident, compared with three per person for the rest of the state. With a population in 1860 of roughly three thousand and hence some thirty-nine thousand cattle, Hillsborough County stood as a potential rival to the fabled cattle ranges west of the Mississippi.[35]

Florida cattle drives of the 1850s often ended in such coastal cities as Jacksonville, Savannah, or Charleston. Cattlemen tended to look homeward for lucrative markets despite the greater distances involved. Wild cowmen up from Florida and their wilder charges became a common sight on the busy streets of Charleston. In an 1856 incident, two animals escaped from their herders and bolted for freedom down Broad Street. Moving at speeds usually reserved for horses, horns at the ready, these Florida steers frightened passersby and their mounts. The break for liberty failed, and the cattle were corralled in the yard of the Charleston Library Society. From there, reported the Charleston *Daily Courier,* they found safe lodging at the city's guard house.[36]

Charleston remained a good market for Florida beef exports throughout the antebellum era despite accidents such as this. Even with competition from cattle driven from Kentucky and Tennessee, Florida beef could be found in the stalls of the local beef market. Beef from the peninsula, however, did have problems contending in quality with meat from these states because of their superior pasture lands, but in Charleston even cuts of the worst meat sold at eight and nine cents per pound. South Carolinians' taste and desire for Florida beef never really waned, and it slowly grew with the coming of the sectional crisis.[37]

Cattle dealers looked even further north than South Carolina for potential customers. In August 1859 the schooner *G. Hoffman* loaded 135 head of cattle at Saint Augustine and then sailed for New York. This was the first known attempt to establish trade in beef with the Northern states before the Civil War. Many hoped thousands of dollars worth of cattle would leave the ports of Florida bound for hungry Northern city dwellers. Business leaders advocated the employment of a steam-powered vessel in this promising new trade, one with the capability of transporting in three sailing days upwards of 200 cows to the shores of the Chesapeake or the banks of the Delaware River. The Saint Augustine

Examiner agreed with the idea that such a ship "would be the most profitable vessel to engage in this business."[38]

Most Floridians, however, believed that the future of the cattle trade lay to the south, not in the urban North. The 1850s marked the beginning of the shipment of beef to Cuba and the rest of the West Indies. *De Bow's Review* as early as 1851 suggested that the Bahamas and the rest of the Caribbean islands were potential markets, "in hope that persons who have large stocks in the northern part of the state and in Georgia may profit thereby, as the price of cattle in these islands may be estimated at twenty dollars per head."[39] In 1858 shipment of these valuable creatures from the port of Tampa to Cuba began, and by 1860 four hundred head a month arrived in Havana butcher shops. Civic leaders in Florida were certain that such commerce was the key to economic growth for small towns like Tampa and the rest of southwest Florida. A local journalist editorialized that, "taking into consideration the capacities of South Florida for stock raising and the number of citizens engaged in the trade, it will be seen that the prosperity of our entire community depends in a great measure upon the success of that branch of industry."[40]

With Florida becoming a potential rival of Texas as a beef supplier, it was natural to make comparisons of the two. In an 1860 article in *De Bow's Review,* for example, the relative merits of Florida and Texas for cattle raising were discussed at length. The author concluded that Florida had the greater advantage because Texas contained vast tracts of arid land unable to support even wild scrub cattle. Florida, on the other hand, did not have any acres so poor that they could not serve as grazing areas.[41]

Southern interest in Florida cattle ranching generated several articles during the antebellum era in respected journals like *De Bow's Review* and the *Southern Cultivator.* These writers described ranges sufficient to feed an unlimited number of animals and explained the small effort that was necessary to maintain beef in a semitropical climate. "The atmosphere is so heavily impregnated with salt from sea breezes," ran one account, "it affords an ample supply of salt for stock, cattle are neither fed nor salted at any season of the year. All the labor and expense in stock raising is to drive up, pen and brand."[42] Another commentator told of large numbers of fat Florida cattle going to market out of the state, even though Floridians seemed to enjoy beef at meals much more than their fellow Southerners. Culinary tastes aside, the amount of beef cattle shipped outside the borders of Florida was undoubtedly large. Readers of these publications could not avoid forming the impression that Florida was a cattle-producing region of major significance.[43]

Travelers often saw many large herds of cattle or were told about them by proud local inhabitants. Often herds grew from hundreds to thousands in the telling. "A stranger would think that cows . . . had special privileges on our highways and by-ways," complained a Florida newspaper editor.[44] A British visitor was informed that one Florida cattle baron paid taxes on eighteen thousand head roaming at large over the peninsula's open spaces, from which towns easily drew for meat. This foreigner concluded from her own observations that the resources of Florida were underappreciated and underdeveloped. Florida cattlemen enjoyed a life of relative plenty despite the "slovenliness, disorder, incompleteness, and discomfort" in the region. This beef industry was as much a part of the culture and economy of the Old South as the more well-known cotton plantations, regardless of such criticism.[45]

If boastful Floridians had tried to document the actual size of their state's cattle herds they would have been keenly disappointed. Data from the 1860 census show that Florida did not hold first position among cattle-producing states in the South. Instead, Florida ranked last, with less than 300,000 head. Reports of large herds, while true, confused total numbers with the number of animals available for slaughter. When stock and yearlings are deducted, cattle productivity figures fall markedly. For example, a herd of 250 head was necessary to produce 50 head for market. Using this formula it can be estimated that Hillsborough County had 6,558 head of cattle for sale in 1860 out of its herds of 32,789. Manatee County, the second largest beef-raising county during that year, produced 6,250 head from herds numbering 31,252. Noncattlemen both inside and outside of Florida failed to realize that large herds did not quickly translate into equally large amounts of meat.[46]

Vast expanses of pine forests presented another field of economic endeavor for Floridians during the 1850s. Lumbering operations sprang up in the northern sections where the woods soon rang with the sounds of axes and saws. During the decade of the 1850s lumber mills processed tens of thousands of board feet of timber annually for export. Pensacola and its environs reaped great benefit from such activity, more indeed than from the shipping of cotton. In eastern Florida Jacksonville and the Saint Johns River region rivaled Pensacola in amounts of lumber harvested and sold each year. Hundreds of small vessels and barges descended the Saint Johns annually, bound for the saw mills and docks near its wide mouth. If Fernandina and Cedar Key are included, Florida exported approximately two millon dollars worth of raw lumber in 1860.[47]

Ships carried this lumber to ports around the hemisphere during the golden age of the American merchant marine. Pensacola pine sold in Cuba and as far away as Rio de Janeiro. Florida cypress shingles adorned houses on the islands of the Caribbean at six dollars per thousand at the end of the decade. Florida wood products also found their way into other parts of the Union on a limited basis. A small but lively trade in cedar grew up between the Cedar Keys area and New York. During the first three months of 1860 no less than seven ships called there for cargoes of cedar boards, and the gathering of this wood provided a good living for many residents along this Gulf coastal area.[48]

During the 1850s it was not lumbering but the production of naval stores that excited many entrepreneurs when they looked to the Southern pine forests for potential wealth. "Turpentine-making is getting some attention in the western part of the state [Florida], where its profits are so large as to draw off attention from the culture of cotton, even at present high prices," proclaimed an 1851 article in *De Bow's Review*.[49] In the pine belt slaves collected rosin in the woodlands as well as picking cotton in the fields. By the mid-1850s the industry had expanded beyond the Carolinas and into the hitherto untapped eastern Gulf states, including Florida. West Florida, especially the Apalachicola region, produced thousands of barrels of rosin and turpentine in the course of the decade. Despite a relatively low level of development in the industry, naval stores from the state went in bulk to New Orleans and from there to the Northern states or to overseas markets. Nevertheless, the Florida naval stores industry, though hobbled by the lack of an adequate transportation system, appeared to have a bright future as a business enterprise. The coming of railroads promised to connect the turpentine camps to the rest of the world with bands of iron.[50]

As Floridians eagerly sought to bring forth all their natural resources, they turned, during the 1850s, to the bounty of the sea. The state's extensive coastline, abounding with fish of many species, offered unlimited employment for local fishermen. Sheephead, grouper, and mullet, caught in nets and traps, both fed the populace and went to market stalls. For example, on the coast around Saint Andrews Bay in western Florida the catch was salted down, packed in barrels, and then hauled to inland vendors. Before the decade closed, twenty-one thousand such casks were sold at from eight to ten dollars each.[51]

Florida fishermen found customers for their catches in the interior of the state and beyond. Planters bought considerable quantities of salted fish for their slave workers in order to vary their diets and cut provision costs. Fishermen sometimes were forced to undertake lengthy trips far from the coast to sell their wares. Wagons carrying two-hundred-pound barrels of Florida fish were frequently encountered on the roads as far north as Columbus, Georgia. Similarly, oysters from Apalachicola Bay, preserved by various methods, found their way to neighboring states and on occasion to the North as well.[52]

Fisheries in the southern half of the peninsula supplied Cuba with their catch. By the late 1850s operations on Tampa Bay and Charlotte Harbor caught and prepared fish for export, and a profitable exchange between Florida and the island began. Some Floridians working the fishing grounds complained, however, that Northern fishing boats and their crews had an inordinate share of both the Cuban trade and the fishing in Florida waters in general. Yankee sailors from New York and Connecticut did indeed work local waters from fall to the early part of May before heading for their home ports.[53]

A considerable amount of Florida fish were eaten or handled in some way by members of Florida's slave population. These laborers helped supply the energy that drove the engine of the state's economy. Without doubt many of the wagons carrying salted fish were loaded, driven, and unloaded by slaves. On farms and plantations they chopped the cotton, picked the oranges, and plucked the ears of ripened corn in the fields at harvest time. They probably joined with whites in herding cattle and hogs in various parts of the region. Defenders of the institution proudly deemed Florida the perfect setting for the slave system because of the tropical climate. Whites believed that slaves thrived and multiplied here as their ancestors had on the African continent. "It is an excellent and cheap climate to breed and raise them," bragged one master. He recommended to prospective sugar planters that they feed their slaves the waste molasses from the refining process. "Offal of the Sugar House fattens them like young pigs" and would guarantee the slaves' health and long lives, he advised.[54]

All chattel owners shared the problem of obtaining foods nutritious enough to keep their slaves content and capable of working at full capacity. While generalizations about the slave experience are risky, it is safe to say that some blacks in Florida subsisted on scanty rations and that food supplies ran low at times during the year. This put them in common with more than a few white farmers. A fixed amount of corn meal and a few pounds of salt pork or bacon were issued to adult slaves on a weekly schedule, supplemented by other fare such as molasses or fish. Florida planters sometimes struggled to secure basic food items, as did their colleagues throughout the lower South. Obtaining sufficient salt pork locally was both difficult and costly because it was not easy to cure pork in the humid climate. The *American Agriculturalist* confessed that Floridians raised adequate corn for food and animal feed, "but [did] not make pork for the people. That [came] from New York or New Orleans."[55]

Florida's reported dependence on nonlocal pork supplies worried Southern nationalists interested in promoting the state's economic independence. Vast sums of money, of which planters and farmers never enjoyed a plentiful supply, left the state each year to purchase hog products. Journalists frequently admonished such importers to raise more pigs of their own for home consumption. Florida bacon, cheaper and more easily obtained in their view, answered just as well as salted pork from other sources. These advocates of self-sufficiency argued that in most sections of the state hogs, fattened on the abundant roots in the pine forests, provided a nutrition source that required practically no labor to obtain. Some agriculturalists did keep hogs for slaughter on their farms and plantations. Few growers ever dared imagine a time when they would be cut off from the major pork-producing regions of Kentucky and Tennessee at a time of unusually high demand. Fewer still thought it conceivable that imports from New Orleans or foreign countries might be denied them by the actions of the national government.[56]

It is hard to generalize about the self-sufficiency of antebellum agriculture in Florida with any degree of certainty. It is certainly true that wandering herders in the south needed little in the way of additional subsistence from outside the confines of the peninsula. Floridians were told not to rely solely on crops of cotton, tobacco, or sugar, but to plant more corn, beans, or sweet potatoes. By pursuing such a course agricultural profits would stay at home instead of lining the pockets of merchants in Charleston, Savannah, or New Orleans. "Florida can produce everything save flour sufficient for her consumption," proclaimed a writer experienced in cultivation. By adopting the doctrine of increased self-sufficiency, prosperity could not be denied to the people of Florida.[57]

Economic progress in frontier Florida required facilities for moving goods into and out of the state inexpensively. Trade with other states could be conducted only when Florida's commodities could be transported to markets with some degree of certainty. Only cattle provided their own locomotion; other items had to be carried by some means of conveyance. Floridians considered the sea to be a highway running around the peninsula and used it accordingly. Her closest trading partners, the British Bahamas and Spanish Cuba, beckoned from across the waves. Vessels plied the shipping lanes between Florida, Cuba, and the Bahamas during the late antebellum years, loaded with cattle, fish, wood, and farm products to be exchanged for sugar, tobacco, and possibly contraband in the form of enslaved Africans. Key West tried to best the Cubans as a supplier of steamers bound for the goldfields of California early in the decade. The tonnage of goods passing between Florida ports such as Key West and the island colony curved upward in the period leading up to 1861.[58]

Coastal vessels also linked Florida with her fellow members of the so-called Gulf Squadron states. Scheduled lines operated among Florida and New Orleans, Mobile, and other Gulf ports. But most of Florida's trade was carried on with Charleston and Savannah. The 1850s brought a gradual increase in commerce with Savannah, along with numerous Georgians and South Carolinians moving to Florida's plantation belt. Passengers and goods journeyed on steamships running directly to Charleston or on smaller ships making local stops along the seaboard. Mail went from the docks of Charleston to Havana via Savannah and Key West twice each month, bringing the citizens of all four urban centers closer together. Florida newspapers praised the commercial and nautical ties with South Carolina in particular as beneficial to both states in many ways and predicted that they were certain to grow stronger with the passage of time. The editor of the Ocala *Florida Mirror* believed that south Florida particularly needed such connections with the Atlantic coastal cities to supplement its trade with New Orleans and other Gulf cities, such as Mobile.[59]

Florida's shallow rivers provided water transportation of limited utility. The Saint Johns, which flowed from the interior of the peninsula, was suitable for steamer traffic. Others, such as the Apalachicola, Saint Marks, or the Suwannee, were used to their fullest potential to ship cotton to market. The port of Apalachicola exported cotton bales from Georgia and north Florida until the 1850s brought a period of decreasing cotton shipments, due in no small part to railroad construction in Alabama and Georgia that diverted the cotton to new destinations. Yet, despite competition from the new rail lines, Florida's inland water system continued to play a vital role in its economic life until the end of the decade and beyond.[60]

Land transportation, on the other hand, remained very primitive during the 1850s. There were no good roads or even fair ones; wagon paths and trails provided the only means to get from place to place. Anyone attempting to convey bulky articles into the central areas of the state faced a very arduous task. One unhappy veteran of wagoning said that "travelling and hauling was hard, slow, laborious, irksome, and expensive."[61] Sand, heat, biting insects, and reptiles plagued teamsters on any trek, particularly in south Florida. The greatest deterrent to settlement and economic expansion of the interior was this lack of a quick and reliable means of overland transportation that would eliminate such hardships. In Florida, as in much of the South in that decade, most leaders believed that railroads were the best solution to the transportation problem.

Railroad construction and development followed much the same pattern in Florida as in the other Southern states. The railways began as feeders to ports or replacements for inadequate water routes, and they generally grew sporadically as capital became available for new construction. Florida rail enthusiasts entered the race behind their fellows in other states and endeavored to make up for lost time. "We want means of communication with the productive soil of the interior," voiced the editor of the Tallahassee *Floridian and Journal* in 1857. Since the existing rivers were not reliable as commercial thoroughfares, they needed to be superseded by railroads, in the newspaper editor's view.[62] Leaders also hoped that railways linking the scattered settlements and towns of their large state would help decrease a lingering internal sectionalism. Such sectionalism hindered economic growth and in some cases led to movements to detach parts of Florida with the objective of splicing onto Alabama or Georgia. The state invested considerable amounts of money in railroad-building schemes, often straining the fragile resources of government in Tallahassee. Notwithstanding financial problems, by the end of the decade of the 1850s a few railroads were completed and operating, with others either started or in the planning stage.

Three significant rail lines emerged from these construction efforts. The Alabama and Florida Railroad, begun in the 1830s, connected Pensacola with the state of Alabama although it did not run much farther than the state line. A second railroad, the Florida, Atlantic, and Gulf line, was built from Jacksonville to Alligator (later Lake City). An extension, known as the Pensacola and Georgia Railroad, was designed to complete the system all the way to the west Florida port city. The initial section, finished by 1860, intersected with a short line running from Tallahassee to the town of Saint Marks. On completion, the project garnered praise as "greater than has ever been done in the same space of time by any other Southern state," and further that it "may well challenge comparison with . . . [such undertakings] of any of the older States of the Union."[63]

The last major railroad enterprise in antebellum Florida was the Florida Railroad, running from Fernandina to Cedar Key on the coast. When the last spike was driven in 1861, it was Florida's largest rail system in terms of rolling stock, and it provided a link between the Atlantic and the Gulf of Mexico. Visions of trade flowing through upper Florida on iron rails naturally excited state businessmen and political leaders. A Tallahassee newspaperman expressed this eagerness by exclaiming that "soon the dim and gloomy recesses of those primeval and almost impenetrable forests will re-echo the startling scream of the locomotive."[64] But a rail network worthy of the name was not a reality despite the flurry of building. In fact the lines existing in Florida in 1861 were connected with only one other state, Alabama. No priority had been given to linking Florida's rails to those of the rest of the lower South, probably because of the influence of merchants in port towns who were fearful of a diversion of trade to the North. At the beginning of the Civil War only Pensacola enjoyed direct access to the rest of the South, by way of Mobile.

Every article involved in the construction of Florida's railroads, with the exception of the wooden ties, was manufactured outside the state. Manufacturing went on only in small shops geared to meeting local needs. The state contained one small shoe factory, a cloth mill, and a scattering of tiny iron foundries. Pensacola did have a brickyard that prospered by filling government contracts for military fortifications. A small-scale ship-building operation existed in Key West during the 1850s, with skilled "mechanics" being imported from South Carolina for the metal work involved in hull construction.[65] Because agriculture so completely dominated the local economy, Florida remained dependent on manufactured goods from other states or from overseas.

One item Florida did produce in abundance was salt. So important in the preservation of food and necessary for tanning and livestock, salt was indispensable for life in the antebellum South. Planters often dispatched gangs of slaves to the coasts to refine salt by boiling seawater in kettles, while those of lesser means carried all manner of vessels to salty water to do likewise for themselves. Large-scale salt production using evaporation was established near Key West in the 1850s and continued operations until the outbreak of civil war. Natural salt ponds scattered on the island issued as many as seventy-five thousand bushels of salt per year, and Key West soon competed successfully with salt from the Turks Islands and Great Britain. Salt makers in the island community managed to undercut such foreign salt from twenty to fifty cents per two-bushel sack by 1860.[66]

Improvements in transportation also helped spur another beginning industry, which had to do with the increasing number of Americans with the means to travel for reasons of health or leisure who found what they sought in balmy Florida. Southerners copied the Northern custom of seeing and being seen at fashionable resorts during the season. That Florida became such a watering place comes as no surprise, considering the legend of Ponce de Leon and the Fountain of Youth. At the start of the decade, however, the state's reputation as a spa and tourist haven was yet to be made. All but the most hardy balked at the discomforts and hazards of travel to the region. In 1851 Solon Robinson described for the readers of the *American Agriculturalist* his journey from Macon to the capital of Tallahassee. It took sixty hours to cover the 220 miles at a cost of 22 dollars, and the weary Robinson summed up the experience with the terse "taverns unimaginable, coaches, horses, and drivers to match anywhere else upon this earth."[67]

Floridians hoped to lure travelers who had in the past frequented Cuba and the other West Indian islands to winter instead in their state. By 1860 many did so, arriving in November and usually staying until May. The flight of these antebellum snow birds was enhanced by improved water and rail conveyances, along with better accommodations for tourists.

Advertising often exaggerated the pleasures of tropical winters in Florida. Nevertheless, one Yankee visitor did write home to Boston that the climate was "superior to Italy in Winter; and it is said to be cool in Summer from the Southern trade winds." Supposedly, such breezes kept this region cooler than Philadelphia or even New York at the height of summer.[68]

Tourism did much to help local economies, and towns like Saint Augustine depended on winter guests to bring infusions of cash. Jacksonville also enjoyed the financial benefits of tourists, aided in no small measure by its status as a sea and later a rail terminus. River excursions up the Saint Johns from the town were popular among South Carolinians, who reveled in the sights and sounds along the exotic river shore. Unfortunately, hopes of such visits growing into an even larger industry that would attract more Northerners were dashed by the events of 1860 and 1861. The unsettling sectional tension, hard economic times, and the atmosphere of distrust and fear confronting those from the North ended a business not to be resurrected for years.[69]

The coming of secession terminated an era in the economic growth of the state of Florida. Evolving along similar lines as neighboring states, it had relished a full measure of prosperity. Its economy of the 1850s was in actuality a dual one, based on planters and small farmers on one hand and the cattle herders, lumberers, and fishermen on the other. Most of these reveled in financial success and expected the 1860s to produce more of the same. The peninsula, with its fields of cotton and corn, was blossoming like a garden, while the natural bounty of the woodlands kept sawmills and turpentine workers occupied. Exports were reaching markets throughout the United States and increasingly were going overseas. Ties were strong with Florida's lower South neighbor states, from which so many settlers had migrated. Stories of lush richness returned with every letter to their old homes and were repeated in newspapers and such leading journals as *De Bow's Review* and the *Southern Cultivator*. Problems of inadequate transportation seemed unimportant and solvable. A clear extension of the Old South, antebellum Florida would share the same fate in the crucible of revolution and war.[70]

2 Secession, War, and the Blockade

The citizens of Florida had observed the political upheavals of the 1850s as partisan spectators, and the majority of them were swept up in the crisis of fear following John Brown's abortive raid on Harper's Ferry, the disintegration of the Democratic Party, and the possibility of a "black Republican" occupying the White House by the decade's end. In the 1860 presidential contest Florida's electoral votes went to Kentuckian John C. Breckinridge, although there were some pockets of support for John Bell's Constitutional Union ticket. When Republican triumph at the polls was assured, Florida political leaders began to lay the groundwork for taking their state out of the Union, though none wanted it to be the first to take that momentous step. Governor Madison S. Perry believed that Florida was not inclined to assume the lead in the secession movement, but that it "will most assuredly cooperate with or follow the lead of any single Cotton State which may secede."

The governor-elect, John Milton, reportedly agreed with Perry, and many state editors wrote that secession was inevitable in any case. Disunionist editorials decried waiting for any "overt act" or other form of delay, which would only strengthen the enemy's hand. A small radical faction of secessionists welcomed calls for a state meeting to debate and decide on a future course of action and were prepared to accept the consequences in the event that policy led to violence. These fire-eaters presumed that Floridians would firmly stand behind other Southerners to resist any Republican-inspired attack. "Our census-taker put down his tally in rather small figures," wrote a resident of Jefferson County, "but you need not be told that size is not always the true measure of spirit."[1]

The Florida legislature, dominated by members known as immediate secessionists and already in session in late November 1860, called for a convention to deal with the question of withdrawal from the Union to be composed of specially elected delegates. This assembly, in the minds of fire-eaters, heralded the beginning of a new era in the history of the Southern states. The forces of immediate secession had failed, however, to receive an overwhelming mandate in the voting. Those candidates representing the opposition "cooperationist" position received between 36 percent and 43 percent of the votes cast on 22 December. The vote reflected the division between the conservative panhandle region west of the Suwannee and the rest of the state. High percentages of Unionists also inhabited Jacksonville and Duval County, plus parts of neighboring Clay County. Regardless of sectional differences of opinion, when the delegates gathered in Tallahassee on 3 January 1861, the main discussion concerned only the how and when of seceding from the United States.[2]

The members of the convention pondered various drafts of an ordinance of secession before voting on 10 January. Meanwhile, important developments occurred as state leaders wrestled with options. Local military forces took over the Federal arsenal at Apalachicola, occupied Fort Marion in Saint Augustine by 7 January, and were threatening to move on other United States property. As a result emotions ran high and no doubt helped the cause of the immediate secessionists. The decree taking Florida out of the Union passed the convention by a vote of sixty-two to seven. In response to the news, joyous crowds celebrated in the streets of Tallahassee and in other towns throughout the state as people looked forward to joining with South Carolina, Mississippi, and the other soon-to-secede states to form a glorious new confederacy.[3]

In order to explain why Floridians took such a fateful step, the influence of South Carolina must be examined. Large numbers of Carolinians had moved to Florida during the 1850s, and they had brought their political proclivities along with them. A similar situation existed in Mississippi, where the secessionist faction of the state Democratic Party controlled the machinery of government. Carolinians themselves had little doubt that their youthful neighbor state to the south would follow their example in responding to Republican aggression, real or imagined. Charleston newspapers carried pieces praising the unanimous support for immediate secession manifested all around the state of Florida, articles no doubt read by many Floridians who may have been influenced by them. Governor Perry had already strengthened the emotional ties to South Carolina by his unofficial pledges of aid to the seceders who met in Charleston in December. Not all Florida citizens, however, agreed that the best policy was to follow in South Carolina's wake. Cooperationists continued to argue that leaving the Union with Georgia and Alabama still members of the United States was sheer economic folly. "This little infant daughter of South Carolina," ran an editorial in the *West Florida Enterprise,* "is not yet out of its swaddling clothes; and its revered old mother is evidently so far advanced in her dotage . . . [that] she needs the succor of some more powerful auxiliary than this little daughter."[4]

The secession of Alabama on 11 January and Georgia on 20 January eased Floridians' fears of geographic and economic isolation. The exodus of the lower South has been likened more to an act of counterrevolution than one of revolution. Grave concerns about what the abolitionist-tainted Republicans might do now that they enjoyed control of the executive branch of the national government chilled Florida residents at all levels of society. Nightmarish visions of scores of John Browns plotting slave uprisings and race war with the Lincoln administration's acquiescence made the risk of leaving the Union acceptable to them. A member of the secession convention expressed these fears by stating, "With our people of course, slavery is the element of all value, and a destruction of that destroys all that is property." Fire-eaters had convinced yeoman farmers that the incoming Republicans planned nothing less than the abolition of slavery and, the worst of horrors to them, racial competition and conflict. In order to be able to continue to live as before and to realize the economic benefits of a separation of slaveholding states, secession from the Union in 1861 seemed necessary and almost prudent to many of Florida's leaders and a large segment of the population.[5]

Representatives from the seven seceded states met in Montgomery, Alabama, on 4 February to organize a Southern confederation and a provisional government. Within three months of Lincoln's election, the Confederate States of America had a constitution, a congress, and, in Jefferson Davis and Alexander Stephens, a president and a vice president. Most important of all, the Confederates had begun to create an army and a navy under the leadership of the former United States senator from Florida Stephen R. Mallory. Their purpose was to defend the new nation's sovereignty and independence. Weapons taken from Federal arsenals and acquired from other sources went to equip the one-hundred-thousand-man force authorized by the provisional congress. The continued presence of United States troops in forts within the borders of the Confederacy made military preparations necessary in the view of state and Confederate officials. The bulk of the soldiers and arms available to President Davis early in 1861 came from the states, each rushing to field as many regiments as possible.[6]

Florida authorities were confronted with several problems when they began to organize a defense of their state. Union forces remained firmly ensconced on Florida soil, and they would have to be ejected. Forts

Taylor and Jefferson to the south were under Federal control, along with the town of Key West. Stronger units occupied secure positions at the vital port of Pensacola. When Florida left the Union, the small Pensacola garrison quickly abandoned installations in the city proper and concentrated themselves at Fort Pickens, located on a lonely spit of sand on the tip of Santa Rosa Island. The guns of Fort Pickens effectively commanded the entrance to Pensacola Bay, thereby closing one of Florida's, and the new Confederacy's, best ports. Furthermore, Pickens, unlike beleaguered Fort Sumter in Charleston harbor, was accessible from the Gulf and therefore easy to reinforce with men and supplies.

In response to a call from Governor Perry, volunteers for the Florida army flocked to Pensacola with the idea of evicting Union soldiers and sailors from their stronghold. Other states, knowing the economic consequences of losing one of the South's major ports, contributed troops and weapons to the growing Confederate army camped around Pensacola. Alabama was the first to send such aid, followed by Mississippi, Louisiana, and Georgia. Raw recruits from these states found themselves in what to many must have seemed an exotic tropical environment. When not sweating on the drill field under the eyes of their commander, the taciturn Braxton Bragg, these Alabama and Georgia farm boys and clerks enjoyed the opportunities to explore the city and the country beyond. Most were favorably impressed, especially by the good quality of the rations they received. "The country about here is very fine," wrote one Georgian to the folks at home; "we are living on fish, oysters, crabs, and have a few vegetables."[7] These soldier-tourists soon settled down into a routine as Union and Confederate forces around the bay attacked and counterattacked each other beginning in April 1861.

Raising, equipping, and feeding the thousands of new soldiers strained the resources of the new Confederate States before and after the firing on Fort Sumter. Florida in particular faced great difficulty in supplying the tools of war, since the majority of goods in the state heretofore had been imported from cities to the north. Besides arms, ammunition, and uniforms, each new unit required tents, kitchen utensils, buckets, shovels, and a myriad of things used by troops in the field. Stocks of these items quickly ran out in Florida, forcing quartermasters working for the state government to look for equipment in Atlanta, Savannah, Charleston, and New Orleans. Although the credit of the state was strained to the limit and beyond, a heady optimism gripped white Floridians. So a scramble to procure military supplies went on continuously during the spring of 1861.[8]

President Lincoln's call for seventy-five thousand men to put down the rebellion after the attack on Fort Sumter and the resulting secession of the

Confederate troops around Pensacola. (Photograph courtesy of Florida State Archives)

states of the upper South only confirmed notions in the new Confederacy that the war would be brief and victory easily attained. Many looked enthusiastically to the future and predicted prosperity for the independent nation. Florida was prominent in such visions of the great days to come for the South. The editor of the *Southern Cultivator* believed that under the Confederate government Florida's economic potential would finally be reached. "She will increase much faster and become of considerable importance in wealth and strength," the journalist concluded in April 1861. As in the antebellum era, the *Southern Cultivator* enhanced Florida's reputation as a garden spot by printing articles and comments highlighting the state's virtues. In June editor Daniel Lee went so far as to proclaim Florida "the healthiest state in the Confederacy." The exuberance that followed secession lost some of its luster, however, when leaders across the South faced the prospect of conducting a long war against a determined foe with numerous advantages. [9]

Cooperation among states obviously was essential to a successful Confederate war effort. Because of Florida's limited military resources it turned quickly and instinctively to its neighbors for assistance. When the peninsula state passed its ordinance of secession, commissioners from Alabama and South Carolina were present in the hall, observing and consulting with local leaders. The Alabama representative, E. C. Bullock, expressed the hope that his state and Florida would "soon be united in the new Union of brotherly love in which a homogeneous people taking their destination into their own hands, . . . [would] exhibit to the world the highest development of free government." Negotiation began at once to create the structures needed by the new government, including a new system of mail delivery. In the midst of cooperative efforts, interest in Florida by contiguous states was more than fraternal. The proposal to annex west Florida to Alabama resurfaced in February 1861. One newspaper editor even suggested dividing the newly independent state into three sections, the panhandle going to Alabama, middle Florida being attached to Georgia, and the area east of the Suwannee being left to fend for itself. Such a scheme would complete "the greatness of two great states" and insure prosperity for all. The movement came to nothing because the attention of Georgia and Alabama expansionists was diverted by the widening war. [10]

The idea of being annexed by other states might have appealed to a few Floridians because it offered some relief from the financial difficulties that plagued Florida after the state joined the Confederacy. The state's banking system was anything but sound in 1861. While as many as ten private banks existed in the state, only the Bank of the State of Florida, located in Tallahassee, and the Bank of Fernandina were of any significance. As the demands of creating an army plunged the state government deeper into debt, Florida officials asked the banking community to support their military efforts with a temporary loan to enable the purchasing of war material in rapidly inflated markets. The legislature turned also to the printing press and authorized the issuance of five hundred thousand dollars in 8 percent bonds. By the end of 1861 Florida banks were forced to suspend specie payments. The only circulating medium was private bank notes and the newly pressed state and Confederate scrip. Since bank notes could no longer be redeemed for gold, they plummeted in value and added to economic uncertainty. The net result of increased governmental spending and governmental responses to it sowed the seeds of an inflationary spiral that in the end crippled the overall Confederate economy.[11]

With the suspension of specie payments by banks, rates of currency exchange fluctuated wildly in many areas. Since the farther one got from Richmond, the higher the rate of exchange for Confederate money seemed to rise, Floridians failed to enjoy much buying power with it in local marketplaces. Both state and national officials were printing more and more paper money, so the money supply increased some eleven times between January 1861 and January 1864. Their futile efforts to shore up the economic front made Confederate secretaries of the treasury appear as little more than Dutch boys with not enough fingers to plug the multiplying holes in the dike. On the subject of the supply of money a Quincy resident wrote in 1864, "It is hoped that the leprosy of Mammon which has been so contagious for the past three years . . . will disappear."[12]

The government of Florida committed itself to retiring its share of the Confederate debt, provided that the burden was shared equally by each state. A resolution to that end passed the General Assembly in December 1862, pledging the state "to the most cordial cooperation with her sister states in the maintenance of the Credit of the Confederacy." The state's commitment to fiscal unity continued after a fashion for the rest of the war, though hindered by the progressively weakening currency. Yet, such handicaps did not prevent an occasional economic victory, such as the one in which the state retired its debt to persons in Charleston and Savannah in May 1863. The Charleston _Daily Courier_ praised this act, accomplished "without the smallest sacrifice either of the credit or securities of the State." Such obligations were paid without a corresponding hike in tax rates, which never matched the needs for revenue created by war-time spending. In fact, the legislature rejected advice to raise taxes during the war years, thereby making Floridians some of the least taxed citizens of the Confederate States of America.[13]

While Florida would make many contributions to the greater Confederate economy during the war, she lacked the financial power to ease the fiscal burdens of the national government. The state struggled to pay the various Confederate levies and to subscribe to the loans and bond drives, but in the end lagged behind the other seceded states. As currency values declined, Floridians turned more and more to a primitive system of barter. Florida gave the war-time South strong support in the form of commodities, which increased in worth as the struggle continued. Her value as a Confederate state lay in these areas and not in the realm of banking and economics. Nevertheless, the state offered to wealthier states like Georgia or South Carolina an example of dedication by claiming its share of the national war debt in the face of limited fiscal means.[14]

Though finances vexed Florida leaders in 1861, the problem of adequately defending the large peninsula still occupied center stage. Newly inaugurated Governor John Milton faced the problem of coping with possible enemy attacks anywhere along the hundreds of miles of Florida coastline with painfully few men or weapons. So many Florida units had left for the fighting fronts in Kentucky, Tennessee, and Virginia that Milton felt compelled to ask Richmond for help in the herculean task. He pointed out to President Davis that the weakened condition of the state rendered it a tempting target for Union advances, from which offensive thrusts could be launched into the heartland of the Confederacy. "As it is, unable to conquer any other State," argued Milton, "may not Florida claim their attention?" Secretary of the Navy Stephen R. Mallory echoed the governor's fears that a nearly defenseless Florida presented an attractive avenue for the invasion of Georgia or Alabama. Yet efforts by Mallory to secure material support from a government with little if any to spare came to naught.[15]

Confederate military and political leaders were hesitant to retain troops in Florida because they were more urgently needed elsewhere and because of a mistaken belief that yellow fever rendered military operations on the peninsula impossible from June to October of each year. So much for the healthiest state in the Confederacy! State officials therefore tried to fill in the military gaps as best they could. Governor Milton worked to scrape together sufficient forces to defend some key points, mostly towns, on the seaboards. Shortages of arms and munitions of all types hampered his efforts to build a state line of defense. Angered by a War Department suggestion that he direct requests for needed weapons to the commanding general of the military department responsible for Florida, Milton retorted that "it would have been almost as reasonable to have referred me to the Emperor of China." The governor wanted batteries of heavy artillery planted at the mouth of every major Florida river, as well as at any other position vulnerable to Federal assault. Milton had a low opinion of the numerous cavalry units springing around his state; he thought them the least efficient means of defending the region. He later assured President Davis that no battle would ever be fought in Florida by cavalrymen.[16]

Florida's war governor wondered late in 1861 why the Union host he so feared hesitated in descending upon his people. Federal troops capturing an entire Confederate state would pose a threat to rebel recognition by Great Britain and other European powers, not to mention the boost it would give to Northern morale after disasters like the battle of Bull Run. "With our feebleness," he confessed, "they are well acquainted . . . [through] those rough traitors, some of whom yet remain among us." Milton knew that Floridians, despite newspaper accounts, were less than solid in their support of secession and war against the North and that such divisiveness would surface many times in Florida during the conflict. The governor overestimated Union resources and misread Union strategy for 1861 but doubted that the state would continue to be unbothered in 1862. Federal planners, as it turned out, were slow in targeting their might toward damaging the Confederate ability to make war. Florida's military weakness threatened to disrupt its economic links to Georgia and Alabama, and the way leaders in these states reacted tells much about the nature of their relationship with the peninsula.[17]

During the antebellum years Apalachicola, at the mouth of the Apalachicola-Chattahoochee River system, was an outlet for cotton to planters in three states. The appearance of Union blockaders off the port town in 1861 threatened to halt any further shipments, as well as stopping imports for the people living along the river corridor. Worse, the river provided a way for Union naval forces to endanger the vital industries upriver at Columbus, Georgia. Numerous complaints to the War Department in Richmond brought sympathy but no additional troops or military supplies. Eventually the city fathers of Columbus took matters into their own hands and voted to have obstructions sunk in the river and other passive defenses constructed to stop any Federal raiders from approaching their town. Governor Milton and other Florida leaders objected to the plan, believing it to be nothing more than a clever ploy by Alabamans to divert trade from Apalachicola to Mobile by making the river impassable to vessels. While wishing to cooperate with the neighboring states, Floridians were reluctant to damage their own economy while seemingly benefiting others. The whole controversy demonstrated Florida's importance to the new Confederate nation in both a geographic and an economic sense. Nevertheless, authorities in Richmond often failed to appreciate its significance.[18]

An indication of this blindness to Florida's economic value came after the Confederate defeats at Forts Henry and Donelson in Tennessee in 1862. After the rebel main line of defense in the west was breached by U. S. Grant's victorious army, the lower South was stripped of soldiers to reinforce General Albert S. Johnston's rebel command. A highly regarded officer, Johnston planned to strike back at Grant before he was joined by General Don Carlos Buell's Army of the Ohio and drove even deeper into Mississippi and Alabama. The Confederate War Department moved most of the gray-clad troops out of Florida, leaving its defense to whatever units the state could raise. General Robert E. Lee, sent by Jefferson Davis to bolster the crumbling south Atlantic coast defenses, bluntly informed Governor Milton on 24 February 1862 that the citizens of Florida must defend their own state from attack. Because Milton was unable to muster many men, the Florida defense forces were compelled to retreat into the interior. Pensacola, Apalachicola, and Jacksonville were evacuated by their garrisons. The economic and strategic costs of losing so many ports on the Florida coast cannot be fathomed or even calculated. The embittered residents of these towns blamed Lee, Johnston, and Braxton Bragg for their plight.[19]

This Confederate withdrawal from the coastal areas of Florida seriously reduced the state's usefulness for blockade runners. Originating with General Winfield Scott's "Anaconda plan," a major war aim of the Union was to cut off all of the South's foreign commerce. While Lincoln's proclamation of a blockade of rebel ports inadvertently granted the Confederacy belligerent status under international law, its slowly growing efficiency unquestionably damaged the war-making capacity of the Confederacy. Historians may argue about the effectiveness of the Union navy's cordon and debate whether it was the most significant cause of Confederate defeat, but none can deny its impact upon the Southern economy. The army in gray desperately needed arms and equipment in 1861 and 1862 that only the factories of Europe could provide, and the Confederacy could pay for such war materials only with exports of cotton. Therefore, all manner of seagoing vessels began breaking what was in the beginning only a "paper" blockade, their captains and owners lured by the promise of large profits for each successful run.[20]

Florida played a role in blockade running from the first days of the rebellion. Pensacola, one of the best harbors in the South, would have been very valuable for such covert shipping. However, it remained under Federal control along with Key West. They were soon to be joined by Fernandina and Saint Augustine, both taken by Union forces. However, there remained the numerous inlets, bays, and coves dotting the coasts on both the Atlantic and Gulf flanks of the peninsula, which were attractive

bases for smuggling. General John K. Jackson of the Confederate army
reported, after a survey of the state in 1864, that "the peninsula of
Florida, preserving as it does not quite one-half of the coast of the Confederate States, affords great opportunities for evading the enemy's
blockaders, and bringing supplies for the Government." Only a handful
of harbors, however, could handle a sufficient volume of cargo to be of
substantial assistance to the rebel cause. Goods landed anywhere in south
Florida stood in danger of being lost, because no reliable means of transportation existed there. Nevertheless, this problem did not deter a flotilla
of small sailing vessels from darting to Cuba or to the Bahamas to trade a
bale of cotton or a barrel of turpentine for consumer goods. Even the
smallest return cargo aided the Confederate cause by helping to maintain
morale among the civilian population.[21]

On the Atlantic coast of Florida the effects of the Federal naval forces
on station were not immediately felt by residents living on or near the
shoreline. During the first months of the war coastal packets continued
their scheduled runs between Charleston, Savannah, and points in Florida. Small craft like the sidewheeler *Carolina* easily evaded the few Union
warships assigned to the area and delivered Florida-grown cotton to the
wharves of Charleston. Another coaster, the steamer *Saint Johns,* managed to complete 486 trips from Savannah into the Saint Johns River
before increasing Federal pressure early in 1862 made such voyages impossible. Thus ended one line of communication and supply with Georgia and South Carolina, which remained broken for the rest of the
conflict. Yet many light-drafted sailing ships continued an erratic trade,
escaping Union detection by slipping in and out of the inland waterways.[22]

Originally, much was expected from the port of Fernandina as a
blockade-runner haven because of its rail link with the interior of the
state. But residents of the town soon became discouraged as disruption of
the coastal trade created shortages and emptied stores of merchandise. In
August 1861, for example, stocks of food shrank to levels sufficient only
to feed the populace for three short days. From their rooftops citizens
watched the blockading ships off the mouth of the Saint Marys River,
and they wondered to themselves how long these hostile vessels would
remain content to cruise beyond the harbor bar. After the withdrawal of
Confederate forces in February 1862 left the port town all but unde-
fended, a Union amphibious attack netted the valuable prize on 4 March.
Likewise, Jacksonville fell to Federal soldiers and sailors, the first in a
series of occupations that eliminated its usefulness as a destination for
smugglers.[23]

Meanwhile, farther down the coast the practically defenseless inhabitants of Saint Augustine waited for the Union invaders to arrive. By September 1861 Federal warships blocked the approaches to its small harbor, although a few daring captains managed to elude the vigilance of the blockaders and reach town. Stripped of soldiers as Fernandina and Jacksonville were, the civic authorities of the ancient city ran up a white flag when Union gunboats sailed up the Matanzas River on 11 March 1862. While many of the town's residents afterward remained loyal to the Confederate cause, others quickly adapted themselves to the new order. The population subsequently enjoyed a higher standard of living than Floridians in the interior. Goods seized by the blockading squadron filled the shelves of stores, and hundreds of Union soldiers walked the streets with greenbacks in their pockets to spend. These uniformed tourists provided the hard currency that the city had depended upon before the war and revitalized the local economy. Saint Augustine continued in Federal hands for the rest of the war and served as a base for raids into the countryside and as a rest camp for Union troops.[24]

Despite its occupation, Saint Augustine was not forgottten by people across the lower South. Southerners were outraged when Federal authorities expelled rebel sympathizers, including the aged mother of Confederate General Edmund Kirby Smith. This incident was eclipsed by a story circulated through the country in mid-1862. In June several newspapers carried a fantastic tale of British warships capturing a Federal transport laden with provisions in Florida waters and their setting up a naval blockade of their own off Saint Augustine and the mouth of the Saint Johns. Union troops, went the story, had abandoned Fort Marion because of short rations and marched toward the broad Saint Johns in hopes of contacting Union gunboats on patrol there. Wishful Southern editors concluded that Great Britain had finally intervened with its navy and was determined to make the blockade of Confederate ports as effective against Northern vessels as the Federals had made it against European ships. In the end the entire story, of course, turned out to be nothing but a wild rumor, but this was not to be the only instance when Confederates hoped for miracles in Florida.[25]

The loss of Fernandina, Jacksonville, and Saint Augustine pushed an obscure anchorage known as Mosquito Inlet into prominence as an important conduit for smuggled supplies. A shallow and difficult harbor, Mosquito Inlet offered shelter for small cargo ships while barring the larger Union warships from entering the bay in pursuit. Goods landed near the town of New Smyrna were hauled by wagon to the Saint Johns and there loaded on small river steamers. After being landed on the west shore of the river, the supplies were carried by a new relay of carts to the village of Waldo on the Florida Railroad line. From there railroad cars, often pulled by horses or oxen, hauled cargoes northward to the junction at Baldwin and then to Madison or Monticello. Wagons ferried the goods into Georgia, where there was an extensive rail system. Products for export, cotton, turpentine, or tobacco, made the reverse journey along this tenuous supply line. River packets like the _Hattie Brock_ and the _James Burt_ also conveyed cotton bales up the river to Lake Harney, located southwest of New Smyrna, and from there they moved to the coast near the site of modern-day Titusville to be placed on shallow-drafted smugglers.[26]

The potential of places like Mosquito Inlet did not escape the attention of the Confederate government in its labors to acquire the tools of war. Early in 1862, arrangements for running cargoes into the inlet and their transportation northward for use by the rebel army were completed by General Robert E. Lee and his naval aide John Newland Maffitt. Lee himself wrote to General James H. Trapier about shipments of arms and ammunition bound for New Smyrna and about the preparations he wanted for their arrival. He suggested that two moderate-sized artillery pieces be emplaced on the dunes to fend off the Union naval forces should they move against the inlet in the midst of unloading operations. Lee concluded that the incoming munitions were "so valuable and so vitally important, that no precaution should be omitted." Earlier, Confederate Quartermaster-General Abraham C. Myers had informed his officers in Florida that departmental supplies were enroute to Mosquito Inlet and had directed them to see to their forwarding as quickly as possible. All such items were to go by boat, wagon, and rail to Quitman, Georgia, on the Savannah, Albany, and Gulf line and then by rail to their final destination, Richmond, via Savannah.[27]

A Federal garrison at Jacksonville and the presence of Union gunboats on the Saint Johns complicated an already nightmarish exercise in logistics. A Confederate ordnance depot used to store arms in transit had to be relocated farther from the river bank to avoid a surprise Yankee attack. This adjustment was made none too soon, for in March the blockade runner _Kate_ arrived in Mosquito Inlet with a load of some six thousand Enfield rifles, large amounts of ammunition, and badly needed items such as medical supplies and blankets. Local residents worked with desperate energy to move the piles of Confederate government property off the exposed beaches to safety. Unfortunately, some of these same civilians plundered the _Kate_'s shipment of new shoes and rifles. Along the route units responsible for guarding these goods equipped themselves with the shiny new weapons with little hesitation. Because of the danger that the entire consignment of supplies might "disappear" before leaving Florida, Governor Milton frantically ordered that all precautions be undertaken to protect the shipment from pilferage.[28]

To make matters worse for the Confederates, the Federals detected the unusually heavy activity around New Smyrna, and on 22 March they launched an attack aimed at Mosquito Inlet, intended to catch the *Kate* and her cargo. Beaten back by Confederate troops, the bluecoats retired to their base. Apprehension that was already felt in military circles from Atlanta to Richmond over the fate of the arms shipment rose with reports of such enemy assaults. Florida officials dispatched at least 150 government wagons from Madison County to the coast to assist in transporting the heavy crates of Enfield rifles. Each wagon thus engaged hauled the boxes about twenty miles. The teamsters then unloaded their goods and left them under guard to be picked up by another wagon with a fresh team of horses. This relay system was designed to remove as much from the dangerous coastal areas as quickly as possible. The difficult task of moving the government stores continued without a halt into April. In spite of a host of delays, Governor Milton promised Secretary of War George W. Randolph that all the supplies would be delivered to the Confederate government as soon as humanly feasible.[29]

With regard to the lost or stolen items, Milton lacked any solid evidence as to the identity of the wrongdoers and requested that Secretary Randolph investigate the matter promptly. Many rumors circulated that all manner of government property was now in the hands of Confederate soldiers or civilians in and around New Smyrna. Milton pledged that Florida authorities would endeavor to reclaim any and all such items. To learn the exact disposition of the *Kate*'s cargo, he dispatched Captain Alonzo B. Noyes, formerly of the Confederate Coast Guard, to follow the supply line southward. Noyes ascertained that Florida soldiers had indeed taken arms from the New Smyrna cargoes and that at least one officer there had sold guns, ammunition, and medicines and pocketed the proceeds for himself. Captain Noyes brought all of the munitions he gathered along the railroad line to the depot in Madison and then had them quickly wagoned across the border to Quitman. Noyes personally accompanied the weapons he collected to their destination, Corinth, Mississippi, by rail via Savannah, Columbus, and Mobile.[30]

Unfortunately for embarrassed Florida leaders, Noyes's journey to Mississippi did not end the *Kate* affair. Attempts to collect stolen equipment and stores produced few results and dragged on into May. Finally, General Joseph Finegan resorted to publicly urging the people of the state possessing, or knowing of others possessing, items landed at Mosquito Inlet to surrender them to authorities or give information as to their whereabouts. Eventually a detailed accounting pinpointed the location of most of the rifles, but other supplies, such as blankets and shoes, were not recovered. The Quartermaster Department's last report on the subject concluded that there was not "a single gun of this cargo remaining in the State of Florida which is not in the hands of a soldier ready to use it in the defense of his country." Some of the weapons brought by the *Kate,* however, were never accounted for.[31]

The circumstances surrounding the 1862 *Kate* affair did not improve Florida's reputation as a secure channel for arms brought through the blockade, since a vital munitions shipment, almost lost to enemy action, was scattered over hundreds of miles because of a disjointed transportation network. Even state troops detailed to guard the valuable cargo joined with teamsters in looting property bound for the Confederate army on the battle line. As a result senior Confederate officials must have concluded that importing military supplies through east Florida was a risky undertaking. Relying upon better organized ports such as Mobile or Wilmington obviously seemed the prudent course to follow. With the government shying away from the peninsula, private blockade-running concerns must also have been wary of using Florida waters for their operations. Yet, despite shaken public confidence, Union pressure on the Charleston port and others, the potential profit, and the desperate need for commodities that could only come from overseas kept blockade runners, public and private, large and small, sailing to and from Florida.

Mosquito Inlet in time became the object of increased attention by the Union blockaders. "A large number of Yankee vessels are now on the Florida coast," reported the Charleston *Daily Courier* in 1863, "and it is difficult for vessels running the blockade to make safe entry." But the Union navy could do little to suppress the trade between the Bahamas and the Florida coast between Cape Canaveral and Biscayne Bay. Indian River, Jupiter, and Hillsborough Inlets gave shelter to dozens of small sloops and schooners that carried cotton and turpentine to Nassau. These craft returned with medicines, coffee, salt, and other items all but gone from store shelves in south Florida. Although records naturally are sketchy, there is little doubt that a considerable amount of smuggling went on in this isolated region. Some might argue that goods brought into Florida in this fashion did little to support the larger Confederate war effort because they were consumed locally. There are two reasons why this view is not entirely correct. In the first place the articles provided by blockade runners enabled rebel sympathizers to continue resisting Federal encroachments in a region of great logistical importance to the South. In the second place, units of the Union navy occupied in chasing the sailboats and small steamers would have been used elsewhere against the Confederates if not tied down on the south Florida coast.[32]

Blockade runners were also active on the Gulf coast of the peninsula. As on the Atlantic side of Florida, the blockade here proved to be porous through most of 1861, but by the following year more and more warships began exerting pressure on shippers. Pensacola, of course, blocked by the guns of Union-held Fort Pickens, had no need for any naval patrols. Farther to the east, Apalachicola became the first Florida port to be officially closed by a naval vessel when the USS *Montgomery* appeared in the bay on 11 June 1861. The commerce of this once-thriving town soon withered and died. Saint Marks suffered much the same fate, and its collector of customs reported to the Confederate Treasury Department in October of that year that not a single ship had departed or docked at Saint Marks since the start of the blockade. For the remainder of the war the anchorage there stayed a secondary port at best for rebel smugglers, and only occasionally did a small vessel manage to land cargoes at the town.[33]

This is not to say that there were no successes, for significant quantities of supplies did land on Florida's upper Gulf coast. In March 1862, for example, the steamer *Florida* eluded Federal ships and entered Saint Andrews Bay with a cargo of twenty-five hundred rifles and sixty thousand pounds of gunpowder. Plantation wagons from as far away as Jackson County rushed to move the heavy munitions to safety inland before they were discovered by the Yankees. The *Florida* also brought consumer goods, and these were quickly bought by eager customers, who flocked to the ship's mooring on Bear Creek just off the bay at Saint Andrews. The rifles and powder, unlike those of the *Kate,* were promptly moved to Columbus. In time, tightened Union patrols ended the career of Saint Andrews Bay as a blockade-runner destination, but, as will be seen, the area continued to occupy the attention of the Federal navy for the rest of the war.[34]

Southward along the Gulf coast were countless small rivers and inlets offering nearly perfect protection for sailing ships and steamers. Frustrated Union commanders, who usually lacked vessels light-drafted enough to navigate in the shallow waters and pilots sufficiently knowledgeable to guide them, were unable to strike at the smugglers. The Suwannee–Santa Fe River system provided a ready route for exporting cotton and moving goods to a point near the railroad running through Lake City. Similarly, cargoes landed on the banks of the Crystal River were hauled inland by horse-drawn wagons that had deposited cotton bales and turpentine for the waiting blockade runners. Considerable numbers of barrels containing spirits of turpentine left the Cedar Key area before it fell under Union control in 1862. The tiny hamlet of Bayport welcomed inbound vessels, as did the town of Tampa, until Tampa Bay came under the guns of the blockaders. Numerous small craft traded along the southwestern coast, especially around Charlotte Harbor and the mouth of the Caloosahatchee River. Even after additional warships joined the blockading squadron, the Union navy remained unable to completely break up this traffic.[35]

Many of these rebel traders sailed between the southwest coast of Florida and the island of Cuba. Ships from Havana bound for ports such as Saint Marks often leapfrogged up the coastline, hiding in sheltered bays and inlets during the daylight hours. Such a trade maintained a commercial relationship with the Spanish island for the Confederacy, and some material from Cuba did reach the South via Florida. Cotton from the peninsula went south in exchange for medical supplies, clothing, Spanish army surplus shoes, and cigars. Despite protests by United States officials, the Cuban government turned a blind eye to such traffic until 1863. The channel of commerce between the mainland and the island, established in antebellum days, appeared impervious to the changes caused by the outbreak of civil war.[36]

The Gulf waters never completely lost their value for blockade running, especially after the closing of primary ports such as Charleston and Wilmington late in the war. Plans to improve facilities at Saint Marks for the purpose of opening a new phase of smuggling from Cuba were initiated in the first months of 1865. The Federals took such actions seriously and reorganized the East Gulf Blockading Squadron into two divisions in March to enable it to cover the Florida seaboard from Saint Andrews Bay to Charlotte Harbor more effectively. Senior officers believed it certain that the Confederates would try to run ships into Florida Gulf waters as their regular ports fell one by one, and they stressed to their subordinates how important it was to capture such vessels. Consequently, Union naval forces kept up the pressure until the surrender of the rebel armies ended the need to strangle commerce by blockade.[37]

While it is probable that the bulk of supplies landed in Florida were consumed in the state, a considerable amount were transported into Georgia and Alabama. Items specifically ordered by the Confederate government, such as munitions and medicines, were moved to their proper destinations in other states with the sole exception of the cargo of the *Kate*. On more than one occasion, government wagons and teams hauled goods from the point of importation in central and south Florida for both public and private owners. Consumer items brought through the naval cordon to Florida were sold as far north as Atlanta. Georgia customers could easily study notices of public auctions of smuggled merchandise. The Atlanta *Southern Confederacy*, for instance, carried an advertisement about such a sale set to take place on 4 June 1862 at Lake City, along with a detailed list of what was for sale. Businessmen could communicate with Florida representatives over telegraph lines linking

Baldwin, Sanderson, Lake City, and Tallahassee about the availability of blockade-run commodities. Such individuals often invested in Florida-based smuggling ventures organized by entrepreneurs such as William A. Swann to supply governmental and civilian needs and sometimes realized handsome profits for their endeavors.[38]

Unsurprisingly, the blockade had a pernicious effect on Florida's economy. By the end of 1862, Union naval power had caused serious shortages throughout the state and had lowered standards of living markedly. In a message to the state legislature, Governor Milton expounded on the damage the Federals had wrought on Florida and its people. "The blockade has cut off all intercourse with other countries," he admitted, "and for the present has rendered useless and valueless the staples by which our people have been able to raise money."[39] One commodity in great demand throughout the South was salt, and sacks brought in from the Bahamas or Cuba were always welcome. Salt from Nassau often filled the small holds of sloops and schooners putting in at Jupiter and Indian River Inlets after eluding the blockaders. Though the Yankees managed to intercept large amounts, a significant quantity of salt reached interior settlements. The availability of imported salt in south Florida eased the hardships of local residents despite its high price. It also freed domestically produced salt for export to states in the center of the Confederacy that lacked the means to make it for themselves in necessary amounts. Along with coffee, flour, soap, and sewing items, salt from abroad helped maintain civilian morale in an area far from the center of the rebel government, isolated also by poor communications.

Even consumers with money to spend had a difficult time finding a store in Florida or southern Georgia containing any wares for sale. Many merchants gave up and closed their doors, especially those unable to acquire any goods from the small stream flowing northward through the state from the coasts. Union naval officers happily reported the distress their presence caused in Florida towns and farms that lacked basic supplies: coffee, tea, and other store-bought provisions. Prices of these items rose to such heights that, in the view of one Federal captain, "large numbers of the people are beginning to become disgusted with so hopeless a struggle." However, this optimistic 1862 prediction proved premature.[40]

The blockade also seriously affected Florida agriculturalists. After being cut off from traditional markets, they sent out on blockade runners staples like cotton, which paid for supplies brought back on the ship's return trips. Cotton was indeed king for Florida-bound captains; no less than eighty-six vessels loaded with it were captured by the United States

Navy before the end of the war. Turpentine ran a distant second to cotton with twenty-one cargoes lost to the Yankee bluejackets. As might be expected some Floridians joined other Southerners in scheming to share some of the enormous profits realized from a single successful voyage through the blockade line. Among them were professionals like William Swann; others were amateurs hoping to cash in on the proceeds of an investment in a single cotton cargo or a share in the ownership of a blockade runner. Such private transactions, combined with stories of outright theft and corruption among Confederate officials inside Florida, did little to enhance the state's reputation. Diarist Mary Chesnut, while on a trip through Alabama in the summer of 1863, recorded the comments of a gentleman about his state's southern ally. He said, "I wish we lived in Florida. It's easy times, they say, down there. They are making money by blockade-running, cheating the government and skulking the fight."[41]

Such words and the incidents that inspired them infuriated Governor Milton. He believed that both government and private blockade running hurt the Confederate cause more than it helped, because, by providing cotton to foreign markets it allowed their leaders to avoid recognizing the South's independence. In 1861 the governor tried to stop vessels from leaving Apalachicola laden with cotton bales and turpentine, but he had to acquiesce to the request of the secretaries of war and of the navy that they be permitted to sail. Milton later summed up his views in a letter to Secretary Randolph dated 25 June 1862:

> After patient inquiry of several months the evidence is such as to admit New York, Havana, New Orleans, and other Southern cities have formed mercantile copartnerships, and for some time past, under pretensions of loyalty to and great sympathy for the South, have realized heavy profits by the most villainous and treacherous arts of traffic. Partners in New York send merchandise to Havana, where, or in transit to, the merchandise is exchanged for cotton sent by partners from Southern ports, and the exchange is made by the management of partners at Havanna or Nassau, and this traffic is not unknown to those in command of blockading vessels. By such base means not only cotton is obtained at New York and other Northern cities, but information prejudicial to our best interests is obtained, our slaves are enticed away, and ignorant citizens corrupted.[42]

Milton proposed a ban on all commercial contacts with foreign countries for the duration of the war as a means to curb speculation and inflation. In the same spirit he refused in 1864 to join with other governors in protesting restrictions placed on state-sponsored blockade running by the government in Richmond. Nevertheless, the pressing need for supplies forced a reluctant Milton to allow the smugglers to continue in Florida waters.

The importation of items not directly useful to the war effort was against the public's interest, in Governor Milton's view. Exorbitant prices for common articles upset him, but the bringing in of liquor to sell at huge profit especially galled the man. He learned from General Finegan in April 1863, for example, that a large amount of West Indian rum, purchased in Cuba for seventeen cents a gallon, was selling in Florida for closer to twenty-five dollars per gallon. Finegan suggested that the "vile article" be confiscated and destroyed before it damaged army and civilian morals. Still worse, eight government wagons in June 1863 carried some 800 gallons of imported rum and 485 of gin from the beach at Bayport to Gainesville. J. R. Adams, chief wagonmaster, had orders from Quartermaster Department officers to personally accompany the important convoy and insure its prompt delivery. Surviving evidence suggests that this alcohol was probably not government property but part of a private shipment involving military officers. Wagons and horses, both in short supply, ended up being diverted from purely official duties in order to engage in blockade-runner dealings, a testament to the debasing effect of the trade on those touched by it.[43]

Historians continue to debate the effectiveness of the Union naval blockade and its part in bringing on final Confederate collapse. Most recently William N. Still, Jr., labeled it a "naval sieve" and a minor contributor to Northern victory. Florida's importance as a haven for blockade runners has been minimized by scholars who counted the numbers of ships captured and the volume of supplies moved through the peninsula to the interior. But the true significance of this traffic can be measured in ways other than by the study of figures on dusty shipping manifests. Although records on Florida blockade running are scanty, many cargoes of vitally needed goods were landed on the Florida coast, and at least part of these goods were sent on into other states. Florida rivers and bays provided shelter for vessels owned by out-of-state investors who lacked the opportunity to import or export anything from their native harbors.

A second significant point to consider is that the state of Florida's viability as a base for smugglers forced the Federal navy to commit dozens of warships to guarding the thirteen-hundred-mile coastline. If no blockade runners had sailed into Florida waters, many of these Union vessels could have been transferred to blockade duties elsewhere and could have tightened the cordon around key ports like Mobile, Charleston, or Wilmington much earlier in the conflict. Furthermore, goods brought through the blockade enabled Floridians in isolated portions of the state to continue resisting the Yankees. Lastly, every sailboat running out a bale of cotton to Nassau and returning with dry goods was an act of defiance against the Federal government, regardless of the profits obtained from such risky undertakings.[44]

Although there is little doubt that Florida's economy suffered because of the Union naval blockade, other aspects of the state's economic structure received war-generated stimulus because of it. The lumber mills of north Florida briefly enjoyed a flurry of government contracts in 1861, before Union forces reduced them to ashes. On the Atlantic coast lumber shippers carried on for a short time but soon turned their attention to the more valuable cotton. As supplies of manufactured goods diminished, home industries sprang up on many plantations and in towns to fashion such essential articles as shoes. Work with leather increased despite shortages of tanned hides that first occurred in 1862. One central Florida resident managed to make thousands of horse collars for the government in 1863, the bulk of which went to rebel forces in Virginia. Countless other harnesses, knapsacks, or parts of uniforms, such as caps, were manufactured on the home front for Florida units serving with the Confederate armies. But no major new industrial establishments grew up in the state during the war, probably because of an inadequate transportation network and a lack of necessary machinery. One small cotton card factory, the Florida Card Manufacturing Company, located in Tallahassee, did turn out some thirty pairs of mediocre quality cotton and woolen cards per day beginning in 1863. Shortages of raw materials, such as metal wire, however, curtailed efforts to expand production further.[45]

The only really significant manufacturing concern in Florida was the Bailey Cotton Mill, located east of Monticello in Jefferson County. General William M. Bailey founded the mill in 1853, but it never enjoyed financial success until the outbreak of sectional war, when demand for cloth kept its machines humming at full capacity to provide for the needs of soldier families and the poorer classes, who were unable to pay for imported cloth. The nationalizing aspects of the Confederate experience touched General Bailey's business before the end of 1864. At that time the Commissary Department tried to gain control of its looms to turn tax-in-kind cotton into cloth for the rebel government. Florida, in the person of its governor, successfully moved to fend off such encroachments on state property and private enterprise. Milton defended Bailey as one of "the most wealthy and patriotic . . . gentlemen in the Confederate States" and argued that his factory should be left in his hands and under his control. The main point in Milton's argument was the fact that Bailey's yard goods sold at a price some 50 percent less than Confederate agents paid for similar material elsewhere in the South. Agreeing that disrupting production by changing management would be unwise, the government ceased all efforts to seize the textile mill. Florida did donate supplies needed for making clothing for Georgians serving in the Confederate service in that year, evidently from the Tallahassee and Jefferson County factories.[46]

The Union blockade not only spurred industrial development in the war-time South but placed a premium on its indigenous resources as well. The hunt for "strategic materials" necessary for building and operating the rebel war machine went on in earnest as the area under Confederate control shrank under enemy pressure. Metals of all types had to be found and recycled into military equipment if the Confederate armed forces were to have a chance against their well-accoutred Federal opponents. Florida proved to be a source of scrap iron that attracted seekers from as far away as middle Alabama. In October 1862 men from "a notorious rebel firm" in Selma scoured the countryside west of Pensacola for old metal, which they took away in wagons for use in their foundry. Iron from antebellum attempts at industry near the village of Bagdad was salvaged until the operation was uncovered and stopped by Union troops. Thus, scrap metal from the Florida panhandle became cannons or the metallic parts of gun carriages.[47]

Nothing was more vital to the Confederate army than a continuous supply of ammunition. Early in the war officials concluded that imported gunpowder could not meet military requirements. The Confederate Nitre and Mining Bureau, a subsidiary of the Ordnance Bureau, was then set up to develop the mineral potential of the South in order to utilize the existing raw materials for a growing domestic munitions industry. An essential ingredient for making gunpowder was nitre, or saltpeter, of which hundreds of thousands of pounds were brought through the blockade. In addition a crash program to produce it at home was undertaken. This effort expanded in 1862 after the loss of nitre-producing caves in Kentucky, Tennessee, and northern Alabama. Bureau chemist and mineralogist Professor Nathaniel A. Pratt surveyed the lower South in hopes of finding caverns suitable for the establishment of artificial nitre beds. His search area included north Florida and its numerous limestone caves. Unfortunately for the Bureau, what some thought to be promising subterranean sites proved unusable because they were too small and too damp. Efforts to recover nitre from plantation earth in the state continued, however, despite the disappointing cave situation.[48]

A nitre bed or "nitriary" did come into being in Tallahassee under government supervision. Lieutenant Charles H. LaTrobe, in charge of Nitre District 2, which encompassed Florida, oversaw the bed and paid

workers there thirty dollars a month in addition to exempting them from
the Confederate draft. The lieutenant diligently launched a newspaper
advertisement campaign offering to purchase nitre, sulfur, or lead from
private citizens upon delivery to the state capital. LaTrobe reminded
residents that nitre could be found or manufactured on every Florida
plantation as well as in towns and that it was badly needed by the army.
Such minerals as he collected went north to the gunpowder works at
Augusta, Georgia, and other places. Governor Milton hoped that the
Nitre Bureau might benefit from a large deposit of galena, a lead ore,
discovered near the Chipola River, and he planned to mine and transport
ore by boat to the industrial town of Columbus for processing. Although
the government welcomed whatever mineral contributions Florida could
make, by the spring of 1865 the Nitre Bureau was expecting officers in
the state to offer little more than food and forage for their Georgia installations.[49]

The Confederate Navy Yard at Columbus looked to Florida as well as
to the Nitre Bureau for material support. Naval agents roamed through
north Florida searching for metals to help in the construction of ironclad
warships. Because the shipyards were desperately short of brass and copper for the internal machinery of such ships, some brave souls volunteered
to slip into Union-held Fernandina to forage among abandoned equipment belonging to the Florida Railroad for such metals. But what naval
engineers wanted most from Florida was not railroad copper but iron rails
to strengthen the hulls of vessels then under construction in the Columbus
yard, for example the CSS *Jackson*. Unused rails from Florida's lines
quickly became very valuable in the wartime environment, with many
government agencies and private companies vying to obtain them. The
rails of the Florida Railroad were subject to attempts by the Confederate
government to impress them for use on a proposed track line into Georgia,
but such plans were delayed for years by the legal maneuvering of railroad
president and former United States senator David L. Yulee. Eventually,
however, some of these iron rails were earmarked for government projects
such as the Georgia link with Florida's remaining rail system and ironclads
under construction such as the *Jackson*.[50]

The war and the Federal blockade reshaped Florida's relationship with
her neighbors and greatly altered her economic life. The peninsula state,
after rushing to secede from the Union, found itself forced to deal with a
strangling Union presence off her shores and in many of her port com-
munities. As the Federal anaconda slowly tightened its grip, Floridians
joined in the task of producing the raw materials of war from domestic
sources. Despite Florida's clear value to the rebellion, Confederate authorities lacked the military force and the will to defend the state properly.

3 Salt Production in Confederate Florida

During the antebellum years, the states that would make up the future Confederacy never lacked for the mineral sodium chloride. Salt "licks," salt springs, and the evaporation of seawater provided pioneers with the essential and at times expensive item until improved transportation and competition from imported salt made it plentiful by the mid-1840s. Cheap, high-grade, foreign salt replaced local products that had been used in the preservation of pork and other meats throughout the upper South and at the pork-packing capital of the United States, Cincinnati. Salt from Great Britain, the Mediterranean countries, and islands in the Caribbean became commonplace in most Southern states, making domestic production all but redundant. Operations like the one located at Key West, Florida, though economically viable, at times barely managed to break even. By the 1860s the only sizable salt sources available were situated in the Kanawha valley near the town of Charleston and in the mines at Saltville, both in the state of Virginia. Goose Creek, Kentucky, rounded out the list of active large-scale salt-making centers. Leaders of the future Confederate States failed to grasp how exposed these salt suppliers were to Northern attack and how much the South depended on such salt for preserving food, for tanning hides, and for other activities.[1]

Few if any residents of the lower South concerned themselves with such mundane topics as the supply of salt in 1861. The heady business of establishing a new nation from the seceded states monopolized attention. Soon, however, circumstances would thrust the subject onto center stage as inventories of salt shrank and deliveries dwindled to nothing. Imported salt no longer flowed from the trade hub at New York to Charleston or New Orleans. Ordinarily plentiful salt grew increasingly scarce as the Federal blockade reduced imports even further and heightened military demand for salted pork hastened the consumption of existing stocks. The realization quickly dawned that neither the new Confederate army nor the nation could long survive without an abundant and sure supply of the mineral once so common. Methods of salt production long abandoned, such as boiling seawater, were pressed into service to meet this new crisis. The state of Florida became an important source of salt because of its long coastline and facilities for salt making. Eventually the manufacture of salt in Florida became a vital industry contributing significantly to the Confederate war economy.

A scarcity of salt appeared throughout the Confederacy before the conflict was a year old. "No cargoes of salt being landed," lamented a contributor to *De Bow's Review;* "the value of this indispensable article [has] increased monthly proportionally to its scarcity." Prices jumped to unheard-of levels for a once-ordinary mineral, and the greed of speculators with access to stocks of salt shocked many consumers. Southerners, aghast at the spectacle of their economy being crippled by the lack of plain salt, complained that the shortage revealed some serious defects in the character and initiative of the people of the new country. "The only trouble is salt," cried the editor of the Macon *Daily Telegraph,* "and to think that salt should be scarce and high with the great Atlantic lime tub on our borders is a reflection upon the intelligence and enterprise of the Confederate States."[2]

Even Floridians were affected by the salt shortage. Many agriculturalists and townspeople found it nearly impossible to obtain salt at reasonable rates, especially after Federal troops holding Key West shut down the salt-making plants on the island. As it became obvious that no appreciable amount would be brought in by blockade runners, Floridians sought sources closer at hand. Farmers and planters first turned to the floors of their smokehouses. The earth inside these sheds contained considerable quantities of salt that could be recovered by several methods of leaching. Some even claimed that salt obtained in this fashion was of a purer quality than that produced from seawater. Unfortunately, the salt-laden soil from the smokehouses was quickly exhausted during the salt famine of 1861. Some other sources had to be found that promised a longer-term solution to the problem.[3]

The best option for Floridians manifestly was to extract salt from seawater, and soon both individuals and private companies began to manufacture the vital commodity on both the Gulf and the Atlantic coasts. Stockpiles of salt had to be accumulated to satisfy the demand of the upcoming meat-salting season in the fall of 1862. By midsummer of that year the Tallahassee *Florida Sentinel* advocated increased salt production along the coastline and urged in its columns that states and the

Confederate government assist those operating saltworks. An editorial pointed out that, although "corn and gunpowder may be necessary articles just now . . . salt is just as necessary therefore let everyone make it who can."[4]

Floridians joined other Southerners in determining the most effective method of distilling salt from seawater. To begin with, there was no consensus as to the proper kind of vessel to be used in boiling salt water. Much depended on the size of the saltworks and on the availability of the metal needed for making containers. Small operations, meant to produce only enough salt for home use, managed by employing one or two old iron sugar kettles. Larger concerns, however, often utilized steamboat boilers cut into two sections or metal harbor buoys converted into vats by local blacksmiths. One observer of Gulf coast saltworks later described them as "unique affairs" that included every conceivable iron vessel that could be pressed into service to heat salt water.[5]

Newspapers in Florida and Georgia printed detailed instructions for novices who wished to make salt. If pinewood was to be used as fuel, they were informed, only three kettles could effectively be heated by one furnace. However, four such furnaces could be connected to a common chimney ranging from ten to fifteen feet in height. Usually a three-foot-high partition ran from the mouth of each furnace back to the chimney to separate and protect each boiler. A pump to raise seawater and barrels or a cistern to hold it were necessary to contain quantities of water obtained at high tide when salt concentrations were at their peak. Dippers and skimmers for removing scum and changing water from one boiler to another completed the list of tools needed by the would-be salt maker.

In order to refine the salt, all the kettles must be filled with seawater and the contents raised to boiling temperature. As the water bubbled, the surface of each vat became covered with a thick scum that salt makers called "scrotch." Such scum was removed with a hand dipper in order to filter out impurities. As the solution in each kettle evaporated sufficiently, it was transferred to the next in the series of kettles serving as crude filters. Workers then began pouring and dipping one into another until the kettle nearest the stack held the concentrated brine. The mixture was considered to be of adequate strength when thin white foam rose to the top and collected on the sides of the kettle. Again dippers were used to scoop out the brine from the vat into barrels containing a small amount of lime, and then the compressed solution was left to settle. After a time a hole was opened in the cask to draw off most of the remaining liquid, leaving precipitated saline particles clinging to the sides of the barrel.

Next, the contents of the barrel were once again heated to boiling in the kettle nearest the furnace, and any resulting scum was removed by hand. The process was repeated until all the water in the brine was evaporated; then the salt was filtered out and placed in baskets to drip dry. Advanced facilities boasted pans and square vats lined with sheet metal for more efficient extraction of the scrotch. But small salt refiners made do with common equipment for what in reality was an uncomplicated procedure. A standard one-hundred-gallon sugar caldron had the capacity to make two and one-half to three bushels of salt in a twenty-four-hour period. Saltworks of any size generally emitted a strong odor from the boiling brine that, along with the smoke from the furnaces, alerted downwind friend and foe alike to its active operation.[6]

With the price of salt rising almost weekly, many Georgians and Alabamans set up operations along the Florida coasts making salt for consumption in their home states without obtaining permission from Florida authorities. Unable to stop such exploitation of their state's natural resources, the Florida legislature in December 1862 issued an invitation to citizens of the other Confederate states to manufacture salt locally. In this manner all those out-of-state salt makers already at work were legalized. On this matter Florida and her contiguous neighbors showed a considerable degree of cooperation: the same legislature that welcomed non-Floridians into the patriotic enterprise had previously enacted laws designed to control the making, sale, and export of high-priced commodities such as salt. These regulations had little impact as saltworks stacks multiplied on Florida's Gulf shores.[7]

Earlier in 1862, when Georgians had begun arriving on the same coastline to reconnoiter and claim prime locations for saltworks, one such adventurer, William R. Barnes, visited Saint Andrews Bay on the panhandle and found it to be well suited for salt production. He reported that the sheltered bay offered such advantages to salt makers as water with high saline concentrations and ample forests for fuel. Various secluded arms or bayous extended from the bay, whose shallow water and sand bars shielded workers from attacks by Union gunboats. Because Saint Andrews Bay was located relatively close to the banks of the Apalachicola River and its steamers, salt from this area could be easily moved into the heart of Georgia or Alabama. Barnes was confident that the site could supply the salt requirements of both Florida and his home state to the north. "If this be true," Barnes concluded in a report of his finding, "operations should be commenced at an early date; the prospect of an abundance of meat next winter is now good, but we must have salt to save it."[8]

Barnes's report, published by newspapers in Columbus, Macon, and Atlanta in May 1862, raised interest in the development of Florida as a supplier of salt for the southeastern section of the Confederacy. Inflation by then had gripped the country, and most cities witnessed rapid jumps in salt prices in the spring and summer. Atlanta offers the best example of the upward spiral in salt costs during the middle months of 1862: In March a single sack of salt cost $22, but by 16 April a similar bag went for $35. In May salt in the markets of Atlanta reached the unbelievable price of $40 per sack, when it could be had at all. A concerned Governor Joseph Brown communicated to the state legislature that such prices and the difficulties in securing a supply were causing unrest among the people of Georgia. Eventually state officials began seizing private stocks to stop speculation and insure a fair distribution of what salt existed within its borders.[9]

The salt famine continued to increase in the lower South despite such efforts as Brown's, and many observers believed it to be more dangerous to the cause of Southern independence than all of Lincoln's armies combined. "We will be in a dreadful condition unless we get salt," an editor of the Atlanta *Southern Confederacy* wrote in May 1862. Other editors urged individuals to go to the coast and make salt for themselves. Every salt consumer, they warned, must become a salt producer either in person or through an agent working the kettles. Only by wholesale public involvement could the estimated twenty thousand bushels of salt consumed daily in the Confederacy be provided at affordable rates. Some Georgians looked to the Atlantic, and others to Florida's long Gulf coast, from which encouraging reports of great salt potential circulated.[10]

Concerned civic leaders cast about for solutions to the salt shortage. They eventually suggested two ways of making the needed salt, by private enterprise and by public ventures. Partnerships conducted for profit seemed too small to meet the needs of the general populace, so calls went out for the formation of joint stock companies to construct large saltworks. Merchants in many Georgia towns, desperate for the mineral, formed such companies, and stock in them was quickly purchased by both patriots and those seeking good investments in the midst of economic uncertainty. Suitable locations for works not exposed to raids by the Federals were eagerly sought.[11]

In Columbus, for example, a Salt Association was founded for these purposes and agents were sent into Florida to survey the bays and inlets for a site for a projected salt-extraction plant. In June 1862, Colonel A. W. Redding of Chattahoochee County reported on his search for a proper locality to manufacture salt for Columbus. He recommended a secluded section of the west Florida coast. Easy access to the site, plentiful wood, ample forage for cattle and draft animals used in hauling, and no heavy tax on salt making caused this Florida location to appear very promising. Redding estimated that the labor of four hands with eighty- to one-hundred-gallon kettles could extract ten bushels of superior-quality salt from seawater each day. The Salt Association's executive committee heartily agreed with Redding's conclusion that the Florida spot offered a cheap, safe, and convenient place for boiling salt water. The owners of the Columbus salt plant, for security reasons, did not reveal the exact location of their establishment to any of the local press, but it was probably positioned somewhere on the shores of Saint Andrews Bay.[12]

In another case George Curtis, a citizen of Augusta, Georgia, approached Governor Milton with a proposal to set up a saltworks on the Florida coast employing at least a dozen laborers. Milton probably gave his official consent to the plan, for salt, boiled not far from the state capital, soon rolled back along the wagon roads to Augusta. A reporter for the Charleston *Daily Courier* witnessed eleven such wagons in November 1862 passing through the streets of Tallahassee on their way from Georgia to the coastal saltworks. These teamsters or their employers paid sixteen dollars per bushel, which was the current rate on the shore at the time, but the selling price in Augusta was no doubt much higher.[13]

Most of the lower counties in southwest Georgia eventually operated saltworks in north Florida. Thomas County, for example, maintained kettles at Deadman's Bay near the mouth of the Steinhatchee River on the Gulf coast until they were demolished by Union raiders in 1864. This and similar works had created thousands of bushels of sea salt by the beginning of 1863, and this salt flowed northward into Georgia by oxcart, mule-drawn wagon, or river packet. One Floridian cashed in on the new boom market by shipping salt from a camp near Saint Marks to Macon, where he sold seventy-five bushels for about three thousand dollars. Government wagons also regularly carried salt to the Confederate supply base at Savannah. By the end of 1862 no Georgian could deny the importance of Florida saltworks to Georgia's economy and the feeding of its people.[14]

Alabamans as well as Georgians turned to Florida as a source of salt when they experienced the same shortages and spiraling prices. In 1861 the state government intervened by seizing fourteen hundred sacks of salt belonging to a group of speculators attempting to convey it across the Georgia border to Columbus in hopes of reaping a huge profit from its sale, while Alabama residents went without. Despite salt boiling along Mobile Bay and a significant concentration of works at Bon Secour Bay, Alabama quickly faced the same situation in regard to salt supplies as neighbor states. Crippling salt deficiencies demanded action by governmental officials without delay. "The salt question is hourly increasing in magnitude and importance," wrote the state adjutant and inspector-general George Goldwaite early in 1862. "Salt is in very great demand

here," he continued, "and every artifice and fraud is resorted to by speculators either in this state or Georgia."[15]

In April 1862 Alabama's governor, John G. Shorter, officially requested
permission from Florida to send parties into that state to create new
saltworks along the Gulf coast. Shorter proposed dispatching armed
bodies of men to make salt; they would be available for use by Florida
authorities against any Federal intrusions. This company had license to
produce salt for distribution by Alabama governmental representatives
only. The Alabaman hoped that the projected saltworks might generate
enough salt to meet his state's minimum requirements at least partially.
Florida's Governor Milton, while sure that he lacked the legal authority
to grant extensive use of any of the state's public lands for such uses,
nevertheless considered that the crisis justified agreeing to Alabama's plea
for salt factories at any point on Florida's panhandle coast. "The people of
Florida," Milton informed Shorter, "will be glad if Alabama shall by her
own enterprise be able to supply herself with salt by manufacture on our
Coast or elsewhere."[16]

As a result of this arrangement Alabama natives, either in state service
or as private workers, made salt in west Florida throughout the remaining war years. They ran the same risks from enemy attacks and enjoyed
the same potential gains as Floridians and Georgians employed in the
same hot work. Many were active on the banks of the western section of
the Saint Andrews Bay, tending their kettles and skimming scrotch.
Their finished product, loaded on wagons, followed the trails to Marianna and then turned north toward Eufaula, Alabama. From there the
salt was shipped to the capital at Montgomery for distribution. Thus,
Florida salt found its way into yet another Confederate state, where it
contributed greatly to the war effort.[17]

Floridians took pride in what was being accomplished along their
seacoasts by the end of 1862. Both the quality and quantity of salt
produced had improved during the past year. The many thousands
of bushels brought into the market tended to stabilize prices in the
Florida-Georgia-Alabama region and even decreased them in some areas.
Surprisingly large numbers of people were boiling their own salt in small
operations at sites where a short time previously there was only empty
wilderness. The editor of the Tallahassee _Floridian and Journal_ urged skep-
tics in December to "visit our bays and see our sturdy farmers with
kettles and furnaces of all shapes and sizes lining the beach, busily engaged in condensing the briny fluid into an article so essential."[18] In this
fashion the war magnified an antebellum enterprise of small scale and
turned it into a major industry of the first importance to the Confederate
economy.

Probably the greatest concentration of salt manufacturing during the conflict was located on or near Saint Andrews Bay in Washington County. This Gulf inlet was divided into three interior bays, into which several creeks or small rivers emptied. These streams ran through numerous salt marshes that were excellent for salt making. A period of drought lasting several years had reduced the flow of fresh water into the bay and increased salinity in the waters of the area. Pine forests stood ready to supply fuel for the fires. Also, a fairly extensive series of wagon trails connected the bays with towns to the north such as Marianna in Jackson County. Significantly, the location was difficult to approach from the Gulf, and attacking Union forces rarely achieved tactical surprise. Try as they might, the Federal naval forces never managed to eradicate the saltworks from Saint Andrews Bay nor to stop the salt from reaching the rest of the Confederacy.[19]

The western arm of Saint Andrews Bay probably hosted the most salt-making facilities of all sizes because of its near-perfect combination of fuel, accessibility, and seclusion and was possibly the best site available in the lower South. "The salt operations are going on at West Bay as extensively as ever," wrote a correspondent to Governor Milton in December 1862. The "very extensive flats there affords ample room for thousands of works, where water is obtained in shallow wells."[20] Large works using steamboat boilers and numerous chimneys competed with temporary plants designed to refine enough salt for family or plantation consumption. Some twenty miles west lay an inlet known as Lake Ocala, which supplied not less than three different establishments that used adapted steamer boilers and seven kettles with a combined capacity of 130 bushels per day. Such an output made the works on the shores of this lake frequent targets for Union sailors bent on breaking up the business, and they suffered from such assaults.[21]

Federal plans to stamp out the making of salt on Saint Andrews Bay proved a herculean task and in the end unattainable. At night from the decks of their ships out in the Gulf sailors plainly saw the glow from the multitude of fires at the works and yearned to wreck them. In 1863 and 1864 the bark USS *Restless,* Acting Master William R. Browne commanding, conducted extensive raids against rebel saltworks up and down the bay. Landing parties cut up or smashed to pieces the boilers and kettles, destroyed stocks of salt, pulled down chimneys and furnaces, burned structures and wagons, and enabled slave workers to escape. Such raids were usually bloodless and uncontested, because the salt workers had ample time to take to their heels and had little inclination to offer any resistance. Despite such devasting attacks, the sites were placed back in operation in what seemed to Union naval officers an all-too-brief period.

But all hoped that their exertions indirectly struck telling blows at the rebel armies.[22]

Acting Master Browne continued his campaign against the enemy ashore, but with saltworks being built faster than he and his men could destroy them, some of the vigor displayed earlier waned under the broiling semitropical sun. After an amphibious sweep of the western arm of the bay in April 1864, he passed along information that several small concerns were boiling salt on the western half of Saint Andrews Bay, but on hearing the rebels intended to construct more elaborate saltworks for the Confederate government, he decided not to strike at them until construction was finished.[23] The crew of the *Restless* learned a month later that even after a new series of raids, two hundred works still functioned on the bay. Even worse, the salt makers now stockpiled large numbers of new boilers to replace any lost to the Yankees before the Federal sailors and marines had a chance to row back to their vessels. Salt produced on Saint Andrews Bay continued preserving food for Confederate soldiers and civilians despite all Union efforts until the conclusion of hostilities.[24]

Moving in a southeasterly direction along the Gulf, Cape San Blas and the inlet it formed were the next centers of salt production on the peninsula. Known as Saint Josephs Bay, its sheltered waters offered many of the same advantages as Saint Andrews, with thick woods and limitless salt water. The abandoned town of Saint Joseph on the mainland provided ready materials for chimneys and furnaces. It soon came to the attention of the Union blockaders that salt for the rebels was boiling near the lighthouse on the cape and along the bay. Action from the bluejackets came quickly. On 8 September 1862, men from the USS *Kingfisher* landed and gave salt makers still present a generous two hours to clear out, which they did, taking four cartloads of salt with them. The sailors then proceeded to smash the two-hundred-bushel-a-day plant. Upon completion the weary men returned to their waiting ship. Putting the best possible face on his success, the captain of the *Kingfisher* in his official report of the action wrote that the raid on the beach at Saint Josephs Bay "created great excitement throughout Georgia and Florida, these works having been the main source on which these states relied for a supply of salt." The officer likened his sweep to a great victory on land. To him it seemed a greater injury to the Confederate cause than if he had captured twenty thousand rebel soldiers.[25]

Union warships continued visiting Saint Josephs Bay well into the third year of the war, in hopes of suppressing the salt makers. One large work that fell victim to their energies consisted of thirty boilers ten to fifteen feet in length set in a foundation of brick. Twenty yards from these boilers lay a vat for holding seawater nearly forty feet in diameter. From

Harper's Weekly *view of a saltworks on Florida's Gulf coast in 1862. (Photograph courtesy of Florida State Archives)*

this container water flowed to the waiting caldrons through five couplings of two-inch pipe. All this ingenuity went under the sledgehammer, and a large wood pile was put to the torch for good measure. Like Saint Andrews, Saint Josephs Bay supplied an undetermined, though no doubt considerable, amount of salt in the face of determined enemy efforts to halt its production. The salt industry displayed a remarkable resiliency in spite of widespread destruction at the hands of the Yankees. Frustrated, the captain of the USS _Ethan Allan_ complained that, while undertaking a cruise off Saint Josephs, his men put out of commission four saltworks, but more popped up along the shoreline daily.[26]

The next salt-producing area on the Gulf coast lay along the rivers, creeks, and marshes south of Tallahassee and west of the Saint Marks River. By the end of 1862 some twenty-five companies operated salt-making equipment in the general vicinity and turned out a product known for its high quality. The banks of a stream known as Goose Creek, combined with the swamps nearby, hosted the highest concentration of saltworks east of Saint Andrews Bay. The Goose Creek wetlands, thousands of acres in size and dotted with occasional small pine-covered islands, contained the saline water needed for the refining process. Workers here dug wells three to seven feet in depth and waited for the rising tide to send water laden with salt oozing into the holes. The best water from such wells yielded one bushel of salt for every seventy-five gallons of water drawn, unfortunately a lower ratio than that for water taken directly from the Gulf of Mexico. "The quality of salt that is made here on this beach varies from the best Liverpool [salt] to a very poor article," reported a visitor to the region.[27]

Such large-scale salt making attracted the attention of the ever-vigilant Union blockaders. In November 1862 one of the warships in the blockade squadron steamed close to shore and began shelling the Goose Creek works with its heavy guns. The naval gunfire, lacking the necessary range, did little to damage the works along the stream, although the peace of mind of those camped near the boilers suffered greatly. Threatened landings created a panic among the workers, who rapidly abandoned their sites, taking their salt and slaves with them. When no Yankees appeared, the men drifted back to the creek and resumed their work. The Saint Marks area, unlike Saint Andrews Bay, lacked the natural protection that gave fair warning of hostile Federal movements. Even the eventual assignment of Confederate troops to guard the saltworks only marginally increased their security. Tallahassee resident Susan Bradford Eppes, whose family operated a site worked by slaves from their plantation, remembered how the coast during this period was "a rather dangerous place to work, for the Yankee gunboats can get very near the coast and they try shelling the works."[28]

Dangers from the sea hardly deterred Floridians or others from this essential and lucrative war industry. Daniel C. Barrow, a planter of means from northeastern Georgia, owned a saltworks near Saint Marks run by an overseer named William Braswell. Barely literate, Braswell laboriously composed lengthy reports from the coast to his employer; these letters paint a detailed picture of day-to-day life at a saltworks in Civil War Florida. With so many individuals and companies interested in establishing their own plants, arguments over claims to land suitable for salt making grew heated and often resembled feuds over site ownership common to the California goldfields of the 1850s. In 1863 Barrow stood in danger of losing a large section of marsh below his works, reputedly one of the best locations on the coast. Overseer Braswell fended off advances of rival salt companies and worked to improve Barrow's plant by constructing crude shanties in the piney woods to house his woodcutters and mules.[29]

January 1864 found little salt manufacturing at the Barrow works, only the chopping and hauling of wood in anticipation of need for the furnaces. Braswell, who managed to sell the last of the salt stored in his sheds, informed Barrow in Georgia that the remaining stock was retailed at the best price available at the time due to lower demand. He assured the planter that he was taking good care of both the mules and the field hands under his control and looked forward to the coming salt-making season. Heavy rains at the time made neighborhood roads almost impassable; empty wagons hardly moved, much less wagons filled with heavy sacks of salt. The primitive roads provided the only means to get salt from the shore to the inland towns desperate for it and return with supplies and wood for the fires. In many cases the condition of roads set the pace of salt production.[30]

Braswell estimated that his people could make an average of 150 bushels per week with a potential of 200. Only the possibility of destruction by Yankee raiders worried the overseer. "I don't fear being taken or losing my stock for we can see them here for 4 or 5 miles," he wrote, but concern about becoming a Federal prisoner crept into later notes. By mid-March Braswell and company had made 764 bushels of salt, a figure that calmed the Georgian and influenced his decision to remain at his post. Salt sold on the coast then for fifteen dollars a bushel, and Braswell supplied Barrow and his partners for the coming year before selling to anyone else. The salt produced here went north to Columbus via Tallahassee and from there to its final destinations. Although arranging for such transportation proved bothersome, Braswell managed to get his product from the Saint Marks marshes to locations deep in rural Georgia.[31]

The Barrow saltworks was only one of many manned by slaves; their labor played a key role in Florida salt manufacturing, as it did in other sectors of the Confederate war economy. Blacks tended kettles and oversaw the various stages of the salt process, usually under the watchful eye of a white overseer. The large amounts of wood needed to fuel the boilers necessitated almost continuous timber cutting. As ready stands of trees decreased, such wood had to be hauled in from ever-greater distances. Slaves spent long hours engaged in this arduous task, as well as in building huts and storage sheds. Many worked at caring for the draft animals as well, and black teamsters drove wagons loaded with salt to sell in Georgia and Alabama and returned with cargoes of provisions and fodder.[32]

In addition to this, many planters continued the prewar practice of dispatching gangs during slack periods to boil salt for their plantations' yearly needs. For example, hands from the El Destino plantation in Leon County spent a week working the kettles in December of 1862. With such a potential for monetary gain, many slaveholders greatly desired to place their slaves in a position to learn the salt-maker's art. Blacks themselves warmed to the idea of earning considerable amounts of cash over and above what their masters received for their labors. A Jackson County merchant, Ethelred Philips, testified that slaves strongly desired to remain at the works and that they enjoyed their toil on the coast. He wrote that several blacks "would be delighted to return after a visit and make salt for they have made near 400 for themselves. . . . They were willing to pay their passage."[33]

Were masters fearful of losing their slaves to Union raids or to desertions to the blockading warships? Philips, for one, believed that such apprehensiveness was unnecessary, based on his personal experiences with slave salt workers. In June 1862 he wrote that he had no concern about the loss of any of his bondsmen, since they relished the work and greatly feared the Yankees. Despite Philips's opinion, with the passage of time defections increased among the slave labor force as a result of more frequent Union attacks near the coasts. By the end of 1863 the merchant Philips sadly recorded the loss of dozens of laborers to the Federals, who often polled captured slaves and took away all of them who expressed a desire to leave.[34] Some slave owners protested when Union forces sheltered escapees from the saltworks. Late in 1862 a Georgian operating a plant on Saint Josephs Bay, for example, pursued a slave attempting to seek refuge in a small boat on board a blockader. After angrily climbing onto the deck of the ship, the white salt maker was confronted by not one but a dozen runaways. When he requested that all persons be returned to their rightful owners, the vessel's captain replied with authority that all who wished to stay aboard would remain because he considered them spoils of war or "contrabands." Later in the war all doubts vanished as to whether slaves working near the coast might flee if given the opportunity to join the Federals. An employee at the Barrow works reported to his absentee superior in 1864, "most any of the negroes will go to the Yankees if they get half a chance. I see a wide difference in them [from] three months ago."[35]

In the spring of 1864 Union forces stepped up strikes on saltworks in the Saint Marks area. One group raiding up Goose Creek in March captured 2,000 bushels of salt, 165 kettles, 43 eight-hundred-gallon boilers, and 98 brick furnaces. A Union officer in this instance noted that works had been destroyed having the capacity of making 2,400 bushels per day. However, saltworks like this one continued to rise from the ruins and quickly resumed production at near their former rate. At the same time the Federals expanded operations westward from the mouth of the Saint Marks River, hopeful that they could frighten some workers into evacuating the coast for good. In other attacks boatloads of blue-clad sailors smashed works located in the marshes of Dickinson's Bay and on the southern shore of James Island, known as Alligator Bay or Harbor. Again, at most of the sites the salt makers returned soon afterward, to the great annoyance of Union naval commanders.[36]

Assaults from the sea were not the only dangers facing salt workers on the Florida coasts. At times the weather posed a deadly peril. On 27 May 1863, to cite one instance, a large tropical storm struck the peninsula without warning and devastated the Saint Marks region. Fierce winds and rapidly rising water caught most of the salt manufacturers by surprise, and they were unable to save much from the flood tides. Furnaces were swept away, and large iron kettles were carried hundreds of yards from the works. Houses, tents, and boats were demolished, and at least forty thousand bushels of salt were returned to the sea. Some thirty-five mules and eight oxen drowned in the floodwaters, and more than thirty salt makers, black and white, perished. Later many dead mules were found still tied to trees where they had been left by owners who were hastily loading salt in a futile effort to salvage something. But the wall of water rushing in from the Gulf left them no chance of escape.[37]

When the killer storm had passed, surviving owners of the flooded salt plants quickly commenced repairs. At the Augusta saltworks, for example, reconstruction proved difficult, as the site had suffered hurricane damage estimated at fifteen thousand dollars. James Barrow visited his father's establishment some weeks later and even then noticed signs of destruction caused by the gale. Furthermore, an outbreak of fever among the Floridians and the Georgians on the coast soon afterward was blamed on the storm and on the flooding of rivers and streams that it had caused.

Another frequenter of the coast recorded in his diary that "down here particularly among the salt makers, an immense quantity of salt was destroyed . . . and worse of all many negroes and a few white people were drown [_sic_]."[38] Nevertheless, the urgent demand for salt left little inclination to mourn the losses.

Some forty miles east of Saint Marks along the curving coastline, another concentration of saltworks added to Florida's production of the mineral. There, the coast of Taylor County, like that of the Saint Marks area, possessed the creeks and swampy flatlands that the salt makers found so attractive. Smoke from the fires of the salt plants filled the air as far south as the estuary of the Steinhatchee River, although the operations in this area tended to be on a smaller scale than those to the west. One estimate of persons engaged in the salt-making business placed the total at near five hundred. Large numbers of dealers from other states constantly came down to the shore for the purpose of purchasing the salt produced by local manufacturers. The Union navy lacked the ships and the men necessary to impede production effectively in this area, but there were occasional attacks. During one raid launched against a saltworks on the banks of the Warrior River in June 1864, the Federals deprived the rebels of twenty-seven kettles of the newest type, each lined with porcelain to speed the filtering process.[39]

Union forces also campaigned against saltworks located in the general region of Cedar Keys. In October 1862 they destroyed at least fifty boilers near the railroad line running toward Fernandina. Confederate troops in the vicinity were able to offer only feeble resistance to such advances, much to the dismay of local residents. After one successful mission the captain of the USS _Tahoma_ bragged that "the rebels here needed a lesson and they have had it."[40] Small salt makers managed to evade the Federals and provide some salt for home consumption. Of course, producers in the Gulf Hammock area contributed little to overall efforts to supply the lower South with Florida salt, but they provided useful service to local farmers depending on them.[41]

Small to medium-sized works sprang up on the shores of Tampa Bay as well, to take advantage of high prices. By March 1864 salt from the plants north of the bay sold for ten dollars a bushel. One of these manufacturers, short of fodder, offered to barter one bushel of salt for two bushels of corn. Another salt plant in Hernando County, capable of making ten to fifteen bushels a day, was offered for sale for eight thousand dollars, payments to be made half in cash and the rest in installments. Other persons constructed works on Tampa Bay itself at places known as Rocky Point and Gadsden's Point. Output from these works was only average, but nonetheless they were noticed by Union blockaders hovering just outside the entrance of the bay. Acting on information supplied by a Unionist resident, boats from the USS *Sunflower* and the USS *James L. Davis* wrecked a total of sixteen boilers and accompanying structures during the month of June 1864. As at the other salt plants on the coast, such damage merely slowed the pace of production and never completely halted it. Yet, Federal naval officers continued to order attacks because they knew just how valuable such places were to the rebel cause. In addition, the raids were a means of occupying their crews during the long periods of inactivity on the blockade line.[42]

Sometimes raids were anything but routine for the Yankee sailors and marines involved. A force sent to smash a work near Rocky Point encountered not only salt boilers but a unit of Confederate cavalrymen, who drove the mariners back to their boats in a disorderly retreat. Six of the luckless sailors remained behind on the beach as prisoners after the Federals hurriedly rowed away from the shore. After this rebuff, the commander of the East Gulf Blockading Squadron, Rear Admiral Cornelius K. Stribling, issued a warning to his captains about being too reckless in attempts to damage enemy saltworks and suggested more caution in the future, regardless of how tempting the target. Such expeditions, he felt, "are too frequently, I fear, undertaken without due caution and without regard to consequences in hope of doing something to get . . . prominently into notice."[43]

While the attention of all concerned with salt making in Florida was directed to the Gulf coast, it is important to remember that salt was prepared as well on the shores of the Atlantic. Eastern Florida suffered badly from the lack of salt throughout 1862 and naturally turned to the sea for relief. The Charleston *Daily Courier* in February proudly carried an item on how a South Carolinian, Major Thomas J. Starke, made salt on the coast near Saint Augustine at the rate of some six bushels per day from his two boilers. Citizens of Volusia County to the south gathered household pots and buckets and rode ox-drawn carts to the ocean in order to boil salt water for the mineral it contained. Fearful of losing their new supply while crossing streams on the journey homeward, many placed their salt in smaller pans or pails and waded creeks with these balanced on their heads. Occasionally blockade runners touching on the same coast brought salt as part of their cargoes, but little reached the poorer classes, who needed it the most. A leading resident of east Florida, James M. Hunter, complained to Governor Milton about some five hundred bushels of such salt abandoned near New Smyrna by the government. He went on to express concern that it would fall into the hands of private speculators and be sold for exorbitant prices unless state officials promptly acted.[44]

Units of the Union navy patrolling off the eastern coast of Florida conducted antisalt operations much like their fellow tars in the Gulf. Well aware of the shortage of salt in the interior, officers felt certain that nothing could strike a heavier blow at the Confederates than the quick and total elimination of all saltworks on the Atlantic shore. In order to accomplish this goal, a force of small and shallow-drafted vessels able to maneuver in the coves and narrow inlets would be required. Such a squadron had the potential of doing great harm to the "Southrons" at a point of perceived weakness. Amphibious raids launched from the blockading ships broke up plants from the mouth of the Saint Marys River to the Indian River Inlet south of Cape Canaveral. Few if any of these targeted operations rivaled the saltworks at Saint Andrews Bay or on Goose Creek; they appear, to a large extent, to have supplied only local needs. The salt they made had only a minimal impact on one corner of the Confederate States of America.[45]

Union attacks were not the only obstacle to Floridians' and others' acquiring salt from the various coastal works. As in other areas of the South, individuals sought to cash in on the war-time shortage of salt and reap profits by purchasing quantities of the mineral and withholding it until demand made any asking price acceptable to desperate consumers. A mania of sorts affected many Confederate citizens to some degree as people invested currency of declining worth in commodities, such as salt, whose value only increased with time. "The truth is," editorialized the Mobile *Daily Advertiser and Register* in 1862, "a wild spirit of speculation and money making seized the public mind." Florida had no special immunity from this unpleasant by-product of the war. Its state legislature in 1861 moved to curtail rampant speculation and inflation through a series of war measures dealing with the economy. Not only were private citizens denied permission to export certain items, including salt, from the state; they were further restricted to a maximum profit of 33 percent on all commodity sales. However, a wide gulf existed between the letter of the law and the government's ability to enforce it, and blatant overcharging never completely disappeared from the marketplaces.[46]

"Florida," said its governor, "will resist to the bitter end speculation and speculation for the benefit of other localities by the sacrifice of the rights of the state." Even with such a clear declaration of intent, Governor Milton and the government of his state faced a determined foe in the struggle to end unethical practices in the salt trade. In 1862 the price of salt rose from three dollars a bushel to as high as twenty dollars in some sections of the peninsula, and hoarding it became an all-too-common practice. Often salt dealers refused to accept currency issued by Tallahassee or by the Confederacy. Prices for land suitable for the construction of saltworks soared as sharp investors bought up previously worthless coastal wetlands and leased them at high rates to salt makers. Finally in 1863 the governor and the other members of the Board of Trustees of the Internal Improvement Fund of Florida halted all sales of such lands in the public domain. This measure was designed to insure that no person could be denied or hindered by such schemes from manufacturing one of the absolute necessities of life.[47]

As in the case of public land policy, many Floridians criticized Governor Milton for not moving more quickly to deal with rapidly rising salt prices and the unavailability of salt for soldier families and the poorer segments of society. Newspaper editors contrasted Milton's record with that of Georgia's Joe Brown, then waging an energetic campaign to release stocks of salt from private hands by seizing it. Such complaints reached a peak in the fall of 1862 during the prolonged salt shortage. In the midst of governmental shortcomings, at least one citizen proposed to deal directly with the salt problem. Joseph R. Lines, a Gadsden County planter, set up a system to sell salt to soldier families at the bargain price of four dollars per bushel. Lines sent his own wagons from his home north of Quincy to the coast and bought directly from the salt boilers. He then sold it to anyone of the yeoman class or lower who was in need, making no personal profit on the transaction.[48]

Not everyone connected with the salt trade was as public-spirited as this Gadsden County agriculturalist. Georgian Daniel Barrow and his partners kept a weather eye on salt prices when deciding whether or not to sell. At the end of December 1861, when rates fell briefly to between thirty and thirty-five cents a pound, one of Barrow's associates asked if it might not be prudent to hold their salt until the spring brought increased demand and raised the market for salt. In a letter to Barrow he reasoned: "Salt will be certain to go up in the spring and can't get much lower than it is now. The present price will not pay me, after expenses are paid it will not net more than $13 to $14 per bushel and we could have sold for that at the works. If you don't need the money now I think it best to hold."[49] Eventually Barrow and company moved their salt from the coast of Florida to Columbus and then to Macon by rail, arriving when market prices had reached the desired level for its profitable disposal.

Many citizens watched such dealings with disapproval and great concern. The Macon *Daily Telegraph* echoed in print this anxiety about the large numbers of Georgians on the Florida coast making salt for purely personal reasons and not for the public good. The newspaper's editor believed boiling seawater for the creation of salt must be done as an act of patriotism and not for speculative gain. Service at a salt-producing plant was in his eyes as noble as raising food for the army.

Despite such appeals, great demand often led to bidding wars at the saltworks that boosted cost beyond the means of ordinary people. These increases in turn inflated the cost of pork, especially bacon, hurting government efforts to procure meat to feed both soldier and civilian. The answer, therefore, according to the *Daily Telegraph,* was for even more persons from Georgia to depart for Florida and work at making salt, in theory decreasing its price by increasing supply. Those so occupied served the Confederate nation as surely as soldiers in the ranks, and in fact they had the potential of making a greater impact on the war effort than those simply shouldering a rifle. Patriotism walked hand in hand with monetary pursuits in many salt enterprises, and those suffering from astronomical prices and shortages continued to grumble about the select few who were growing rich at their expense.[50]

Salt production had effects on the economic health of Florida and her neighbors beyond that of the commodity itself. The hundreds of horses and mules used in hauling salt and provisions needed at the works consumed large amounts of fodder in the form of hay and corn. Soon the price of these feeds rose in relation to demand, hurting small farmers who were trying to compete with salt makers for grains needed for their livestock. Salt workers also bid against the government for such things as draft animals, wagons, and especially rations for hungry men laboring on the coast. A large portion of the scanty meat supply in west Florida went to the hundreds employed at saltworks instead of to the Confederate armies. Later in the war shortages of goods hindered the provisioning of many salt camps, and the deteriorating economic structure reduced many to bartering salt for essential ration items. Braswell, the overseer at the Barrow works in 1865, loaded a wagon with salt and headed inland hoping to trade with a farmer for corn to feed his mules. He later complained to his employer that a lack of adequate teams kept considerable amounts of salt on the shore in danger of capture by the Federal navy.[51]

The problem of defending saltworks in Florida was an issue that reached across state lines and involved the government in Richmond. After a series of assaults in September 1862, the governor of Alabama urged that the War Department send troops to guard against the enemy's disruption of salt making by Alabamans on the Gulf coast. Alabama eventually raised volunteer companies to defend its own salt interests in Florida out of frustration with tardy Confederate responses. Florida itself acted when its General Assembly gave Governor Milton the authority to appoint officers to organize all the salt workers, excluding slaves, into a self-defense force. Any salt maker failing to participate faced possible ejection from the area and a ban on future salt making in the state. Milton called on Richmond as well to reorganize the command structure in the panhandle so as to better utilize the few regular troops in the region and thus improve the degree of protection for those occupied in the vital industry. The chief executives of both Alabama and Georgia added their vocal support to this request, fully aware of the importance of Florida sources of salt to their respective states.[52]

The remaining military reserves of Florida, much to Governor Milton's disappointment, were not used to their fullest extent in defense of the saltworks. Salt speculation and the exemption of salt makers from the 1862 Confederate draft angered many Floridians, who asked why they should be called upon to defend individuals who were reaping large profits at their expense. One gentleman, D. W. Everett, suggested a possible solution to the problem of providing a credible defense in the face of public disapproval. He proposed a new 30 percent tax on all salt made, with the revenue collected being used to defray the costs of stationing troops near major salt areas. Increased security should encourage more people to refine salt at those places, thus driving down prices and eliminating some of the animosity between salt makers and the general populace. Milton supported the plan, knowing that something had to be done before the enemy stopped or greatly reduced salt production and therefore, in Milton's words, caused "much suffering among citizens and soldiers for want of beef, bacon, and pork."[53]

In 1863 the salt workers, formed into companies, began receiving the rudiments of drill and military training. The final result did little to inspire confidence in these reluctant soldiers' ability to withstand the Federal naval attacks. Lieutenant William Fisher, commander of the salt-worker force, had some 485 men but only forty-three firearms and practically no ammunition. From his position at the Barrow plant, Braswell, the overseer, feared for his safety and at first doubted that these poorly equipped amateurs could withstand the Yankees. He grumbled, "We are not protected and I don't think we will be. . . . Fisher is trying to organize all the salt makers but what good will that do." Later the nervous overseer calmed a bit and grew more confident in the unit to which he now belonged. He felt certain that he and his fellows could defeat any crew of Union tars sent against them. But on the other hand, should a large body of troops threaten the works from the interior, Braswell and the others planned to beat a hasty retreat with as much salt and other property as they could move.[54]

The conscription status of salt workers, so unpopular with the bulk of the population of Florida, plagued salt refining throughout the rest of the Civil War. Because the Confederate Congress exempted men in war-related occupations, salt boiling, like other deferred forms of employment, offered a tempting haven for many who sought to avoid being forced into one of the fighting regiments of the Confederate army. More than a few headed for Florida with this goal in mind. Governor Milton sadly admitted that possibly thousands of able-bodied young men from his state and others loitered on the coasts pretending to make salt; he knew personally of one group of ten men who had not one single sack of salt to show after more than a month at the works! These frauds enjoyed their masquerade, unaware that the Union navy considered all persons at or near the shoreline to be abetting the rebel cause, and if captured they were to be treated as legitimate prisoners of war.[55]

The dangers of enemy attack in some ways aided those using salt making as a means to evade service in the Confederate army. One salt maker, Joshua H. Frier, remembered that "one of the principle charms of the salt works was that it was too near the gun boats for enrolling officers to be meddlesome as they were making themselves in the interior. To a good many they were making life a burden by threatening and pretending they were going to send them off. Of course they were not subject to the conscription act but they knew the Government hated to lose the opportunity of an able-bodied man."[56] Conscription officials in Florida, under pressure to find men for the ranks as the war entered its third year, longed to induct as many salt workers as they could locate. The Richmond government shared this desire and at the end of 1864 issued a War Department general order giving enrolling officers the power to draft salt makers on the Florida coasts.

Realizing this new policy would hinder if not cripple an essential war industry, civilian and local military leaders on the peninsula rallied to stop the government from breaking up experienced teams of salt workers. The commanding officer of the Florida Reserves, General William Miller, warned that Florida saltworks produced nearly all the salt consumed in southern Georgia and Alabama, as well as providing large quantities directly to the Confederate government. In the face of Miller's arguments the exemption was restored, but enrolling officials watched the workers carefully to insure that all indeed boiled salt regularly. An investigation of several of Captain Fisher's newly promoted men began late in April 1865 in hopes of uncovering a few "lay outs" for the shrinking rebel battalions. General Miller again intervened and directed that Fisher be allowed to carry on with his business until a further inquiry could be concluded. Since there was still urgent need for salt, the general wanted agents responsible for conscription to be as liberal as possible in granting deferments and keeping men at the works.[57]

Army needs for manpower impacted the Barrow works as it did all the others in Florida. Braswell, still in charge in the spring of 1865, had a dispute with the owner over the condition of the works. Colonel Barrow

had received reports describing the plant as being in a dilapidated state
with cracked kettles and boilers. An associate of the planter's, J. W.
Williams, after inspecting the work, estimated that an average of two
bushels per day might still be expected after an overhaul of the plant's
equipment. Salt prices promised to remain high, because many salt
makers were abandoning the business on account of increased difficulty
in acquiring provisions in the western section of Florida. Braswell himself left the salt trade, probably aware that Barrow was on the verge of
discharging him, and entered the Confederate service. A replacement put
the works in order and refined pounds of salt through the month of
April, shipping it by the regular route northward into Georgia.[58]

Union naval forces kept up the pressure on salt makers by raids until
the end of February 1865, then practically ceased such operations. With
the war seemingly already won, captains may not have wished to risk
their ships and personnel in attacking shore installations no longer important to victory. Many of these same saltworks ironically outlasted the
blockade itself and continued making salt well into 1866. Then more
traditional sources made the enterprises unprofitable, and they faded
away from the economic landscape of the postwar South. So ended Florida's most successful manufacturing endeavor during the Civil War.

Why the government did so little to protect and promote salt making
in Florida remains a question that probably will never be completely
answered. In any case the industry seemed by nature almost destruction-
proof; works wrecked numerous times somehow managed to return
to production after quick repairs. The Union forces learned, as would
others in the future waging economic warfare against an enemy, that
industrial targets large or small require constant attack to end their productivity and that the only definite means of ensuring such a goal is the
actual occupation of the sites by land forces. So it was with the saltworks
in Florida, which Federal troops never permanently captured.[59]

The manufacture of salt, in monetary terms, was Florida's most important contribution to the Confederate economy. At times thousands of
workers produced and forwarded salt from the coasts that went deep into
Georgia and Alabama to ease the burden of shortages among the people
in those states. So much salt left Florida that in fact natives often had
to struggle to secure some of it for their own use. An estimated ten to
twelve million dollars were invested in saltworks, and remarkable ingenuity was demonstrated by Southerners in providing essential materials. Whether motivated by patriotism, personal need, or desire for gain,
salt workers in Florida played a key and often underemphasized role in
the Confederate war effort.[60]

4 Florida Agriculture and the Confederacy

With the coming of civil war, all members of the newly formed Confederate States of America found themselves quickly forced to evaluate their material resources for an armed conflict with the North. When the road to victory and independence grew longer and more difficult than anticipated, the agricultural value of the lower South to the rest of the Confederacy rose with each Union land advance. Under the circumstances Florida's worth as a granary and butcher shop for the rebel cause increased markedly. In the beginning the peninsula's possible contribution to the South's war effort was exaggerated by prewar tales of balmy climate and agricultural abundance. Whether the state could actually live up to the high expectations placed upon it as a source of food was a question yet to be answered. Change bordering on revolution swept through its farming economy as Florida's experience in the end mirrored that of other Southern states. Heretofore, scholars have generally neglected to assess fully the extent to which Florida contributed the bounty of its lands to the rebel government and to the armies striving to give the Confederacy legitimacy as a separate country.

Although the industrial weaknesses of the Confederate States in 1861 were a source of general concern, the agricultural strength of the region led Southerners to believe in the ultimate success of their movement. In the months after Fort Sumter, editors bragged of the new country's ability to produce all the breadstuffs needed along with ample supplies of beef, pork, and bacon. These confident pronouncements were echoed even in the journals published in the North. The *Knickerbockers Magazine,* for example, examined the South's agriculture and recommended that the truncated United States make peace with the Confederacy as soon as possible in order to avoid the prospect of starvation in the Northern states. Another article, in the New York *Journal of Commerce,* reprinted in the Saint Augustine *Examiner,* dealt with the southernmost of the Confederate states directly. It concluded that Florida was well adapted to the production of corn and wheat in abundance. The writer found no reason for supposing that any sort of famine would occur in the South, even if the war turned out to be a protracted contest.[1]

After the eventful summer of 1861 both Confederate and Union forces were content for several months to plan and enlarge their armies for future campaigns. In the same period the civilian population attempted to adjust to war-time conditions. Southern cotton growers were particularly hurt as the tightening Federal blockade hindered their trying to market bumper cotton crops. Especially troublesome for them, the American merchant fleet, based for the most part in New England, would no longer be carrying their bales to the mills of Great Britain and the rest of Europe. Southern leaders advised that cotton production be reduced so as to entice the British or the French into intervening on the side of the Confederacy to ensure their cotton supply. Also, vacant lands could be converted to growing food crops.

"Farm products will be in demand," the Atlanta *Southern Confederacy* promised planters, "and every bushel of corn or pound of meat will bring the best of prices." Many Florida growers responded to this advice by voluntarily limiting their acres sowed in cotton in 1861. Patriotism combined with potential profits held down the number of Florida long- and short-staple cotton bales harvested, although King Cotton did not abdicate his throne without reluctance. Wise agriculturalists simply opted for more diverse crops in the midst of uncertain times and markets.[2]

By the summer of 1862 the volume of Florida cotton was showing a steady decline, but rumors of peace in early 1863 led many growers to increase their cotton acreages in expectation of a resumption of the bull market of the 1850s. Self-regulation by Florida farmers failed when they were faced with choosing between the interests of the Confederacy and those of their own plantations. Although a widespread campaign by state newspapers and civic leaders against overproduction had some effect, Florida's increasing importance as a food supplier for the Confederacy prompted the legislature to follow Georgia's example by enacting laws in 1863 that set limits on nonfood crops. Under this legislation no more than one acre of cotton and one-fourth acre of tobacco per field hand could be legally cultivated, with violators facing a one-thousand-dollar fine for each acre grown that exceeded the acreage restrictions, taking into account any exemptions that had been granted. The Gainesville *Cotton States* ironically declared in its columns that victory over excess cotton growing had been achieved in 1864, claiming to "hear nothing about cotton planting these days, which we regard as a good sign."[3]

One might well ask why anyone would continue to raise cotton at all in the face of considerable public and governmental pressure not to do so. In fact, planters could offer several valid reasons for cultivating cotton despite the drive to convert the Confederacy's agriculture to foodstuffs. First, many believed in 1863 that the war would end soon and that on news of an armistice between the sections cotton would quickly flow again from Southern ports. As things stood, no Confederate law prohibited exporting cotton to Europe if a means could be found to convey it there. Second, growers in Florida and other Deep South states reasoned that cultivating a number of acres in cotton would provide them a ready cash crop needed to pay their taxes and other debts. A third motivation to continue cotton growing was the need to ensure a supply of fresh cotton seeds for use in the anticipated postwar return to King Cotton. Lastly, cotton planting offered a means for the larger planters to keep their whole slave-labor force occupied, something the less labor-intensive corn could not do.[4]

Despite crop restrictions, Florida lands remained in demand as investments for Georgians and South Carolinians throughout most of the war years. In 1863 some thirty-three thousand acres were offered in Charleston for sale to any seeking business opportunities in Florida. In the same year ninety thousand acres along the railroad line in Suwannee County went on the market. Called "one of the best and safest investments in the Confederacy" by its owners, this parcel's chief selling point was the possible yield of seven hundred to one thousand pounds of long-staple cotton to the acre. "There is more money to be made by planting on these lands than on any other in the South," ended a glowing advertisement for these sections in the Charleston *Daily Courier.* In contrast, Floridians at the time had difficulties with real-estate transactions in states like South Carolina because of the uncertainties of war-time currencies. Some even refused to rent Carolina lands to Florida citizens who intended to raise quantities of corn on them.[5]

The Confederate government was interested in Florida cotton lands as well as in the fibers they provided. Although planters faced limits on their acreages, those specifically supplying Confederate agents were free from any state crop restriction. Most of the cotton was acquired for outward-bound blockade runners leaving Florida waters. For example, the Confederate Surgeon General's Office allocated fifty thousand dollars for the purchase by a representative in Florida of an amount of cotton to be shipped and sold for the purpose of buying medical supplies. Government teamsters hauled the valuable bales to points along the coast where vessels engaged in slipping past the Federal warships waited. Since all ships competed for these prime cargoes, officials eventually established a first-come, first-served policy to guarantee fairness for all. Traffic in cotton by sea declined by 1864, mostly due to the increasing effectiveness of the Federal blockade. An agent of the Ordnance Bureau sadly reported to his Richmond superiors in February of that year that he "deemed it entirely inexpedient to make any purchase of cotton, as there exists no reasonable prospect of its exportation now, no vessels being looked for at any point on the coast pending the military operations in progress."[6]

In addition to government agencies, private individuals sought to purchase cotton, usually for speculative purposes. Governor Milton decried such "villainous traffic" being carried on by cotton traders running the blockade; he believed it to be a fundamental cause of inflation. Such activities tended, in his opinion, to encourage planters to grow additional acres of cotton in defiance of the laws, to the detriment of the general welfare. Undeterred by Milton's indignation, cotton dealers such as Savannah's Gazaway B. Lamar continued to buy cotton in north Florida in small lots of twenty to fifty bales. His Importing and Exporting Company of Georgia used warehouses in Thomasville and Quitman to store purchased cotton until it was loaded on cars of the Atlantic and Gulf line bound for Savannah itself. North Florida cotton growers readily sold to businessmen like Lamar. Charles P. Chaires of Leon County, for example, let Lamar have 172 bales at 12½ cents a pound in December 1863. Profits resulting from dealings of this type, sometimes totaling tens of thousands of dollars, kept planters willing to continue cotton as an important crop in the face of official disapproval.[7]

As in the case of cotton, tobacco growing in Florida suffered from the drive to convert to food crops. With production limited by law to a quarter acre per hand, tobacco planters faced economic extinction, and in Gadsden County a way of life ground to a halt. Nevertheless, the exportation of Florida tobacco went on well into 1863, albeit at nowhere near antebellum volume. As late as November 1861 leaf wrappers from its fields, considered choice by those experienced in the tobacco trade, still graced markets in New Orleans. Charleston, however, captured the bulk of war-time tobacco exports from its rivals. In that city, S. Wyatt and Company of East Bay Street acted as agents for the majority of Florida growers and retailed their 1861 crop. Those knowledgeable of tobacco markets suggested that South Carolinians quickly buy up this fine-quality leaf before the raising of the Union blockade created a larger demand and higher prices. While this prayed-for event never occurred before Charleston itself fell to the Federals in 1865, tobacco shops in the city had Florida cigars to sell as late as May 1863, at prices ranging from fifty to one hundred dollars per thousand.[8]

Demand for tobacco led at least one Floridian to ship it into Georgia in hopes of reaping a substantial profit. H. L. Hart, sometime agent of the Confederate Quartermaster Department, hauled a quantity of tobacco in one-pound "plugs" from Gainesville across the state line to Thomasville. Here a $.90-per-pound "chew" sold for at least $1.60. Such activities declined, however, as less and less tobacco was planted and harvested, and eventually Confederate troops stationed in Florida either received tobacco with their rations or went without. Before the end of the war, Florida, in fact, became a tobacco-importing region, with the government sending thousands of pounds into the state from Georgia fields. Like the other traditional Southern cash crop, tobacco became increasingly irrelevant as Florida endeavored to adapt itself to a new set of economic and agricultural priorities.[9]

As the rebellion continued, Florida agriculturalists placed a new emphasis on growing all the corn needed to feed both men and their animals. With corn such a prominent fixture in the Southern diet and outside sources no longer dependable, it was essential that domestic corn production be expanded. Corn crops across the lower South, including Florida, were bountiful and of high quality early in the war, easing fears of immediate food shortages. Reports from the Florida peninsula of bumper crops added to the existing rampant optimism; one newspaper editor even went so far as to predict that Florida corn reserves alone would negate Federal efforts to starve the South. "Old Abe's blockade will not have the slightest effect in this respect. Florida will much more than feed herself," concluded the Macon *Daily Telegraph* in July 1861. But before the end of that year Floridians realized that they must depend on their own resources, because government requirements absorbed much of the 1861 harvest all over the country. Cavalry and artillery horses, not to mention draft animals pulling supply wagons, consumed small mountains of corn and other grains each day. Despite his understandable concern for an adequate defense of his state, Governor Milton soon complained that cavalry units in Florida were devouring thousands of bushels of maize. In 1861 government purchases to feed cavalry mounts drove the price of corn from fifty cents per bushel to close to two dollars, not including the costs of transporting the grain across the state.[10]

Demand for corn remained strong into 1862, with Florida growers supplying markets beyond their own borders. At this time shortages of grain appeared in Georgia and elsewhere in the lower South, and corn from the peninsula made up deficits caused by crop shortfalls or problems in the distribution system. "Unless the Confederacy can raise Indian corn enough to feed herself," editorialized the Macon *Daily Telegraph,* "she may fight till doomsday and never be independent."[11] Predictions of large crops in Florida calmed apprehensions in Georgia and South Carolina that there might be a corn famine. In fact, South Carolinians owning Florida lands ordered cotton already standing in the fields to be plowed under and the acres replanted with corn, a desperate policy motivated by patriotic zeal and rising grain prices. Newspapers carried reports of farmers constructing new cribs in west Florida to store the expected large corn yields. By July growers began delivering bushels of it to points along the Florida Railroad for shipment northward, and at least a portion of this crop continued into Georgia and beyond.[12]

Optimism over food supplies in the Confederacy faded by year's end because of a prolonged drought that ruined cereal crops in an arc from Virginia to Alabama. The resulting shortages in southwestern Georgia encouraged speculators to purchase as much corn as they could locate, leaving army quartermasters with empty cribs. Fortunately, grain from Florida fields was sufficient to make up for deficiencies in part of Georgia and neighboring Alabama. Even as wagon loads of corn left the state, Governor Milton issued a warning to the War Department that the amount of grain in Florida was far from limitless. If Florida corn fell into enemy hands or, according to his opinion, was wasted nourishing idle cavalry nags, none would be available for export to other states. Shortages of bread might well lead to real suffering even among Floridians. Brigadier General Howell Cobb, then commanding the Military District of Middle Florida, concurred with Milton that corn stocks were in danger of running short or of being seized by the enemy. This threat and accompanying crop failures compounded the problem of providing soldiers and civilians with a basic staple.[13]

By 1863 the diversion of cotton acreage to corn in Florida underscored the increasing importance of the state to Confederate logistical planners. As legal crop restrictions took hold, many planters reluctantly switched to corn and grains, products that, though profitable, lacked the attraction of King Cotton. Governor Milton reminded agriculturalists in February that a failure to make full crops might mean the subjugation of the Confederacy, along with the loss of slaves and all other real property. As far away as the Confederate capital, officials expressed great interest in Florida staples, especially with the outbreak of food riots in Richmond and other major Confederate cities in the spring and summer of 1863. Jefferson Davis himself was pleased with Governor Milton's efforts to boost grain yields, and he hoped that the crops planted in his state that spring would be furnished to the government. Unfortunately, by October reports of inferior harvests in many sections of Florida reached Tallahassee, forecasting that shipments to other states might have to be curtailed and that Floridians themselves faced the possibility of serious shortages before the end of the year.[14]

In the last half of 1863 corn prices reflected the poor harvest, with the cost of a single bushel of corn going from $1.50 in June to as much as $3.00 in December. The coming of winter redoubled the need for the grain everywhere, forcing the government to increase its collection efforts. Such distant counties in south Florida as Hillsborough, Polk, and Manatee provided some 15,000 bushels of corn under the tax-in-kind program that December, but on the whole Florida suffered from a dearth of maize, the likes of which had never been seen before. A minister from Calhoun County complained to Milton that several soldier families in his flock had not seen a grain of corn since September and that without some sort of aid they faced at least another three months without a single kernel in their homes.[15]

The hardships caused by the substandard crop harvest continued into 1864. Citizens from many counties reported that their poorer neighbors were completely out of corn. The governor energetically sought relief for such individuals, asking the Confederate government to release some of the corn from its tax-in-kind warehouses scattered across the state. Having such grain rotting in cribs while people went hungry made no sense to Milton, and he asked for at least ten thousand bushels from government stockpiles. South Florida particularly needed such assistance to ward off famine among the yeoman classes, where crops were barely one-third of their usual size. Pleas for immediate delivery of one thousand bushels to ease the acute suffering appeared in at least one newspaper. The Gainesville *Cotton States* continually reminded Floridians of how much the southern half of the peninsula had contributed to the war in terms of men and provisions and that "in her hour of calamity her voice should be heard." Grain from government sources helped the people of Florida's less productive districts survive a trying period; however, no one dared predict what assistance might be expected if corn crops failed again, or from where it might come.[16]

Food shortages in Florida, chronicled at length in the state's newspapers, failed to diminish the region's exaggerated reputation as a land of abundance. At the height of the corn crisis the agricultural periodical *Southern Cultivator* printed an article written by recent visitors to the peninsula. The authors rhapsodized that: "Florida appears to us to be the granary of the Confederacy—at least there is more to eat than in any other portion we have visited. . . . Emphatically Florida is a great country—all the blessings and few of the evils of life are to be found within her borders. Flowers and pretty maids, and hog and hominy, alligators and mosquitoes."[17]

While this account may well have been written in 1863, it points out that the fundamental perception of Florida's agricultural capabilities remained alive and was exercising some influence on Confederate planning. Even the severity of the 1863–1864 corn famine and the participation of numerous farmers in the Confederate army failed to downplay the impressions lingering from prewar days. From early signs the prospects of the 1864 crop seemed good, much to the relief of Florida leaders. Supply officers particularly welcomed the news, especially those operating in the state of Georgia. The Army of Northern Virginia relied heavily on Georgia for corn and fodder because their usual sources in the Old Dominion and in North Carolina had begun to fail. Georgians could afford to be liberal in their contributions of grain, inasmuch as they knew that Florida had corn ready to forward in the event of any shortfalls. In anticipation of such demands, calls went out from Tallahassee to all working to raise corn on the peninsula to produce as much as humanly possible. Such increases might offset losses caused by Union forces operating in Georgia who cut lines of communications and ravaged food-producing areas.[18]

Despite expectations, however, Florida's corn harvest proved to be too small to meet all the demands placed upon it in the fateful year of 1864. South Carolina officials who requested a grain shipment in April to help feed the population of besieged Charleston came away empty-handed. Floridians declined to fill this order because troops then in Florida itself, especially mounted units, required much more grain than was readily available in government warehouses. Through the summer months agents combed the Florida countryside searching for corn and other types of fodder, which farmers were increasingly unwilling to sell. In July planters in Marion County reported that there were significant amounts of corn in this area of the state, but that it was held by individuals who were reluctant to let it go for any price. A great quantity of corn lay hidden and had to be ferreted out by officials. By 1865 it had become even more difficult for Confederate authorities to acquire grain, for farmers had by then mastered the art of concealing it from the eyes of probing commissaries.[19]

An offshoot of war-time corn growing in Florida involved the distilling and exportation of various types of alcohol. This time-honored solution to the problem of transporting heavy corn was utilized once more as alcohol prices soared and supplies grew short throughout the South. In a time of food shortages, however, this activity was frowned upon, and in 1862 the Florida legislature prohibited whiskey making unless under official contract. In spite of the ban, many Florida natives wished to operate stills, with or without a legal permit. Requests for exemptions arrived regularly at the state capital and in most cases were approved. An Alachua County man, for example, in August 1862 wished to convert some of his area's surplus corn into grain alcohol for civilian use. The applicant argued that the high price of transportation precluded shipping any of the corn to market and that it could be distilled to supply spirits for Floridians who had no other source because of the naval blockade. Governor Milton gave his consent, on the condition that medical alcohol alone be made. Government contracts occupied most of the distillers in Florida, whose arrangements with agencies of the Confederate War Department proved to be most lucrative. In one case a resident of Columbia County landed such a contract to supply the Confederate States Navy with seventy-five to one hundred barrels of whiskey at $4.50 a gallon. The finished product was to be delivered to Columbus, Georgia, beginning on 1 February 1863.[20]

In that year suppression of illegal whiskey selling and manufacturing became a priority of Florida state officials because rebel demands on the state's stockpiles of corn had intensified. If this distilling were to go unchecked, thousands of bushels of badly needed grain would be wasted, and the state would be denied even the chance to tax the illicit alcohol. Governor Milton charged that many persons who were seeking such contracts were attempting to avoid military service. He ordered military units to destroy any unauthorized stills, but the campaign proved less than effective. One can only imagine the flood of volunteers from the soldiers' ranks who were more than willing to seek out the potent brew!

In October Milton proclaimed that no lawfully licensed distillery operated in Florida, with the exception of one in Liberty County. However, the demand for alcohol of all types tempted unscrupulous persons with access to corn to engage in this business. Furthermore, the Confederate government freely signed contracts for the manufacture of alcohol with Floridians. In the same month that Milton issued his declaration on whiskey, Richmond contracted with one William H. Johnson of Madison County to make and deliver ten thousand gallons of it at the rate of three hundred gallons each week. Johnson agreed to transport his spirits to a designated point on the Pensacola and Georgia Railroad for five dollars a gallon. The contract also required him to sell to the government any hogs fattened on the slops left over from the distilling process.[21]

The Confederate Surgeon General's Office was the largest buyer of corn liquor in Florida. Beginning in 1862 the agency sought permission from Tallahassee for citizens to deliver as much whiskey and alcohol as could be produced for use in hospitals and also requested that whiskey makers not be impeded by the ban on grain distillation. State officials were aware that doctors depended heavily on whiskey to ease the pain of the wounded in the field when no other drugs were available, an all-too-frequent state of affairs. It fell to the Medical Purveyor for Florida, John

E. A. Davidson, to secure medicinal spirits from the local people. By 1864 sufficient contracts had been negotiated to supply all the stimulants required by army surgeons in Florida itself. In fact, so much alcohol existed that the Surgeon General's Office ordered increased purchases from Davidson's district in order that surplus whiskey could be sent to Confederate military hospitals in Georgia and Alabama. During the 1864 seige of Atlanta, all the liquor that could be spared went to depots in Augusta for distribution. Florida distillers were also urged to produce as much corn whiskey as possible to maintain the ready alcohol supply in Georgia for the fighting fronts.[22]

In addition to forwarding whiskey, Florida helped Confederate medical officers to obtain needed drugs. As noted earlier, cotton from the state was used in payment for medical and hospital supplies run through the blockade. Vital medical articles like drugs or surgical instruments were carried by couriers to district warehouses in Savannah and Macon, and these messengers returned with any items needed in Florida hospitals. The state may even have played a part in the actual manufacture of medicines for army use. Under the direction of Surgeon General Samuel P. Moore, pharmaceutical laboratories were constructed all over the lower South, and one of these may have been located in north Florida. Private citizens also contributed to this campaign by searching out herbal substitutes for drugs. Florida ladies, asked by the government to join their sisters in other states, grew garden poppies from which opium was extracted. Anyone interested in rendering such "essential service" to the Confederate cause received poppy seeds and instructions on how to cultivate and harvest the narcotic plant.[23]

Medical officers sought to cure the sick with improved diets as well as with traditional medicines. Fruit from Florida citrus groves was shipped to other Confederate states and to the army for this purpose. Oranges, lemons, and limes were in demand from the very beginning of hostilities, with various efforts made to secure them for the market stalls in Southern cities. At least one merchant vessel traveled between Charleston and New Smyrna, returning with its holds filled with lemons and limes, until it was captured by the Union navy in September 1861. War-time demand caused many owners to reactivate abandoned citrus groves, and calls for the planting of new trees did not go unanswered. Many new groves sprang up conveniently near existing railroad lines. Observers predicted that Florida could furnish Charleston, Savannah, and portions of other Southern states with oranges. "We hope the wise will have an eye to this important matter," ran a Gainesville *Cotton States* editorial, "for money can be made without much labor or outlay."[24]

The Confederate government became a major customer for Florida citrus growers, purchasing large quantities of fruit for army hospitals. Wagons hauled oranges from the trees in Marion County to Charleston for use by military doctors, while boats were loaded with lemons and limes from groves along the rivers and creeks. In one instance a Lake City planter entered into an arrangement with the Surgeon General's Office to furnish orange juice, orange syrup, and peels in large amounts for issue by medical officers as far away as Richmond. This grower charged ten dollars for each gallon of juice he delivered to the government at Macon or Savannah. There is also evidence that considerable amounts of Florida orange products left the state in barrels during 1862 and 1863. Citrus fruits did help soldiers who were suffering from vitamin deficiencies caused by unbalanced army rations. However, citrus proved not to be as effective a substitute for quinine as some rebel physicians thought it to be.[25]

The cold winter of 1863–1864 damaged many Florida citrus groves, with freezing temperatures killing fruit-bearing trees in the northern sections of the peninsula. At the same time, soldiers serving in Florida regiments in winter camps far from home included pleas for packages containing fruits, in their letters home to family and friends. One officer wrote to relatives in Quincy that the sending of such food "would be of incalculable benefit to the country and especially to those with whom provisions are very short." Later, when the railroad system began crumbling under war-time pressure and mail deliveries grew erratic, fewer and fewer soldiers or civilians enjoyed fruits from Florida. As late as 1865, some with means continued their efforts to supply relatives in other states with what had become a luxury item. Hunger for Florida citrus products in the long run proved of lasting benefit to an agricultural industry that would prosper during the Reconstruction era.[26]

Two other commodities produced in Florida that suddenly became scarce and expensive throughout the Confederacy were sugar and molasses. The Federal blockade prevented much from being imported through Southern ports, although some sweets were brought in by blockade runners. Domestic cane growers in Louisiana suffered greatly from the loss of New Orleans to Union troops in April 1862 and the subsequent evaporation of credit from the city's banking community. As Union forays into the Louisiana countryside disrupted the labor system on sugar plantations, many despairing planters switched to cotton or food crops. One student of the Louisiana sugar industry emphatically affirms that the coming of civil war all but obliterated sugar cultivation on a large scale in the state. Southerners eventually either turned to growing sorghum cane as a substitute or sought to buy sugar from cane-growing areas still under rebel control. Such war-time demand injected new life into Florida's moribund sugar plantations.[27]

When Florida sugar planters found their cane to be highly prized, they increased acreages to meet the new civilian and military needs. The state government bought many hundreds of pounds of raw sugar and gallons of syrup for consumption by its troops, yet enough surplus remained to allow shipments as far away as Savannah. These hogsheads, holding anywhere from 63 to 140 gallons each, were sold at auction and earned a healthy profit for their owners. In mid-1862, Florida sugar sold in Savannah for from twenty-three to thirty-three cents per pound, although in Florida state agents could purchase it for as little as eight cents a pound. Floridians with the means to get the heavy sugar casks to any spot on the Georgia railroad network had an opportunity to garner the proceeds from a rising sugar market that peaked during the winter of 1862–1863.[28]

Georgia continued to suffer from a shortage of reasonably priced sugar during 1863, which eventually prompted governmental action, as had been the case with salt. Officials seized the bulk of the sugar stored in Atlanta and offered its owners seventy-five cents per pound as compensation. They refused and subsequently filed a lawsuit against the state asking relief. Meanwhile, Florida products could still be had in Atlanta, but not in the quantities necessary to fill the orders of all wishing to buy. In one instance one hundred barrels of Florida syrup, offered for sale by the commission merchants Anderson, Adair and Company, quickly disappeared from its warehouses. Civilians in Georgia and the other Confederate states were not alone in suffering from lack of sugar. In October 1863 the Confederate supply system ceased issuing sugar to soldiers as a part of their regular rations. This ban included troops stationed in Florida, despite the presumably better access to thriving sugar-cane fields. Prices for staples like syrup soared at the same time inside Florida itself, and many government representatives voiced concerns about these high rates and their effect on supply.[29]

The counties of Marion and Alachua in middle Florida were the center of the state's war-time sugar industry by 1864. Commissary officers worked these two areas heavily to secure as much of the sugar crop as possible for the army. One planter having a surplus of fifty-four thousand pounds of sugar received curt orders not to remove or sell any because it was required by the armies of the Confederacy. At that time sugar was subject to impressment if not willingly sold. Eventually the government took possession of the lot in question, along with a quantity of sugar syrup at six dollars a gallon. Barrels containing such wares traveled by wagon or small river craft such as the steamer *Silver Springs* and then by railway boxcars to the front. Agents often left local inhabitants tiny amounts of sugar for use in bartering for such manufactured goods as cloth, because sugar proved to be a more useful currency than any circulated by the Confederate States.[30]

The most famous incident concerning the Confederate government and Florida sugar involved the former United States senator David L. Yulee. Although he was an ardent secessionist and president of the Florida Railroad, Yulee refused, like many people in the South, to place the needs of the government above his private property rights. In July 1863 Yulee possessed sixty-four hogsheads of sugar, weighing roughly fifty thousand pounds, that were stored in a warehouse in the hamlet of Waldo on the Florida Railroad line. An agent representing the city of Savannah offered to buy about fifty of the large kegs from Yulee. The Georgian agreed to pay the former senator and his associates one dollar per pound on delivery, a fair price, considering the high rates prevailing in the retail sugar market at the time. Before the transaction was completed, a Confederate supply officer, Major Antonia A. Canova, learned of the sugar in the Waldo warehouse and took steps to obtain it for the government. Canova proposed that Yulee sell his crop for forty-five cents per pound, a figure Yulee summarily rejected. The major then ordered the entire lot impressed and placed under armed guard.

Confederate impressment schedules of prices fixed sugar at seventy-five cents per pound, a figure Yulee also refused. He then brought suit in a Florida court asking for the return of his property and damages from the government. After losing this case, Yulee appealed the ruling to the state supreme court. The justices on the high court agreed with Yulee that states' rights and private property took precedence and rejected the lower court's decision. The supreme court ordered the government to pay the sugar's owners an amount closer to its true value under current market conditions. *Yulee v. Canova* set an important precedent by determining that the state courts could limit the authority of supply officers applying the Impressment Act within its borders. Since no Confederate supreme court was ever organized, there was little recourse available to the government. This so-called sugar case generated interest throughout the southeastern Confederacy; a reporter for the Charleston *Daily Courier* praised the lawyers involved and thought "the speeches on both sides quite interesting."[31]

Despite such legal entanglements, sugar grown in Florida made its way to many places in the Confederate States during the second half of the Civil War. Confederate government estimates predicted that the state would produce one hundred thousand hogsheads of sugar in 1864 in addition to approximately one hundred thousand gallons of syrup. Some of this sugar crop was earmarked for use by the soldiers of the Army of Northern Virginia. Because the railroad connections with the Virginia theater of war were frequently broken during 1864, Lee's tattered troops probably received little if any Florida sugar in their rations. In fact, transportation bottlenecks caused many barrels of syrup to be issued to men based in Florida in lieu of meat to prevent it from being wasted due to spoilage. Nevertheless, senior officers in Richmond did not lack for sweets from the Florida peninsula regardless of transit difficulties. Commissary-General of the Confederacy Lucius B. Northrop, for one, took delivery of private shipments of hundreds of pounds of sugar and gallons of cane syrup for his own table. The flow of sugar and its by-products to the rest of the South continued intermittently until the final collapse in 1865. When Savannah fell and the rail corridor to Virginia was cut, Confederate supply officers moved the yearly crop westward to Chattahoochee on the Apalachicola River and then transported the sugar and molasses by boat to Columbus. Such activities ended, of course, with the surrender of the rebel armies in North Carolina, Alabama, and Mississippi.[32]

As previously mentioned, the policy of impressment played an important role in procuring sugar for the government and its armies. The Impressment Act of 1863, designed to meet military needs and foil speculators, greatly eroded popular support for the Davis administration in Richmond. In many instances planters and farmers refused to cooperate with commissary officers and thereby generated shortages and increased inflation. However, quartermasters and commissaries maintained they could only gather food for the army by confiscation. Yet, as in the *Yulee* sugar case, when states' rights collided with the national government's military requirements in Florida, the state usually triumphed. The task facing staff officers assigned to collect rations was especially difficult because Florida's large underpopulated areas and the generally poor communications made fraud and questionable practices hard to detect. Some unscrupulous businessmen even succeeded in passing themselves off as government agents vested with the authority to assemble the tax-in-kind produce and impress agricultural products.[33]

Probably no governor of a Confederate state cooperated more fully with Richmond than Florida's John Milton. Nevertheless, public resentment against impressments forced him to disapprove this policy publicly. On 23 November 1863, he addressed the state legislature to charge that both quartermaster and commissary officials were exceeding their authority and complying with orders not consistent with acts of the Confederate Congress. He particularly objected to notices given to planters and farmers stating that they must either sell surplus meats, grains, or sugar to the rebel government at fixed rates or have their supplies appropriated. Although he did not seek special favors for Floridians, Milton did demand fair treatment for his people from the Confederate government and its representatives. He painted the impressment notices as "incompatible with the rights of citizens and insulting to the men who know their rights and have proven their loyalty to the Government established by them for the protection of their rights." To Milton it seemed much better that Florida become a "waste of flowers, enriched with the blood of her brave citizens than to be inhabited by them as slaves."[34]

In accordance with Governor Milton's recommendation, the General Assembly passed a law intended to shield residents of the state from abuses of power by Confederate impressment officers and punish any who overstepped the bounds of his authority. Agents who were charged with collection for the army promised in return that they would never take supplies necessary for the basic survival of the property owner's family or slaves. Honest citizens, according to these officials, need not fear them, for their targets were those speculating in farm goods. They reminded Florida representatives that, while property rights were critical, Florida and the other Southern states were fielding armies that must either be fed or disbanded. No other option existed for the South. For these agents impressment was only a tool used as a last resort to secure

Governor John Milton. (Photograph courtesy of Florida State Archives)

vital provisions for their soldiers. Despite such words Floridians never truly reconciled themselves to the policy of confiscating supplies.[35]

Tensions between Tallahassee and Richmond over impressment remained evident into 1864. In an effort to appease angry Floridians, the War Department praised their patriotism and spirit of self-sacrifice and acknowledged their contributions of essential provisions to the government. Also, the department pointed to several general orders issued by the Adjutant and Inspector-General's Office setting clear guidelines for officers in the field and placing limits on what could be impressed. But the Confederate spokesmen nevertheless hinted to those who complained about the impressment policy that armies could not be sustained without it. They realized full well that the seizing of items in Florida and other states had a depressing effect on agricultural production generally, undermined faith in the system, and sapped the will of the people to continue the struggle. "Nothing so rapidly over-spreads with the evidence of dilapidation and decay as these wholesale robberies of the farmer by insolent minions of the Government," concluded an editorial in the Charleston *Daily Courier* on the necessary evil of impressment. Such sentiments were readily discernible among the Florida population.[36]

As Florida's semitropical climate enabled it to be a good source of sugar and citrus, fisheries on its lakes, rivers, and seacoasts served as a hidden resource for the rebel forces. Using salted fish for the army was neither a novel nor an unpractical idea, but the Confederate government turned to it with little speed or enthusiasm. As late as 1863 a Tennessean presented a plan to officials to develop fisheries as ration sources for Confederate soldiers. He recommended that men and boys not needed in the ranks, wounded veterans, or slaves be employed in catching and preserving fish for military consumption. In reply supply officers reported that efforts along this line had already been undertaken with only marginal success. Federal raiders had targeted many fishing camps for destruction, and the enterprise had suffered from shortages of tackle and the all-important salt.[37]

From the outbreak of war Floridians looked to their waters as a reservoir of potential provisions, causing the legislature in 1861 to enact a series of laws designed to protect the state's fish supply. Nonresidents were prohibited from establishing fisheries on any coast; from being employed in taking fish on any sea, bay, river, or harbor with the intent to export to another state; and from marketing fish in Florida without a license. Violators of the laws faced a one-thousand-dollar fine and the seizure of boats and equipment. Despite these measures Georgia urged the government in Tallahassee to allow the development of a large fishing industry. In September 1861 a correspondent of the Macon *Daily Tele-*

graph suggested that Floridians begin catching large quantities of mullet and shipping them northward. In his view such fish, marinated with molasses, offered an excellent substitute for the bacon currently being consumed by slaves and was far better for the health of blacks than pork. As stocks of other staple foods shrank and prices climbed, demand for Florida fish increased. Sea creatures taken off the coast, sharks for example, also yielded oils needed for lubricating machinery.[38]

During the war years fisheries sprang up along the bays and inlets of the Florida peninsula alongside the saltworks, with the majority located on the Gulf coast. Camps on the Saint Johns River did catch fish into 1862, but Union gunboats on the wide stream gradually terminated their operations. In the winter of 1863 James McKay, a prominent citizen of Tampa, responded to the ongoing army-ration problem by offering to set up a fish-packing concern capable of catching and salting one thousand pounds per month. Salt could be obtained from the works operating along Tampa Bay, and the staves needed to fashion barrels were available in the cypress swamps in the interior. Unfortunately, such plans in south Florida were hampered by difficulty in transporting kegs of the finished product out of the state. Probably salted fish from this area were eaten by civilians and by the few soldiers on duty there.[39]

The center of Florida's war-time fishing industry lay along the creeks and bays on the Gulf of Mexico south of Saint Marks. It is no coincidence that these fisheries were established near one of the state's major salt-making regions, inasmuch as a steady supply of salt was vital for preserving the catch. By 1864 at least four fishing concerns operated here, with each netting mullet at the rate of forty barrels a day. Soldiers fortunate enough to be guarding the fishermen had a welcome opportunity to send some of the salted fish to their own families. Often these troops were pressed into service in the processing operation when the fisheries were short of labor. As a general rule, available workers preferred employment with neighboring saltworks because of their promise of large profits. Threats of Union assaults also discouraged workers from coming to the coast.[40]

The Florida fisheries peaked in importance in 1864, with an estimated annual production of one hundred thousand barrels, equal to twenty million pounds of fish. John S. Wright, the state Superintendent of Fisheries, oversaw operations and endeavored to increase production. Wright frequently communicated with government officials in Florida, Georgia, and the capital in Richmond about the state of the fisheries and about the problems of conducting this needed enterprise. In a general order dated 20 January 1864, Secretary of War James Seddon, also responding to ration shortages in the army, directed that all old and new government fisheries be worked to full capacity. Superintendent Wright earnestly struggled to comply in the face of nagging difficulties. Hampered by the persistent shortage of laborers for the fishing camps, Wright drafted slaves being held as prisoners at Camp Lay in Madison County. Thirty of these reluctant workers were marched down to Saint Marks, where nets waited. Thereafter, numerous barrels of salted mullet packed by slaves were transported into Georgia well into 1865. These shipments, welcome as they were, made only a small contribution to the overall rebel economy. A senior Confederate recalled that in the matter of fishing, for a time "much was expected from those in Florida." Little, however, was actually achieved.[41]

Black Floridians, whether catching fish, boiling salt, tending corn crops, or laboring on government projects, made important contributions to the state's economy and war effort. Slaves continued to toil on plantations and farms with relatively few interruptions throughout the years of war, since the area of highest slave population, north central Florida, never came under direct occupation by Union troops for any considerable period of time. Hardships caused by the war, such as food shortfalls and the lack of cloth for the yearly issue of new clothing, weighed heavily on master, mistress, and slave. Nature also took its toll. A storm striking the Gainesville area of east Florida in 1864 killed numbers of slaves and their owners as it carved a path of destruction during its inland flight. Because a high percentage of its white male population was off in the Confederate army, Florida could not raise enough food for home consumption and exportation to other states without the tacit cooperation of her African-American community.[42]

Slaves provided yet another vital service through their employment by various Confederate government agencies. Many blacks, leased to the War Department by their owners, drove wagons loaded with supplies everywhere in the state. In 1862 a slave teamster even delivered a load of arms and ammunition to a military post without white supervision, something unheard of in the prewar South. The Confederate Commissary Department made particular use of slave labor at its numerous warehouses and installations in Florida, paying their masters the maximum rental fee of twenty-five dollars per month. In February 1865 the department utilized more than fifty such individuals in its daily operations. The Quartermaster Department also pressed into service as many slaves as could be hired (owners were becoming increasingly reluctant to exchange the labor of their slaves for Confederate scrip). As early as 1863 eight slaves appeared on the list of employees at the Quartermaster depot in Lake City, and several remained there throughout the war. The government's need for able-bodied men not eligible for conscription led also to the drafting of free blacks for the duration. A quartermaster officer in need of such men simply had to make an application to the commander of Camp Lay, and black conscripts would be assigned to whatever duties he required.[43]

Slave laborers worked to build fortifications and maintain existing railroads; they also worked in warehouses and in fish camps. In August 1864, for example, slaves removed a section of unused railroad track southwest of Fernandina in Duval County so the scarce iron rails could be used elsewhere. Joshua Frier, a young conscript soldier acting as a guard on the project, marveled at the black men's ability to perform such tiresome work on scanty rations of beef, stale corn, and a little salt, and still have enough energy left to sing and dance after a long day under the broiling Florida sun. In the end the teenage Confederate came to admire these railroad "bucks" for their perseverance. Such men comprised the majority of laborers used on various railroads in the state and on the maintenance gangs that kept the roadbeds of the few functioning railroads in repair.[44]

That Floridians of color neither revolted nor refused to work at their war-time occupations does not mean they all docilely accepted their lot. Instead, many escaped to the Union lines after the Federals established themselves on the coasts in 1862. Others fled from the saltworks to blockading warships. The white population, especially the families of absent soldiers, lived in fear of revolts or attacks by gangs of runaways. Brutal punishments failed to prevent these breaks for freedom. In one instance a group of seven slaves from Marion County in August 1862 made a desperate dash for the safety of the Union camps east of the Saint Johns River. Overtaken by a unit of Florida cavalrymen, known as the Marion Dragoons, the black men surrendered only after one of their number received wounds from a shotgun blast. The runaway, named only Gus, was treated by a white physician on the scene. After recovering, unfortunate Gus paid for the failed escape with his life when he was hanged by members of the Marion Dragoons. A white observer familiar with the incident considered the execution necessary and wrote to an associate that "if they are going to do it the sooner the better." He placed the real blame on a mysterious white and a free black who allegedly had enticed Gus and the others to flee.[45]

Along with the possibility of slaves running away, slaveholders during the war also faced the problem of feeding their charges during a time of agricultural change and scarcity. Pork, the mainstay of the Southern diet, became more difficult to obtain because of military demand and the lack of access to hog-raising areas in the border states. In Florida, during an unusually warm winter in 1861, spoilage during the butchering season caused the loss of great amounts of pork. Nevertheless, the annual ritual of butchering continued seemingly unaffected by the coming of sectional war. An 1861 visitor to Governor Milton's own plantation in Jackson County described the work: "Those killing days were horrible. You could not look out of a door or window without beholding cartloads of slaughtered pigs being carried to the yard to be cut up. Then you could not venture a step beyond the threshold without perceiving this cutting up process, when all sorts of appendages were strung upon lines to be dried, and a whole row of negroes were engaged before boards and benches in salting, packing, and drying these portions of pigs, which made one feel one never wished to behold a porcine dish in one's life again."[46] Although a townsman might be repelled by the sights and smells of the slaughter yard, rural Floridians, both black and white, looked forward with anticipation to the supply of hams and bacon the butchering and salting of hogs provided.

In Florida shortages of pork made themselves felt from the start of the Civil War, serving notice that the region's food-producing capacity was indeed finite. In the summer of 1861 the state government had to seek outside Florida for pork products to feed the regiments then being raised. For a while, troops on the peninsula subsisted on hams imported from as far away as Charleston and Wilmington, North Carolina. Soon, however, such sources began drying up. Consequently, most cities and towns throughout the lower South were reporting shortfalls and unbelievably higher prices. All efforts to boost hog production depended heavily on the conversion of farms and plantations from cotton to corn, and the change could not be made earlier than the 1862 planting season. Advances by the Union army that coincided with further epidemics of hog cholera compounded the problem. "We want meat," cried a correspondent of the Atlanta *Southern Confederacy* in 1862. "Our Army cannot be kept up without it."[47]

Before the end of that year, Confederate supply officers in other states began inquiring whether there might be any pork in Florida available for the government to purchase. The head of supply in South Carolina asked in December if bacon could be cured in Florida and shipped directly to Charleston. From Richmond rebel authorities suggested that Florida pork be obtained to make up for short rations given soldiers stationed in the lower South. Everywhere throughout the Confederacy salt meats, especially bacon, remained in great demand. As the area under Confederate control diminished, the number of hogs to pick from went down as well. Subsequently, letters calling for conservation and improved packing techniques to reduce waste due to spoilage filled newspapers. Obviously not a pound of meat could be spared if the Confederate army was to continue to be an effective fighting force.[48]

In 1863 the task of providing pork supplies for soldiers and civilians grew more problematic. Many Florida farmers who had surplus hogs refused to take them to market out of fear of losing them by impressment at less than current prices. A writer in a Tallahassee journal charged in April 1863 that there were large amounts of bacon in Leon County that should by rights be impounded for the public good. The onset of fall added urgency to the efforts of government agents to collect such meats and forward them to the fighting fronts. Commissary officers roamed through the state searching for hogs, along with representatives sent down from Georgia. Florida commissaries received strident requests for pork and other supplies to be sent without delay to north Georgia and Virginia to help ward off hunger in the army camps. Governor Milton himself joined in the work and did what he could to provide rations during the near-famine. Unfortunately, his state lacked the numbers of hogs to supply two Confederate armies and its own civilian population. [49]

That the number of pigs in Florida was not very large did not deter many from coming to the state in search of pork. In one case the president of North Carolina's Sapona Iron Company visited the peninsula in 1863, hoping to purchase some forty thousand pounds of pork for the hands employed at his foundry. A representative of the Raleigh and Gaston Railroad who accompanied the iron maker was just as eager to buy at least sixty-five thousand pounds. Supply officials complained that such efforts as these complicated the problems of obtaining bacon for the government by running up prices. While the companies mentioned above were never formally charged with speculation, in the words of a senior commissary officer, "the desire to save the immense difference in the cost of their supplies here and at home, is the next of kin to speculation and is the true reason in my opinion why they are here." [50]

The Confederate military units in Georgia claimed much of the ready pork exported from Florida in 1864, since that state's reserves of hogs were unable to meet demand. The situation forced a general reduction of the daily army ration to four ounces per man per day in the Georgia–South Carolina–Florida theater of operations. To combat the crisis Florida bacon was rushed northward by all available transportation, with some even going as far as Richmond. Georgia officials naturally protested against sending it on to Virginia, as the army in their state was in such dire need that no pork could be spared for that front. Intent on obtaining as much pork as possible, a government commissary agent in Thomasville established a system of barter with his counterpart in Tallahassee, trading cloth, yarn, and thread, probably from the mills of Columbus, for salted meat. In the exchange, 1 bunch of cotton yarn was worth 16 pounds of bacon or lard, and 1½ pounds of pork bought 1 yard of osnaburg, a coarse canvas-like cloth material. Other rates of exchange included a bunch of thread for 12 pounds of tallow or a yard of finer cloth for 1¼ pounds of pork.[51]

Speculators were numerous in the war-time South, and they infected the Florida pork trade with their dealings. In January 1864 a man calling himself Gaming arrived in the state from Savannah, claiming to represent the Confederate States Navy on a search for provisions. He managed to purchase some twelve thousand pounds of bacon before anyone checked his credentials and authority to engage in such procurements. Florida officials suspected that he was an imposter and asked the proper naval authorities to ascertain his true identity. If this man was a fraud, he picked a very good alias, because the Confederate navy maintained several plants in Georgia handling pork supplies. Instead of saying that he came from Savannah, however, Gaming should have claimed he represented the naval depot at Albany, since this base processed tens of thousands of hogs into sailor rations during the second half of the war. Chances are that Gaming was exposed as a fraud, but not before he absconded with some six tons of vitally needed bacon.[52]

Even in the face of illegal purchases of pork, Confederates very optimistically estimated that Florida might produce as many as 100,000 hogs in 1864. These could translate into roughly some 1,000,000 pounds of bacon. Gathering and moving such numbers of animals proved difficult for the government. For example, a rebel agent in Gadsden County tried with little success to obtain a wagon and team when he wanted to go into neighboring Liberty County to collect hogs. Some 25,000 to 30,000 pounds of pork could be had there for the army he believed. A similar lack of teams and carts hampered operations in agriculturally rich Gadsden County, costing the government at least 150 hogs. Ironically, teamsters in Florida at this time subsisted on very slim rations of bacon while they were hauling government stores of pork. Nevertheless, thousands of pounds of Florida pork continued to be exported right into 1865. This small but significant contribution to the war effort might have had a more positive impact if the Confederate food distribution and transportation system had been more efficient.[53]

Although hog owners and other agriculturalists felt the heavy hand of the Confederate government in many ways, the Quartermaster Department influenced the lives of Florida farmers more than any other branch of the rebel republic. Representatives of this agency collected the so-called tithe, the tax-in-kind on farm produce. Its agents concentrated on gathering corn, potatoes, beans, and peas for human consumption, and hay and other fodder for draft animals. The Commissary Department, its counterpart, specialized in securing bacon, sugar, and beef, which also became army rations. Headquartered in Lake City, the Quartermaster Department maintained warehouses in Milton, Marianna, Quincy, Tallahassee, Monticello, Baldwin, Starke, Gainesville, and Tampa. Second only to Lake City, the quartermaster depot at Gainesville served as the most important collection point for goods sent from the interior of the state. The value of this base was well known to the Unionists, and it even received mention in Northern newspapers. The *New York Tribune* referred to the town as "a place of some importance as a depot for Confederate government stores, and as the residence of many wealthy rebels."[54]

Agents operating from Gainesville and the other quartermaster bases in the summer of 1863 found collecting the tax-in-kind impossible in some cases because of Federal military activity. These officials had to reluctantly abandon Escambia, Santa Rosa, Walton, Taylor, Lafayette, Levy, Putnam, Duval, and Saint Johns Counties in June of that year. Thus, the proximity of Union troops denied to the Confederates a significant portion of Florida's agricultural resources. A distressing lack of coordination between the quartermasters and other supply agencies operating in Florida continued to exist, leading to untold complications in the field. The scanty surviving record of communications between senior officers in charge of the departments in question suggests that they were not informed of each other's activities. The Quartermaster Department, like its commissary companion in Florida, was severely handicapped by inefficiency, corruption, a population at times almost hostile, and the lack of a good railroad system.[55]

During the early months of 1865 the quartermasters diligently gathered crops and forwarded them to the hungry gray-clad armies. When owners of horses balked at renting them to the government for fear of permanent forfeiture, the officer in charge of the depot in Lake City told a subordinate, "If you cannot hire any teams *impress them.* . . . The Government's supplies must go forward and no obstacles can be permitted to stop it." The fall of Savannah diverted the flow of agricultural products for the Quartermaster Department westward through Gadsden County to the Apalachicola River, then northward by river boats. Despite the disintegration of the Confederate economy, the department's forces in Florida managed to assemble substantial amounts of provisions for man and beast. Between 1 January and 4 May 1865, the Lake City depot handled some 856 bushels of sugar and molasses and approximately 12 tons of fodder (23,729 pounds). When Tallahassee surrendered to Union troops in May, its storehouses bulged with government food supplies. Obviously, Florida's contribution to the ration reserves of the Confederate military and civilian population had been truly significant, making the state a valuable member of the Confederate States.[56]

Throughout the period of the conflict cotton, corn, sugar, citrus fruits, fish, and pork were exported from Florida in considerable quantities, along with distilled spirits and medicines for use by both soldier and citizen. Yet these shipments, as extensive as they were, could do little to prevent suffering from hunger in the ranks or in the urban areas of the war-time South. Despite some success at converting from cotton production to corn, farms and plantations in the state never lived up to what was expected of them. Demands upon Florida's resources continually increased as the Confederacy's agricultural base shrank under Union assault.

Floridians of both races labored to meet the challenge as well as they were able, and they could take satisfaction in knowing that a supply network still functioned when Federal troops arrived after the capitulation of General Joseph E. Johnston's battered command in North Carolina. Historians have noted that stocks of food could be found in parts of the Confederacy right up to the very end, but that inadequate transportation facilities and inefficient supply arrangements prevented provisions from reaching the army. As will be seen, the lack of a rail connection with Georgia until late in the war impeded furnishing of beef cattle, grains, and pork to the government. But failures to meet all the demands placed upon the people of Florida should not overshadow their very real accomplishments. Obviously, the small population of the state could not be expected to feed the Confederate armies in the Southeast and beyond by themselves.[57]

5 Rebel Beef: 1861–1863

The Swiss military strategist Antoine Henri Jomini, one of
the formulators of nineteenth-century military thought, once
speculated that the pressing wants of an army for food could be
satisfied by using available cattle on the hoof. These existed in
most populous countries in sufficient number to provide rations for limited periods. Baron Jomini warned would-be great
captains, however, that this source of food would soon be exhausted, giving troops the choice of going hungry or plunder-
ing the countryside. He advised that "requisitions for cattle
should be well regulated and the best plan is to supply the army
with cattle purchased elsewhere."[1] Jomini's classic *Art of War*
(1834), read at West Point before the Civil War, conceivably
influenced many officers who went on to hold senior positions
in both the Union and the Confederate armies. In questions
of tactics as well as logistics, the master's dicta commanded
respect. But the American Civil War did not follow the
Napoleonic model, and both sides faced the task of supplying
field armies of unprecedented sizes. Past military experience
offered no answers; nothing in the history of the United States
matched the scope or the complexity of the operations conducted during the war of the rebellion.

The Confederate Commissary Department encountered little difficulty in providing rations for the growing rebel armies
during· the summer and early fall of 1861. Troops in Tennessee
and Virginia consumed, among other things, cattle procured
locally from abundant sources. Supplies gathered via purchases
on the open market were plentiful, and most people believed
that the South had ample means to meet both army and civilian
needs for a brief, glorious war of independence. Texas exported
considerable numbers of beef cattle into the eastern half of the
Confederacy, thirty-eight thousand head reaching New Or-

leans between April and December 1861. Another fifteen thousand
passed through the city before it fell to the Federals in April 1862. Commissary officials claimed to have placed orders for an additional two
hundred thousand Texas cattle, but the lack of funds for advance payments hampered delivery. The presence of beef stock in the lower South
softened this shortfall, which did not immediately impact Florida.[2]

Florida beef being used in the Confederate war effort in mid-1861 went
to feed state troops within the state's borders. Many cattle were purchased to supply troops positioned at places like the Cedar Key area,
where Union attacks were expected. The beginnings of the devastating
inflationary spiral so crippling to the Confederate economy were evident
in the rising price of cattle bought by these Floridians. In May 1861 beef
went for six cents a pound, but by September it cost the state government eight cents per pound and remained at that price well into 1862.[3]

The coming of hostilities did not halt the flow of Florida beef northward by sea all at once. The steamer *Carolina,* for example, landed fifty-
one head of Florida cattle on the wharf at Charleston in mid-May 1861.
Such imports were welcomed, since military demands on all types of
food created shortages of increasing severity. Planters depending on purchased beef to make up shortfalls found themselves scrambling to find
cows for sale. Some cattle owners in the lower South attempted to increase the production of beef from their own herds, but cattle suitable for
slaughter took time to raise. Deficiencies of grain and the lack of practical
experience in serious cattle breeding made it hard to increase herds in
relation to the heightened need for meat.[4]

In an effort to boost the army's beef supply, the Commissary Department in Richmond began awarding contracts to civilian agents to locate
and drive cattle for military consumption. These men received orders not
to buy any secondhand beeves but to purchase them directly from
ranchers, the object being to discourage inflation and speculation. Such a
contractor system seemed natural for Florida, a state whose large herds
were well known. Jacob Summerlin became the person charged with
furnishing Florida beef to the Confederate forces. Summerlin, a larger-
than-life figure on the Florida frontier, claimed to be the first white born
on the peninsula after it became American territory. Other sources place
his date of birth between 1819 and 1825 at the settlement of Alligator
(later Lake City). At the age of twenty Summerlin traded a number of
inherited slaves for six thousand head of cattle, thus beginning his career
as the foremost cattleman in south Florida.[5]

A taciturn man who neither drank nor gambled, "Uncle Jake" had
sufficient business acumen to parlay his lean range cows into an empire
stretching across the state by the end of the 1850s. The 1860 census listed

him as a farmer and butcher with real and personal property worth over ninety thousand dollars, enriched further by his participation in the Cuban cattle trade along with James McKay. With the outbreak of the war he opted to support the rebel cause and accepted an appointment as commissary sergeant of the first volunteer company raised in Tampa. Because he was the largest cattle owner in the state, the Confederate government deemed him more than able to fulfill a contract to supply beef. Summerlin jumped at the offer and went to work in the fall of 1861.[6]

Sergeant Summerlin set up his headquarters at Fort Ogden (in present-day De Soto County) and organized a group of drovers. His cattle drives followed the old trails from Fort Meade to the settlement at Brooksville. The cattle then turned toward the large range known as Payne's Prairie, located just south of Gainesville. From this rallying point they pushed northward until reaching the railroad terminus at Baldwin, west of Jacksonville. From here the beef moved to Confederate supply depots in Georgia and the Carolinas, on foot or in railroad cars once in Georgia itself. The entire trip could last as long as thirty days, with fourteen to twenty miles per day being the average rate of travel. About six hundred head a week left the state in this fashion.[7]

Florida cattle drives hardly resembled their Western counterparts. On the first day of a drive herders roamed the bush gathering all the cattle in the immediate area and moving them into holding pens constructed of pine logs. These moved on the next day to another such enclosure about a day's ride along the trail, with any cows found included in the growing herd. Droves expanded in this manner from a few dozen to sometimes thousands by the time they reached the Georgia border. Often as many as 150 head would be lost enroute, but the cowmen managed to get the bulk of their charges to their final destination. They faced the ever-present dangers of the trek: snakes, sudden thunderstorms causing stampedes, lack of water, and sawgrass marshes that cut both man and animal as they tried to pass through.[8]

Richmond's arrangement with Summerlin called for him to deliver at least 25,000 head for army use. Prices ranged from eight to ten dollars per cow, depending on age and condition. Cattle brought by their owners to the rail line near Gainesville usually received the greater amount. Until 1863 Summerlin kept consignments heading north, but he questioned the method by which he was being compensated for the meat he obtained for the government. For his first year of service he received crisp, new Confederate currency, and "Uncle Jake," ever the shrewd businessman, doubted the real value of this scrip. He personally made a trip to Charleston to exchange his rebel dollars for bonds redeemable in gold. Not

Jacob Summerlin. (Photograph courtesy of Florida State Archives)

totally satisfied with the arrangement, the cattleman continued working for the government out of a sense of patriotism if nothing else. Unfortunately for him, the Confederacy collapsed before he could convert his bonds into specie, so he realized very little profit from his association with the Confederates.[9]

Other Florida ranchers felt uneasy selling to the rebel government and were never monolithic in support of the cause it symbolized. Hillsborough County herders, for example, had to choose, as others did, whether to retail their beeves to a government seemingly unable to pay in any secured currency. In spite of a daily increasing demand for cattle, the number of residents in that important beef area showed a marked decline. Registration of new brands, a status symbol for cattlemen, dwindled from twenty-five in 1860 to eleven by 1862. There were other factors involved, such as the absence of potential ranchers who were in the army and the slowing of the lucrative Cuban trade because of the strengthening Union naval blockade. But the fact remains that the war, although bringing increased need for Florida beef, was not a stimulus for many natives to capitalize on the new market by becoming cattle raisers. This is true despite the exemption from Confederate draft that all cattlemen enjoyed. Many prominent Hillsborough herders did become directly involved in the war effort in different capacities, as shown by comparing brand records with army muster rolls.[10]

The fall of Saint Augustine in March 1862 hindered Summerlin's efforts to gather beef in the northeastern corner of the state. Citizens here, steeped in Southern ideology and the rightness of the cause, sold cattle to the government with less trepidation than those in the southern half of the peninsula. Cattle owners in particular suffered from Union raids designed to release slaves and confiscate cattle, the Saint Johns being a natural avenue for strikes into the interior. Its significance as a beef region did not escape officials in Tallahassee. One such representative told Governor Milton that if the Saint Johns remained in rebel hands, beef enough for ten thousand troops might be brought out during the forthcoming summer.[11]

The summer of 1862 witnessed the first in a series of meat shortages in the Confederate army. Units in the western theater, later to become the ill-starred Army of Tennessee, suffered from a lack of fresh meat while campaigning in Tennessee and Mississippi. The army's new commander, General Braxton Bragg, fumed at his Tupelo headquarters about the vital matter of subsistence. He had only sixty days' rations of salted meat available and slim prospects of acquiring more. Fresh beef was limited in supply and becoming harder to obtain; Texas beef no longer arrived on a regular basis. Bragg's commissaries looked to the pastures of southern

Alabama, Georgia, and Florida as possible meat sources, and newspapers asked owners in these states to sell only to authorized government agents and not to private individuals, regardless of what they might offer in return. Rebel cowboys also rode into the Florida panhandle to drive cattle back into Alabama to feed men at Bluff Spring and Pollard during the lean summer months.[12]

As Union armies advanced in the west, Florida grew increasingly important in Confederate logistical considerations. The significance of the state's beef reserves was not lost to Federal forces conducting aggressive missions along the coasts. Commander Maxwell Woodhull of the gunboat USS *Cimarron* reported to his flotilla commander what he learned on a cruise up the Saint Johns in October 1862: along the river he picked up rumors that the cattle herds in Georgia, Alabama, and the Carolinas were dwindling at a rapid pace. With Texas cordoned off, "the whole dependence of the Confederate Government to feed their army now rests in this state." Woodhull learned from reliable sources that rebel agents covered the peninsula, buying all obtainable cows at any price.[13]

The failure of Bragg's thrust into Tennessee and Kentucky only exacerbated supply problems. By entering Kentucky, Bragg hoped to subsist his men from the agricultural richness of a near-pristine region. During the campaign and after the retreat following the clash at Perryville on 8 October, Confederates enjoyed plentiful amounts of fresh beef, especially since the herds grazed within easy march of their camps. But the future of beef supplies, according to Commissary Department reports, was anything but bright. Referring to stock in Georgia and Florida, one statement ran that the "country through which the cattle must be driven is not a good one to subsist them on in winter . . . and cannot be relied on as a source of supply."[14] This sentiment was underscored in another report that fully two-thirds of the cattle being slaughtered for army use came from Tennessee, the remainder coming from Virginia and other places. Since Robert E. Lee's Army of Northern Virginia consumed one thousand head per week, no exports from that area could be expected. If the key beef areas stayed under rebel control, no meat shortage loomed on the horizon for late 1862 and early 1863. If not, difficulties seemed unavoidable.[15]

The loosely knit commissary scheme then existing proved far from efficient, as army officers frequently competed with other officials operating under direct authority from Richmond. Competition of this type in middle Tennessee during the winter of 1862–1863 made gathering supplies of all kinds all the more problematic. Commissary-General Northrop admitted in November 1862 that he could not safely meet army requirements unless he traded cotton for beef and pork on the black market in Union-held Memphis. He informed President Davis that projections of the lower South's ability to furnish meat were unrealistic and "it has been erroneously supposed that South Georgia, Alabama, and certain portions of Florida would afford large amounts of stock, but they have not done it. They have not even fully fed those posts which from geographic position would naturally draw from them, and they cannot do as much in the future as they have done in the past."[16] Northrop's lament that Florida failed to live up to its potential to provide beef cattle later proved false.

One reason for Confederate problems in securing cattle in Florida was competition from other markets. Many recalled the profitable trade with Cuba in the 1850s and thought possible gains outweighed the risks of running the Union blockade. And risks did exist, for taking cattle to the island meant breaking both Federal and Confederate laws, since it was illegal to remove beef from the state for private transactions. Legal entanglements hardly slowed Samuel Mitchell from trying his luck against the blockaders. A Manatee County resident and brother of a future state governor, Mitchell successfully slipped through and returned with badly needed staples. He also brought back large quantities of Cuban gold coins from the sale of his cattle.[17]

Jacob Summerlin also remembered Cuba and its taste for Florida beef. Disheartened with the Confederate bureaucracy, he left its employ on the expiration of his contract and turned his energies to smuggling and blockade running. A hotel at Punta Rassa served as his headquarters, complete with a dock suitable for loading beef onto ocean-going vessels. From there his stock of beef bought from other settlers left the state bound for the island and its market stalls. Summerlin ran the gauntlet of the blockade at least six times on the ship *Scottish Chief,* operated by James McKay. The *Chief* and other McKay-controlled craft carrying the animals skirted the Florida coastline from Boca Grande to Charlotte Harbor and then darted across the Gulf for Cuban ports. Flour, sugar, salt, and other staples returned aboard these ships and were sold to residents or traded for more cattle. Such exchanges took place near old Fort Ogden on the Peace River.[18]

The Cuban government allowed this trade to continue, based on a desire to maintain commercial ties with the South regardless of the fate of the Confederate States. Cuban leaders did not want their island's economy damaged any more than necessary, so cattle boats from Florida enjoyed warm welcomes as long as they kept a low profile. The *Trent* affair and the growing Federal naval presence on their minds, Cuban officials maintained contacts with the rebels until the issue of the war had been clearly decided. After 1863 only limited quantities of cotton were accepted in exchange for supplies, but no limit on the importation of beef seems to have been in place. The war only intensified the demand, making the risks of blockade running acceptable to Florida cowmen.[19]

It is a wonder that the slow, smelly, and bulky cattle boats managed to repeatedly slip past Union warships. Expert knowledge of local waters and more than a little luck explain it in part, but not completely. The Federal fleet kept several ships patrolling the southwestern coast and the approaches to Cuba. Swift blockade runners fell prey to them on a fairly regular basis, but no mention of the seizure of cattle-laden vessels appears in any official reports. The Union sailors knew of the unusual activity in the immediate vicinity of Punta Rassa and on the Caloosahatchee River, but they never managed to suppress it. Perhaps their officers turned a blind eye to it because they had no desire to stop the flow of beef *out* of Florida and out of the reach of the Confederacy. Each cow landed in Cuba was one less feeding the rebel armies, so why not let them be removed from the country? Also, a shipload of cattle would not bring the kind of prize money that a shipload of cotton would when seized as contraband. Any staples brought into south Florida as a result of smugglers' activities were for the most part consumed locally anyway and did little to aid the rebel war effort.[20]

The year 1863 began with the thunder of massed guns and the anguished cries of the wounded and the dying as Union and Confederate armies battered each other at the battle of Stones River or Murfreesboro. After three bloody and inconclusive days, Bragg's Army of Tennessee retreated southward in the general direction of Chattanooga. Troops on this march nearly starved along the two-hundred-mile route because middle Tennessee, effectively scoured by Commissary Department agents, had little left in the way of food to offer, especially beef cattle. As Lee's army in Virginia enjoyed priority on rations in late 1862, Bragg's famished men had to fend for themselves. The main depot in Atlanta presented a gloomy picture in the limited stocks on hand for issue. Major John F. Cummings, in charge of the facility, had four thousand head of cattle, but they were only a small fraction of what the Army of Tennessee needed in the weeks and months ahead. All his salted provisions, earmarked for shipment to Virginia, did not offer a solution to the pressing deficit. Scarcity for all approached unless energetic steps were undertaken.[21]

Newly appointed Secretary of War James Seddon assured the new overall commander in the west, General Joseph E. Johnston, that the entire Confederacy was being ransacked for supplies for his waiting troops. Any shortages of rations would be made up from other sources that at that moment the Commissary Department was trying to develop.

Cummings, one of the best and most efficient commissary officers in the service, could be trusted to collect and forward the necessary commodities. General Johnston believed in Cummings, but faith alone could not feed his soldiers. Bragg estimated that his army required 400,000 pounds of meat of all types to fulfill ration needs for the month of March 1863. Cummings sent only 191,000 pounds and had little hope of sending more at any time soon. As supply officers desperately pondered their few options, memories of Florida's large herds of cattle and other animals generated notions that enough beef grazed there to more than ease present shortfalls. If meat did not come in from somewhere, the Army of Tennessee could no longer be adequately fed, and the disintegration of a major Confederate field army thus hung in the balance.[22]

The hungry Army of Tennessee was not the only body of rebel troops looking to Florida for help. The Military Department of South Carolina and Georgia included middle and eastern Florida in its jurisdiction. Its commander since August 1862, General P. G. T. Beauregard, expected Union attacks on either Charleston or Savannah and tried to build a force capable of withstanding these anticipated Yankee onslaughts. Increased numbers of troops strained supply networks in both South Carolina and Georgia, causing heightened food shortages and inflated prices in the coastal cities. The Charleston _Daily Courier_ reported in January 1863 that even poor-quality beef in the city market sold for seventy-five cents a pound when it was available. The newspaper's editor concluded that "the price of provisions of all kinds is becoming a serious matter." The War Department sent agents into east Florida to purchase cattle and drive them back to Beauregard's command in Savannah and Charleston. One official engaged in this operation complained that finding and moving Florida beef was "a most arduous and extremely troublesome business." But the work went on regardless of such difficulties due to the gravity of the ration situation.[23]

As commissary officers cast eager eyes on the peninsula and its resources in 1863, an era in the cooperation between Florida cattle traders and the Confederacy came to an end. Cattle smuggling greatly expanded in scope, and the open market–contract system fell by the wayside under the pressure of war-time demand. Florida no longer remained a secondary source; it now moved into the forefront in plans to keep the rebel armies fed and fighting. A new centralized system of commissary agents, designed to maximize collection and shipment of cattle and other products, would be created. Increased activity meant increased scarcities: beeves became harder to find as stocks diminished and the Confederate economy began breaking down.

April of 1863 ushered in the new organization, upon which so much depended. Food shortages during the lean winter demonstrated the need to overhaul the existing logistics scheme. Strategies based on a short war were scrapped in favor of a more comprehensive arrangement capable in theory of gathering all available farm and range production. The government in Richmond responded with what it hoped met military and civilian needs in a fair and reliable manner. A myriad of problems stood in the way of success and plagued the transportation of Florida beef until the final days of the war. Unrealistic expectations of existing stock and dwindling support for the Confederate cause were definite factors, along with rampant speculation. Officials faced shortages of trained drovers and lacked the rudiments of a railroad system. The flow of cattle was under constant threat by Union troops and their sympathizers, rebel deserters, and even a possible Seminole uprising.

Commissary-General Northrop optimistically unveiled his new program on 15 April. Each Confederate state was to have its own chief commissary officer to control collection and shipment of all food supplies. This officer dealt with both the Commissary Department and supply personnel in those armies operating in or near his state. He enjoyed the authority of being able to divide his particular state into as many districts as he thought necessary to achieve maximum coverage. An assistant commissary in each of the districts would be required to submit detailed reports on purchases and supplies on hand every ten days. Northrop thought that once the new order was in place no portion of the Confederacy would fail to contribute to its utmost for military use. A network of energetic officers, he reasoned, guaranteed that wherever rebel armies moved, "all the supplies of our country will be tributary to their use."[24]

This stream of supplies, however, was not to be as deep or shoal-free as the commissary-general thought. Though this new situation brought direction and thoroughness, it also enlarged the tangle of bureaucracy. State commissary officers in many cases now found themselves in competition with their opposite numbers in the various armies for ready agricultural products. Charged with securing enough food for their own units and stockpiling for future campaigning, they had little motivation to defer to other representatives because they might have a higher priority. Such competition led to infighting and inefficiency, neither of which the Confederacy could afford if it hoped to survive as a nation.[25]

By the coming of spring the food situation in the Army of Tennessee showed signs of improvement. Three thousand head of cattle, mostly from the Florida peninsula, were on hand in Georgia to subsist the troops. Spring permitted the cattle-driving season to commence, and the ration outlook appeared favorable for at least the next several months.

But events to the west altered even further Florida's position in the rebel supply equation. Union divisions moved down the Mississippi River valley and slowed the trickle of beef coming from the trans-Mississippi section of the Confederate States. As such imports decreased, the high command urged that efforts to bring them across be stepped up. Commissary-General Northrop, in a moment of reflection, stated that it might be worse for the Confederacy to lose access to the trans-Mississippi states and their cattle than to lose cities like Charleston and Savannah to the enemy.[26]

The first priority of Florida leaders was to reorganize the state along the lines of the Northrop plan. Someone had to be found to take the thankless post of chief commissary, a position offering great responsibilities and few chances for martial glory. On 26 June 1863, Pleasant W. White accepted a major's commission and the title of chief commissary of Florida. A Quincy native, White was both a successful lawyer and an ardent Confederate who soon earned a reputation as a talented and zealous administrator, inspiring to his subordinates. Making his headquarters in Quincy, he worked and continued to live with his family there for the rest of the war.[27]

White no sooner had settled into his assignment and begun the task of setting up his state as a rebel storehouse, when a blow of far-reaching consequences struck the rebellion. On 4 July the Confederate garrison of Vicksburg capitulated after a long siege. The Father of Waters did indeed now flow unchecked to the sea. Federal patrols ranged up and down the river and stopped any attempt to move supplies of any kind across. The Confederate leadership now found itself depending on Florida beef to subsist its soldiers as it never had before. The loss of the Mississippi, coupled with occupation of the bulk of Tennessee by the Yankees, tightened the screws on the South and made it increasingly difficult for the Commissary Department to provide any sort of rations.[28]

The military activity on all fronts strained supply lines and heightened tension between officials during the crucial summer of 1863. The Army of Tennessee, grappling with General William S. Rosecrans's bluecoats and being pushed back ever closer to Chattanooga, suffered shortages because of pressures on nonfecund eastern Tennessee and the demand for agricultural surplus in Virginia. Preferential treatment of the Army of Northern Virginia worsened an already serious morale problem in Bragg's troubled command. In June, theater commander General Johnston ordered the main depot in Atlanta to release nothing for his old army in Virginia until the needs of the Army of Tennessee had been met. Almost one thousand head of cattle and one hundred thousand pounds of cured beef, no doubt mostly from Florida, ended up on the western front per Johnston's instructions.[29]

In the meantime, Major White completed his plans for dividing Florida into commissary districts. Because of the huge territory involved, he organized the state into five areas and appointed army officers and civilians to administer them. The panhandle region became the First District, covering all the counties west of the Apalachicola River. Captain J. D. Westcott commanded here, with a staff of six assistants under his orders. The Second Commissary District encompassed the region between the Apalachicola and the Suwannee Rivers, and Captain Alonzo B. Noyes, the former state agent, was in charge.

The Third District comprised Suwannee, Columbia, Baker, Bradford, Nassau, Duval, and Clay Counties. Major Joseph P. Baldwin was the senior officer and had the services of one assistant. The eight counties of north and central Florida became the Fourth District under local-planter-turned-soldier Major A. G. Summer. The fifth and last area contained the major cattle-producing counties of south Florida: Hernando, Hillsborough, Manatee, Polk, Brevard, Dade, and Monroe. Captain James McKay, the logical choice to command here after Summerlin, accepted on the condition that his son James, home on sick leave from the army, be assigned as his aide. This was ordered after McKay took charge of cattle gathering and shipping from his Tampa base.[30]

Not all of the new district commanders expressed confidence in their ability to accomplish what many believed was an almost impossible mission. Major Summer, experienced in the troublesome cattle trade, anguished over whether or not to accept the post. Wishing to do his duty, Summer finally agreed to be placed where he would be of most use to the Confederate cause. White comforted Summer by assuring him that the Fourth District need forward to him only as much cattle as needed for relay to Charleston or Savannah. White thought Summer to be loyal and hardworking and his district rich enough in the precious beef to make his assignment successful.[31]

White soon called on all his district officers as army needs were translated into specific requests. The chief commissary of Georgia, Colonel Joseph D. Locke, estimated that Florida must ship one thousand head per week to meet the ration requirements of Generals Bragg and Beauregard. "This requisition," wrote Locke, "is indispensably necessary for the public interest." A general reduction in the meat allotment to one-fourth pound per day in July underscored the urgency of the situation. Richmond officials were forced by events to admit that no more beef could be reasonably expected from Mississippi, Tennessee, and parts of Alabama and Georgia. The effectiveness of the Union blockade made attempts to import such foods in sufficient quantities a questionable undertaking. The commissary-general, in his usual manner, minimized the shortage by saying that European peasants rarely ate meat and the people of Hindustan never touched it. But in private he pondered what would happen after the thirty days' supply of rations left for the entire Confederate army was consumed.[32]

As operations continued, Major White grew to respect the work and character of James McKay. The Scot seemingly proved his loyalty to the South when he and his steamer *Salvor* were captured trying to run the blockade with a large cargo of arms and ammunition. After a personal interview, White came away convinced he was the best available man for the job. The major, however, was not so naive as to believe that he had no worries about the honesty of all of his officers. Some used their positions, according to White, "only for the purpose of putting money in their pockets." A high priority for White, after stamping out corruption, was to restore the confidence of the people of Florida in their government and its representatives. This was essential if the target figure of three thousand to four thousand cattle a month for the army was to be met out of the estimated forty thousand east of Tampa Bay.[33]

White quickly realized that supply needs depended on the utilization of rail transportation to expedite beef deliveries. A scheme to connect Live Oak with Lawton, Georgia, appeared a sure way to speed the movement of cattle and other supplies and link Florida directly to the rest of the Confederacy. The proposed road, already graded by a private company, lacked only iron rails to be complete. White urged Richmond to use its offices to find rails and pressure all involved to hasten their labors. "The preservation not only of the beef cattle in Florida," wrote White, "but the integrity of our state and its inhabitants, and all its resources" depended on finishing the line in question. The possibility of railroad cars hauling beef from Florida nonstop to the fighting fronts led the major to redraw district boundaries on 14 August. As a result the Fourth District was divided, a portion going to Major Baldwin's Third District. A section of McKay's large area was added to Summer's in an effort to simplify future shipments.[34]

By the end of August, Florida supply agents knew that cattle left the peninsula in record numbers, but not at the rate of three thousand a week as the army had requested. Collecting and driving the semi-wild beef needed the services of experienced wranglers, and requests for detailing such men for duty in Florida in many cases went unanswered. In spite of obstacles, cattle did arrive in the camps to the north. Between fifteen hundred and two thousand reached Bragg's army from the depot in Madison, Florida, during one five-week period. August traditionally ended the cattle season, as trail conditions made it impractical to move beeves considerable distances. However, the pressures of war changed normal practices in this as in so many other facets of Southern life.[35]

On 25 August an urgent message from Bragg's command came to White's Quincy headquarters. The loss of Tennessee beef deeply cut into ready meat stocks, and Georgia sources proved unable to make up the differences. Soldiers suffered from pangs of hunger as they never had to date. Could Florida help? White wasted no time in responding, and an extra six thousand to eight thousand head were purchased and sent on their way toward Georgia. White wrote Bragg that he could expect one thousand beeves per week, but the approach of fall made it unlikely that such an amount could be maintained. Commissary-General Northrop's only contribution from Richmond was to blame the shortages on a Union policy of deliberately destroying or capturing rebel agricultural products. He sternly advocated putting Federal prisoners of war on a diet of bread and water in retaliation.[36]

Confederate soldiers were not alone in lacking beef for their meals in the fall of 1863. The superintendent of the Georgia State Lunatic Asylum, located at Milledgeville, reported that his patients hungered for fresh beef, not having seen any for several weeks. Officials in that state, pressed to fill army orders, declined to provide anything. Thomas F Green, head of the hospital, turned to Florida's Governor Milton for aid. The governor cheerfully gave his permission for Green to buy one hundred head of Florida cattle and drive them back to the asylum. Milton justified this breach of export laws with the rationale that Florida had several inmates there and therefore had a special interest in the institution's welfare.[37]

South Florida could do little to alleviate the crisis because of heavy rains that halted cattle gathering for almost a month. Captain McKay advised that the shortages spawned a new wave of speculation in beef throughout the country. Near Charlotte Harbor two-year-old beeves sold for as much as forty-five dollars each, and McKay felt obligated to outlaw such flagrant black-marketeering in his district at all costs. Such activity, in his mind, necessitated a new state ban on cattle sales to anyone other than authorized commissary officers. White urged both McKay and fellow district commander Summer to make an all-out effort to collect numbers of cattle as a reserve against future emergencies. Any campaign aimed at speculators would have to wait; both leaders were to devote their attentions to meeting the one-thousand-head-per-week figure needed for Bragg's army. White also knew that General Beauregard's forces at Charleston, under constant pressure by besieging Yankees, depended on him for their beef rations and might make even greater demands.[38]

Major Cummings in Atlanta doubted that all possible measures for securing the vital animals were being undertaken by White's men. His agents in the state told him of an abundance of cattle, "but the people are indisposed to sell them for our currency and drivers canot be found." Cattle could be herded in Florida, but a proper organization and more energy must be added to existing methods. Cummings requested and received permission to use his own troops in collecting Florida cattle and bringing them back to Georgia. Despite high hopes, he soon found that nothing could be accomplished without more men and more cooperation from Floridians. White defended his methods in the face of Cummings's criticism by emphatically stating that the pressing demand on his re-sources from the Army of Tennessee could only be satisfied with beef from south Florida ranges. Since the bulk of the state's remaining beef grazed there, the time involved in filling orders for the army must natu-rally increase because of the distance from the front. It seemed that only Florida natives truly understood the logistics of cattle gathering in their large state, and sniping from officers like Cummings helped little.[39]

The food shortage plaguing Confederate soldiers around Chattanooga continued while supply officers bickered. Forced by the gravity of the situation, White reluctantly agreed to the sending of a number of Cummings's men into Florida to collect cattle from its herds. Captain Charles F. Stubbs acted as Cummings's agent and received beef to be turned over to the Army of Tennessee or to General Beauregard, or both, as the case might be. Later representatives from Alabama got permission to cross into the First Commissary District and drive cattle back across the border for government use. Beauregard's commissaries in Florida operated under White's overall direction for the purpose of collections. Requests for additional herders to work the ranges in the south for the purpose of driving beeves northward fell on deaf ears, however. Confed-erate commanders failed to fully grasp that without manpower, army supply needs could never be met.[40]

East Florida soon fell behind in filling its expected quota of cattle because of shrinking herds and decreasing desire to sell to the govern-ment. The Fourth District, relied upon by both Bragg and Beauregard, also lagged behind, and district commander Summer complained that too much was expected from his area. The Charleston garrison alone consumed one hundred head a week, a number Summer could not sup-ply. A lack of skilled drivers hampered his work even further, as it did in all the districts. His men were forced to move their herds all the way to the point of delivery deep inside Georgia, detaining trained cow handlers for long periods.[41]

Summer and others also battled speculators who paid higher prices and left smaller herds for the government to tap. The activities of one individ-ual, S. W. Sanchez, raised the cost of beef some twenty cents per pound in the Fourth District by September. Summer retaliated by impressing all beef in Sanchez's possession and sending it north to Bragg. He came away convinced that cattlemen in his district were the "most slippery in Florida." Another cattle owner, after losing some of his beef in the same manner as Sanchez, gained their release after promising to deliver as many cattle as needed to the Georgia town of Valdosta personally. White heartily approved of such measures and advised Captain Westcott in the First District to end competition from speculators by impressing any cattle that they might be inclined to buy before they had the chance to do so. Only what was needed for immediate use should be spared; with Bragg's thirty-five thousand soldiers on the edge of starvation, no tactics appeared too draconian.[42]

In spite of such vigorous action, cattle still left the state illegally in private hands. Georgia troops, at Major White's urging, patrolled the border with Florida in hopes of interdicting cattle being removed by private parties. Agents of that state stopped and inspected all droves passing through and detained any lacking proper authorization. Florida drovers had to carry the correct documents or risk field arrest on the trail. One such cattle owner, Francis A. Hendry, charged the government $22.50 per head to deliver eight hundred head of his cattle from Hernando County to the depot at Madison. Hendry only reluctantly entered into the arrangement, convinced that he did so at a net loss. Willing or not, an experienced rancher like Hendry was a welcome addition to the droving forces.[43]

Acute shortages of drivers curtailed operations in the large Fifth District even with Hendry's help. A sailor turned cowboy when James McKay himself led a party forty miles from Tampa to bring in a herd of 290 head. He expected some 400 more early in November from Manatee County, where he maintained several cattle pens. Herding cattle in the late months of the year tended to be even more time-consuming because the cows were scattered over wider areas than in the spring. The fall of 1863 in south Florida had been very rainy, raising creeks and slowing the work pace. Communications were poor; it took twenty days for a letter from White to reach McKay in Tampa. Frustrated, White journeyed south himself in September to have a firsthand look at conditions in his primary cattle region. He made the arduous trip with the goal of speeding up the beef shipments. After meeting with McKay and surveying the condition of the country, White came away convinced that all possible efforts were being made to maintain the flow of cows northward. If he entertained any doubts about the Scot's competence or commitment, White never expressed them.[44]

While records are far from complete, there is evidence that significant numbers of Florida bovines went to feed rebel troops and help fuel the Confederate war machine. During the second half of September 1863 over 2,000 head were purchased in the Fourth District alone. Some 1,420 ended up in South Carolina, and 706 stayed in pastures fattening for future use. Curiously, the bulk of the district's beef went to General Beauregard's command even after the Army of Tennessee received a priority on all Florida shipments. A new appeal came on 2 October from the head commissary of that army, pleading for something for his gaunt soldiers. Apprehension existed in Atlanta and elsewhere that White's organization would fail the army in its time of crisis. [45]

Chief Commissary White in response urged his district commanders to do everything in their power to increase purchases even if their other duties suffered as a result. Moving cattle must be "first and paramount for the next two months" to enable the Army of Tennessee to follow up its bloody victory at Chickamauga on 20 September. McKay tried to make a new arrangement with Jacob Summerlin, Francis Hendry, and a few of the other large stock owners to bring their cattle directly to the Madison depot. Instead of waiting for detailed soldiers to assist in the driving, McKay was to employ "citizens or negroes as can be had." An address to the people of south Florida asking for increased support in the name of those defending all that the South held sacred circulated among ranchers and settlers. White summed up the situation when he told McKay that "all eyes are on us for help." [46]

Confederate forces at Charleston also depended heavily on Florida during the same period. Colonel Locke of Georgia practically begged White to put every agency at his command into motion to send him beef, which eventually would go on to South Carolina. Fresh meat, rare in the besieged city, was seldom seen by members of the garrison. Locke confessed that his state's cattle supply neared the point of exhaustion despite Commissary Department actions. South Carolina's head commissary, Major Henry C. Guerin, joined in placing all hopes of feeding his charges on Florida beef. "Our situation," he wrote, "is full of danger . . . from want of meat, and extraordinary efforts are required to prevent disaster." [47]

Tensions among the various commands heightened after yet another call from the officers of the Army of Tennessee for all possible cattle to be forwarded at once. White testily responded that he had no way to anticipate such a large concentration of troops near Atlanta, which made these new requisitions necessary. If the army had taken him into its confidence, possibly some of the shortfalls then occurring could have been lessened. The Floridian explained how he had traveled to south Florida and "ridden through mud and water by day and night among alligators and insects" to speed collections and driving. In this same combative tone he asked the commissary-general why all district commanders in Georgia held the rank of major and not all of his men in Florida had been so advanced. "I suppose the reasons for this promotion," asked White, "could be equally applicable to those in this state."[48]

The chief commissary also communicated to Richmond on the state of Native American relations that he had observed during his trip down the peninsula. He personally saw ragged Seminoles in dire need of cloth for clothing and ammunition for use in hunting small game. White felt that these people had a strong attachment to the rebel cause, since they had not taken advantage of unsettled conditions and sought revenge against whites. Nothing showed their inclination better than the Union's lack of success in trying to persuade them to engage the Confederates. A lack of badly needed staples, however, might swing them into the Federal camp out of sheer necessity. Their location in the heart of beef country gave them control of the balance of power in the region, if they chose to exercise it. As enemies they could sweep cattle herders from the ranges and stop the vital flow of beef altogether. As allies the Seminoles potentially impeded any Union plans to stop such traffic despite their small numbers. A new government agent, in White's view, should be appointed to cement relations by negotiating a new compact with them as soon as possible.[49]

Rumors of possible Indian uprisings notwithstanding, supply problems continued at the top of the agenda. Braxton Bragg complained bitterly to the War Department about the scanty rations remaining in the Atlanta depot, which were in danger of running out in a few short weeks. No meat had been issued to the men for days, and he demanded immediate action from the commissary-general personally. Northrop sharply replied that Bragg himself was to blame for the crisis because of his hasty evacuation of Tennessee, leaving behind enemy lines untold cattle and other provisions. If the general wanted more provender for his army, he should redeem Tennessee as quickly as possible. Meanwhile, stories made the rounds about millions of pounds of meat, stripped from Georgia and Florida, being sent to Virginia while the Army of Tennessee languished. Bragg, dependent on both states, also suffered from the inadequate rail system, which again and again failed to deliver what food was available to the places where it was needed.[50]

A commissary officer on leave from Bragg's army gave White a first-hand account of the torment he had witnessed on a daily basis in the camps and how it eroded morale. Stocks of beef and bacon, once so plentiful, now were greatly depleted throughout much of the Confederate States, and the army depended solely on weekly collections for rations. A knowledgeable soldier lamented that "starvation stares us in the face; the handwriting is on the wall." Major Guerin in Charleston had close to forty thousand troops and laborers in his charge, and the cattle grazing in South Carolina were only a fraction of what was required to feed them. Under pressure to help, Florida commissaries combed the brush seeking beef, only to come away with a handful of undernourished cows for their trouble.[51]

Demands by General Beauregard for Florida beeves became much more strident near the end of October. White met his wrath by reserving a full one-third of his inventory for direct shipment to Charleston in hopes of meeting the need of four hundred head minimum. When the promised beef was slow in arriving, Major C. McClenogham was dispatched to Florida with orders to look into the delays and get things moving at a faster pace. Once in Quincy, he found the chief commissary absent from his headquarters on an inspection tour. Later McClenogham caught up with the busy officer and came away with the impression that White was both competent and a hard-working official. Charges that Bragg's representatives caused delays by diverting Carolina-bound cattle for their own army's use were quickly laid to rest. With an organization both new and incomplete, the staff officer wondered to himself how White and his men had managed to accomplish so much in the short time since commencing operations. McClenogham left with assurances that the promised one-third of all cattle forwarded would go to Beauregard and none other.[52]

Six hundred beeves arrived in Madison from the south Florida prairies, bound for the armies, in the first week of November. McKay reported that the cattle he saw on the whole looked worse than they had in years, mainly because of the rainy weather. Ten to twelve miles a day marked the limit they could be driven in their weakened condition. Also, some south Florida stock owners, increasingly less eager to sell their cattle or have them impressed, hid cows deep in the interior or asked scandalous prices. Future profit, it seemed, meant more to such ranchers than the good of their new country. In all the commissary districts, except the Fifth in south Florida, cattle collections fell to record lows. "If it were not for you," White admitted to McKay, "I do not know what the army would do." The government desired beef herding to be continued until the end of the year, and the bulk of it would have to be done by McKay and his drovers. Any and all cattle gathered in the First District, plus two-thirds of that obtained from the Third, Fourth, and Fifth, were already assigned to the half-starved Army of Tennessee.[53]

November, a fair month for cattle despite the lateness of the season, was a busy time in south Florida. Captain McKay sent 387 head to Charleston via the pastures around Madison. Major Summer in the

Fourth District purchased a total of 566 head during the same month; 326 fed soldiers in South Carolina, and 175 waited at the base at Quitman, Georgia, to continue their journey to the slaughter pen. An additional 68 plodded northward toward the waiting butchers of the Army of Tennessee. Private individuals contributed to this effort, such as a cattleman near Ocala who managed to round up and deliver some 200 beeves to the yards in Madison. After receiving payment for his herd, the cowman declared the cattle season of 1863 over and headed for home.[54]

Unfortunately, the fighting to the north did not cease on such a seasonal schedule. The Army of Tennessee reeled from a series of battles fought around Chattanooga in November that culminated in the Union attack of 25 November on Missionary Ridge. The "miracle" of Missionary Ridge turned out to be anything but that for the rebels. After the center of their lines collapsed, Bragg's men broke and, in a panic, stampeded back into northern Georgia. Taking stock after rallying at Dalton, the hard-luck army of the Confederacy found its losses at more than six thousand men. One is left to wonder how much of this crushing defeat can be blamed on months of poor and irregular rations. Perhaps the seeds of this disaster can be found in the lack of Florida beef and other supplies and not altogether in Union élan. The cliché about battles being lost for want of a nail might be valid in this particular case.

Defeat did nothing to ease the burden on Florida supply officers to provide beef and other stores; if anything, demand increased. Problems multiplied in driving livestock because trail routes by December lacked sufficient forage, as the grass withered under winter temperatures. Very heavy frost compounded the problem of lack of feed and ended beef herding until spring. Trail conditions terminated McKay's plan to deliver cows from the ranges south of the frost line, and the first two weeks of December saw no cattle arrive from his district at all. The situation was slightly better in the panhandle, for the First District exported 340 head of cattle to Eufaula, Alabama, for the government. But most officers worried about how future needs could be met, for example the district commissary who shared his concerns with his superiors: "Beef is becoming a very serious consideration . . . for the balance of the winter. I fear we shall be unable to keep up a supply for the troops."[55]

By late December all district officers agreed that the cattle in their respective areas of responsibility never could survive a drive to army depots. White reluctantly ordered a halt to all beef operations until the animals gained enough strength to endure the trip into Georgia and beyond. He hoped not to begin again till spring, but again events altered his plans. Orders arrived from the Army of Tennessee headquarters for twenty thousand head to be moved northward immediately. Such a fantastic figure was impossible to meet, but the major decided that Florida must at least try to contribute something for the soldiers to ease their suffering. "The cattle will arrive in bad condition," he warned, "yet I do not see how I can get along without them . . . we must continue the supply no matter how poor or how bad their condition."[56]

The last month of 1863 also saw a change in the command of Florida's largest beef consumer. General "Joe" Johnston replaced the discredited Bragg at the head of the Army of Tennessee on 6 December and faced the task of leading men who had undergone both defeat and months of near famine. Secretary Seddon warned Johnston that he faced serious difficulties in providing for the subsistence of his troops, promising him, however, that the Commissary Department had orders to aid energetically in meeting ration needs. The general, true to his combative style, stingingly replied that under Northrop's present system he enjoyed little if any power to procure supplies in his own right. He was forced to depend on "three majors" in each state, none of whom owed him direct obedience. Johnston himself lacked interest in logistical work but believed he should have the responsibility instead of a number of junior officers "who had not been thought by the government competent to the duties of high military grades."[57]

Johnston's remarks, besides being unkind, showed an unusual lack of tact for a man in his position. The officers he thought so deficient held the fate of his army in their hands. Florida beef at that moment moved toward his forward supply centers long after the beef season should have ended. Orders to continue driving until Christmas showed a poor understanding of winter conditions and their effect on cattle operations on the Florida peninsula. Major White, on his own initiative, placed those beeves unable to complete the march in pastures in Taylor and Lafayette Counties until springtime, when they would be moved on to Charleston. This was not the act of an incompetent officer, and the general's outburst may only reflect the frustrations of a proud man losing a war.[58]

A survey of rations on hand brought little holiday cheer to state supply commanders. The projected amount of all types of meat obtainable by taxes-in-kind, impressments, and purchases filled army needs only to May 1864. These calculations included not only Florida, but what remained of the Southern Confederacy east of the Mississippi. Speculators, like birds of prey, waited in the wings ready to reduce amounts even further and fuel the rampant inflation weakening the economic health of the country. White totaled private applications to buy and remove supplies from Florida and found that they were the equivalent of the state's entire agricultural output for the whole year. Parties making such requests so far outbid the fixed schedule of prices offered by commissary agents that impressment frequently became the only sure means to acquire provisions. White asked the War Department for the authority to eliminate such competition once and for all and let the government be the sole player in the marketplace. Secretary Seddon agreed with the Floridian that the existing laws on the subject needed revision but stated that until that happened they had to be obeyed.[59]

A year-end look at a single Florida commissary district shows the extent of cattle shipments to the Confederate armies in 1863. Charleston received 5,679 head from the Fourth District that year, while Savannah took delivery of 899. The Army of Tennessee consumed some 3,564 cows during the long campaign ending in the debacle around Chattanooga. When requisitions for units stationed in Florida itself are included, this one district sent over 10,000 head of beef cattle to the Confederate forces. Major White estimated that around 30,000 bovines left the state during the year; how many exited illegally was anyone's guess. Projections for 1864 painted a gloomy picture, with only 20,000 head of cattle expected for army use. Stock bought in Florida found its way to troops in Charleston, in Savannah, on the coasts of South Carolina and Georgia, and in parts of Alabama. While data is far from complete because of scanty records, it is safe to conclude that Florida beef kept a considerable number of Confederate soldiers fed, albeit poorly, and therefore in the ranks.[60]

6 Cattle for the Confederacy: 1864–1865

By the end of 1863 many Floridians had come to the hard realization that their state stood practically defenseless before their Northern enemy. Pensacola and Saint Augustine, already occupied, served as ready bases for Yankee thrusts into the interior. Even when such Union raiders encountered superior local Confederate forces, they could easily retreat back to their strongholds with captured cotton, freed slaves, or cattle.

Beef was especially prized by Union garrisons, which were always in need of fresh meat, and by sailors on blockade duty. The Federal military presence also encouraged Unionists and other Floridians weary of war to offer greater support to efforts aimed at securing the state for the Union. When the then-unoccupied Fort Myers fell without a shot to the bluecoats in December 1863, the newly arrived troops included several companies composed of native Unionists known as the Florida Rangers. These Rangers improved the fort's defenses and constructed a new long wharf for loading seized cattle onto ships. Local stockman Francis Hendry estimated that as many as forty-five hundred head of cattle destined for the rebel government were lost to forays emanating from Fort Myers.[1]

Confederate deserters roaming through various parts of Florida also appropriated cattle. Soldiers on the run from as far away as North Carolina made their way to the sparsely populated region to avoid capture. Operating as organized bands in some counties, they drove away citizens loyal to the Confederacy and generally looted the countryside. Cattle herds served as particularly tempting targets for these marauders, who could sell the stolen animals to the Federals. Stealing beef was relatively easy because so many wandered at large without any sort of protection. Major White complained to Richmond that the army had taken so many men from south Florida that neither women and children nor the vital livestock were safe. "Our cattle are valuable to them," said a correspondent of the Gainesville *Cotton States* of the deserters, "as they certainly are to us, and we should protect them by all means."[2]

Impressment of cattle and other agricultural products by Confederate authorities created hardships for the inhabitants that directly influenced the rate of desertion from rebel military units stationed in Florida and in other parts of the South. The Impressment Act passed by the Confederate Congress in Richmond in March 1863 empowered commissary officers to confiscate supplies at fixed prices that most often were less than current market values. Many a family milk cow, drafted for the duration, left barnyards in this manner. Governor Milton received numerous complaints from the Fifth District region that cattle, regardless of age, were being taken from local residents. In many cases soldiers' families lost their sole remaining source of fresh meat to the government, leaving them to face hunger if other staples were also taken. Florida troops grew angry upon learning that area commissary agents were taking food from their wives and children at home. One leading citizen warned that if the Confederacy resorted to wholesale impressment of cattle "which are so necessary to the support of our country, then I say God help us, for starvation must be inevitable."[3]

The Conscription Acts, again approved by Congress, were another cause of desertion and disaffection in Florida. The Bureau of Conscription in Richmond lacked accurate knowledge of conditions existing in the hard-pressed state. No one was more aware of this than William Miller, Commandant of Conscription for Florida and later commander of the Florida Reserves. From his Tallahassee office Miller informed his superiors that the remaining men in his area were more valuable raising and collecting food, or boiling salt, for the army than they would be carrying rifles. The War Department, Miller concluded, must recognize the fact that "a sterile and non-slaveholding country deprived of the labor of its men from sixteen to fifty-six could not long exist." An offer of amnesty was made to draft evaders and deserters who would sell their cattle to the government and agree to work gathering food for the army. However, this measure generally failed to entice many men in from the bush.[4]

Disrupted social and economic conditions in the Florida peninsula were only a small part of the tribulations facing the embattled Confederate States in early 1864. The Army of Northern Virginia suffered acutely from a lack of sufficient rations, more so than at any previous time. During this crisis President Davis told General Lee that the emergency more than justified impressing supplies from Virginia farmers without restraint. Alabama reported that its small agricultural surplus, urgently needed by troops defending strategic places like Mobile, could not be exported to other areas. Georgia officials estimated that their state contained no more than three weeks worth of foodstuffs, and Governor Brown admitted to the War Department that Georgia's remaining cattle herds were tiny compared to demand. The news from South Carolina was equally grim, with its chief commissary detailing how future prospects were poor because of the scarcity of beef and other edibles. Angry shouts in the Confederate Congress continued to ring out, but Jefferson Davis continued defending his old friend and fellow West Pointer Commissary-General Northrop. He called him "one of the great geniuses in the South" and claimed that, had Northrop the physical ability, he would surely serve the cause not as a supply officer but as the commanding general of a Confederate field army.[5]

In the meantime, the movement of Florida cattle to those armies slowly ground to a halt. The beeves actually delivered came in so lean that they provided very little meat. Major White, trying to maximize the food value of such emaciated cows, used idle drivers to slaughter and salt beef in Jackson County. Lack of barrels or boxes and the materials from which to make them slowed efforts in this direction, but White still hoped to get a few pounds of meat to hungry men on the firing lines.

The town of Gainesville hosted an operation that prepared beef for shipment in much the same way. Meat was pickled or "jerked" in eight-to-fourteen-inch strips. Slaves were employed in this endeavor, as they were in so many war-time Florida enterprises. It was difficult for the army to obtain their product, however, because swarms of eager consumers scooped up every box as quickly as each was filled. Agents from the state of Georgia, representatives from the city of Savannah, commissary men from several other states, and a legion from the Nitre and Mining Bureau and various railroad companies continued competing to buy up all the beef, fresh or salted, that they could get their hands on. None of these purchasers stopped to inquire about whether their transactions were legal under Florida law. State supply officials, however, were forced to contend with them and accordingly found it exceedingly laborious to obtain or even impress beef. Of course, the activities of these unwelcome visitors created higher prices and decreased stocks of cattle.[6]

As serious as they were, Florida's problems paled in comparison to those in South Carolina. General Beauregard, acting on his own authority, discharged the state commissary, Major Henry Guerin, believing that he lacked administrative ability. But what the South Carolinian truly lacked was Beauregard's confidence, and Guerin provided a convenient scapegoat for all the supply snags of the past year. Commissary-General

Northrop leaped to defend his subordinate and longtime friend, charging that Beauregard had failed to realize that both Georgia and Florida had recently dispatched large quantities of beef to the Army of Tennessee that under normal conditions would have gone to Charleston. Had Guerin executed Beauregard's orders regarding the management of stores, "it would have been impossible to keep up the supply of beeves from Florida as long as has been done." From Florida, White had earlier warned Carolinians that the movement of cattle was likely to be disrupted at any moment, further adding to bureaucratic tensions. Despite the cloud that hung over the Commissary Department in South Carolina as long as "Old Bory" remained in command, Guerin, later reinstated to his post by presidential order, loyally stayed at the thankless assignment.[7]

During the first cold days of 1864, recriminations over ration shortages echoed throughout the entire Confederate high command. General Lee, usually the last to voice a complaint, claimed that his army's beef supply was exhausted and that already-diminished rations were even further cut while troops in other sections of the country fared much better. He grumbled that General Johnston's regiments received full amounts of meat, plus luxury items like bread, rice, molasses, and even corn whiskey, but that soldiers in the Army of Northern Virginia counted themselves fortunate to be issued three-quarters of a pound of any sort of meat a day. "All ought to fare alike," he concluded, "if possible. It stops complaint and produces more contentment." At one point Lee brought the cattle reserves of Florida to the attention of President Davis, believing that they held the key to ending his soldiers' sufferings. Davis referred Lee's suggestion to the beleaguered Commissary Department for possible action.[8]

Richmond's demands for Florida beef only increased during this period, seemingly in direct proportion to the number of criticisms transmitted from the field armies. Northrop decided that all would be well fed if the flow of cattle from the peninsula state continued uninterrupted through the winter months. Surely, he reasoned, a state supposedly so rich in beef would be able to spare another thousand or so head until summer. Major White, weary of explanation by this time, reported back to his superior that the cattle that could safely and economically be moved were already in the hands of the army. While south Florida might contribute a few more, the long drive from the range to the nearest railroad line would tax the weakened creatures beyond endurance. Florida, unfortunately, had reached its peak potential as a beef supplier for that season. Even Governor Milton expressed surprise upon learning that the number of beeves in his state was not as high as he had imagined. Nevertheless, various schemes for collecting and pasturing cows for the spring continued to be implemented, because of the knowledge that active campaigning always increased the need for rations.[9]

White spent the period before cattle operations commenced in the spring of 1864 seeking additional military protection for the south Florida ranges. In several letters to General Beauregard, the departmental commander, he discussed the potential dangers of the current situation there. Union forces from Fort Myers, he said, were actively raiding far into the interior of the state and threatened to cut off the region entirely from the rest of the Confederacy. If Tampa or the Gulf coast town of Bayport, in Hernando County, fell to the Yankees, the vital beef area would be completely isolated. White also feared that Federal agents might subvert the Seminoles in the south and bring them into the Union camp. Thus, access to the estimated twenty thousand cattle south of Gainesville was in grave peril. Beauregard sympathized with White but spared no troops for duty on the southern half of the peninsula.[10]

Confederate military units in north Florida ultimately confronted invading Federals in the battle of Olustee, fought on 20 February 1864. Soldiers from Georgia, rushed south to meet the threat, found themselves eating local beef during their stay in Florida. A Georgian remembered that during the Olustee campaign his regiment consumed meat from a drove of cattle so lean that not a single ounce of grease or fat could be found on any of the bovines. The butchered meat appeared blue in color, and the men amused themselves in camp by throwing their beef rations at brick walls to watch them stick like tar. Eventually, a steady diet of such poor fare came close to starting a mutiny among these Georgians. A great irony with regard to the importance of Florida beef in the rebel war effort was that while the generals begged for the meat, their men preferred something a little more tasty.[11]

Even though the Union army suffered defeat at Olustee, their push into Florida temporarily disrupted the Confederate supply lines and increased privations among those under siege in Charleston and Savannah. There the regular ration provided beef four days out of every ten, but in February no meat at all enlivened the soldiers' meals. Major Guerin was not certain when beef might again be issued to the garrison on a regular basis or whether any from further south would ever arrive at any time. Commanders in the Charleston defenses complained that soldiers must have protein in the form of beef or pork in order to stand the rigors of combat. Guerin responded that he hoped all of them would soon see Florida beef in their mess tins, since he depended entirely on that state to furnish the summer's meat ration. "If that should fail," he wrote, "the privation, I fear will be greater." Major White knew full well that units holding Charleston went without meat and that a similar fate awaited the Army of Tennessee. The twenty-five hundred–odd Confederate troops in Florida were placed on short portions of stringy winter beef for a time in order to free supplies for those actually under fire. "Let us send," White remarked, "to those who deserve it our best meat." Commissary Department men gladly accepted the discomfort, White believed, because they served out of a sense of duty, and not for mundane reasons.[12]

While Florida troops were tightening their belts, another group of government charges found little comfort in this spirit of sacrifice. Union prisoners of war were at the end of a protracted list of people depending on Confederate logistical arrangements for food. Roughly a week after the clash at Olustee, captured Federals began a forced march to a new prison camp located in the piney forests near Americus, Georgia. Officially known as Camp Sumter, it soon was known simply as Andersonville. During the weeks that followed, captives from other prison camps throughout the South entered Andersonville at the rate of nearly four hundred a day, severely straining an already overextended ration system.

Captain A. M. Allen, the commissary officer of the district that included the camp, could procure no beef in Georgia for his hungry prisoners. On 15 March he turned in desperation to Florida and Major White for help in avoiding a potential catastrophe. Allen sought some twenty-five hundred head of cattle to subsist the growing population behind Andersonville's pine-log stockade. In the event that he failed to locate such beef, Allen confessed to the Floridian, the prisoners would be issued bacon that should go to Confederate soldiers actively engaged at the front. White responded that he had no cattle at all on hand to forward, citing the emaciated condition of the herds and the cold, continuous rains gripping the region as reasons for his noncompliance. Allen could expect no assistance from Florida before the end of April.[13]

As the time approached for the 1864 cattle-driving season to commence, fears that Florida would not be able to supply meat on the same scale as in the past troubled officials at many levels of the rebel command structure. Threats to the supply route posed by Union military forces, pro-Unionist Floridians, deserters, and plain outlaws loomed larger than ever. South Florida in particular was almost isolated and in danger of being completely severed from the rest of the Confederacy because of poor communications and the nagging absence of railroads there. Captain J. J. Dickison, already famous as a cavalry leader in north Florida, summed up the difficulties of conducting military operations on the southern half of the peninsula. Without better lines of communications, "an expedition to that field was one attended with great inconvenience and fatigue." While more troops were needed there, Dickison thought it imprudent to send any reinforcements "while threatened by so formidable a force of the enemy" in the upper section of Florida.[14]

The return of warm weather in the spring of 1864 spurred the Federals and their supporters to step up attacks on the cattle herds being rounded up in the south. James McKay knew that something had to be done to regain control immediately of the countryside and the beef it contained. Venting his anger at the inaction of the Richmond government in a letter written to White on 25 March, he complained that "the government is certainly very blinded to their interests in leaving this country as they do." McKay went so far as to hire additional men at his own expense to help protect the important animals. By the end of the month he had formulated a plan to cope with the pressing problem. He sent a proposal to the War Department via Major White, urging that a special military unit be organized to gather cattle and provide security for the herds. Under Chief Commissary White's command, this battalion-sized force would be able to defend itself and insure a continued and certain flow of beef for army use. Attempting to drive cattle without such protection, he cautioned, would be "extremely precarious," and the chances of rations getting through to either Beauregard or Johnston very slim indeed.[15]

While plans for the new special unit were under consideration, collecting and herding commenced once more in earnest. Details of mounted men combed the northern counties in hopes of finding substantial quantities of beef on the hoof. In most cases they came away disheartened, for the upper section of east Florida, after more than two years as an exporter of beef cattle, stood depleted of cows. West Florida could provide a few head, but these animals had to be grazed for a time before movement northward could continue. In April four to five hundred of such poor-quality beeves were driven to feed the wretched inmates of Andersonville. Yet, in the face of dim prospects, beliefs that there were still great untapped and easily accessible herds were entertained by ranchers and commissary officers. In one instance an Alabama man maintained that he and he alone had the means to bring out eight thousand head from Orange, Brevard, and Volusia Counties. All that was required was for Major White to assign him a few hands to aid in driving the cattle. Apparently, White never replied to this unrealistically optimistic proposition.[16]

The first appearance of elements of the newly formed battalion of cow drivers, commanded by a Georgian, Charles J. Munnerlyn, energized activities by Commissary Department personnel. In two districts they spent over $165,000 to purchase beef, of which 1,120 head were ready to move by the end of July. West Florida contributed 800 cows, a fairly impressive number, considering the diminishing number of animals in the First Commissary District. Many good-quality cows in Lafayette County still waited for roundup, but by midyear the former agricultural leaders, Jefferson and Gadsden Counties, were depleted. North Florida no longer contained the reserves of beef cattle that previously had enabled that section to match south Florida in contributions of meat to the war effort.[17]

While Confederates struggled with the wild Florida cattle, Union prisoners in Georgia faced a daily battle to simply remain alive. In May an urgent request for beef arrived in Florida to help feed the almost fourteen thousand men now held in Andersonville. Although some beef made it to the prison camp, supply never kept up with demand. By 30 June the camp's population had expanded to twenty-six thousand, and commissary officer Allen was forced reluctantly to detach prison guards to drive cattle back to the base and to the Southwestern Railroad station at Albany. Major White ordered all available head, about 1,170, to be turned over to Allen's men. Despite all such efforts, not enough fresh meat reached the cantonment to slow the staggering death rate inside the stockade that ran into the hundreds each day in the hot summer of 1864. A Confederate officer at Andersonville reported to Richmond that at one point during that period there were "29,400 prisoners, 2,650 troops, 500 negroes, and other laborers and not a ration on the post. There is great danger in this state of things."[18]

Allen urgently petitioned Georgia Governor Brown for more men to serve as cattle drovers to speed up deliveries from Florida, but none could be spared from the heavy fighting raging around Atlanta. Because of ongoing battles the demand for provisions never slackened, and those responsible for finding supplies were taxed to the limit. Allen wrote to White that "nothing but full energy and all doing their best will save us." Furthermore, the battles in Georgia during the fiery summer of the war's third year disrupted normal logistical lines and communications, further increasing supply snarls. By mid-August 1864 more than thirty thousand Union men languished at Andersonville, subsisting on handfuls of rice, peas, and some Florida molasses, courtesy of Major White. Only a radical improvement of their diet could slow the frightful rate of death and put an end to the tragedy. Unfortunately, little could be done for them when Confederate soldiers at the front saw meat only two days out of ten. Allen continually begged White for help all through September; at the end of the month he was down to twelve days' rations on hand with scant prospects of securing more.[19]

September 1864 also saw a change in command of a key Florida supply district, when Major A. G. Summer stepped down as head of the Fourth

Commissary District. Summer, no stranger to controversy, was accused of questionable practices in the performance of his duties. In the fall of 1864 charges that there were discrepancies between the number of cattle he purchased and the number he actually delivered to the army forced an investigation. While undergoing an audit, Summer requested a lengthy leave from duty for reasons of health. Because of a bout of hepatitis and fever, Summer's doctor certified that he needed at least sixty days' rest in a climate healthier than central Florida. Summer left his post under a hint of scandal, something not new to the Florida cattle trade. White replaced him by putting James McKay in charge of his district as well as his own until a permanent substitute was named. Obviously, when White doubled McKay's area of responsibility, he showed that he still had great confidence in him; his action also showed that this cattle-rich area was far too important to the rebel war effort to be entrusted to inexperienced, incompetent, or untrustworthy officers.[20]

White was encouraged by the conduct of Major Munnerlyn's cattle battalion and generally pleased with his state commissary forces. Florida's chief commissary, convinced that desertion and skulking in the region had been checked, overlooked the forces' less-than-perfect military appearance and discipline. Indeed, the cattle battalion resembled a cavalry unit in name only. It was in actuality a quasi-military detachment raised for a specific mission, the duration of which no one could even guess. Commissary-General Northrop warned all of his subordinates throughout the shrinking Confederacy, including Major White, that the prospect of a protracted conflict loomed before them and that all planning should reflect this hard reality.[21]

Commanders of combat units looked upon Munnerlyn's battalion and the men assigned to Commissary Department duty in Florida as sources of manpower to replace battle casualties suffered during the summer. General J. Patton Anderson, commander of the District of Florida from February to July 1864, was sure that far too many men remained in the state herding cattle at a time when soldiers were desperately needed in the ranks of fighting regiments. He pressed White to comb out the underutilized extraduty men from his depots and departments at once. In a July letter to White he explained: "I lay claim to some knowledge of the importance of supplying our armies in the field with beef. Three years of service with one of those armies fully enlightened me on that subject, I hope those armies never again suffer the wants and privations in the way of a supply . . . unfortunately I have seen the want too, of more men in the ranks, to stand up in the hour of trial, *to be shot at.*"[22] Anderson felt certain that no specific skill was required to work the cattle ranges and that far too many able-bodied males were avoiding combat service in this

General J. Patton Anderson. (Photograph courtesy of Florida State Archives)

fashion. Only his transfer back to the Army of Tennessee at the end of the month stopped Anderson's campaign against the Commissary Department in Florida.

Another threat to White's manpower came from the bureaucracy in far-off Richmond. The War Department ordered all troops detached from Confederate units be returned to their regular assignments now that the Florida cattle battalion was in the field. Next, a move was made to eliminate the draft-exempt status of men serving in the battalion itself so that they could be brought into the regular rebel forces. This change threatened to strip Florida of the armed men necessary to keep the army supplied with beef cattle. Sherman's successful drive to seize Atlanta, which fell on 2 September, combined with the intense fighting around Petersburg, heightened demand for more soldiers to replace those lost to wounds or death. Regardless of the value of the work being done by rear echelon formations, pressure built to bring as many of them to the front as possible.

Commissary-General Northrop personally argued for an exception in the case of the men in Munnerlyn's battalion. He highly praised its performance and emphasized the caliber of the service it rendered in south Florida. The battalion provided "a nucleus for the militia of the region," which checked the rate of desertions and helped restore a portion of the people's confidence in the Confederate government. He summed up his case with a plea to the Secretary of War: "Take away these detailed men and you destroy the battalion, virtually lose possession of the country and certainly all the cattle in it. It is with confidence claimed that nowhere in the Confederacy can the services of these few detailed men be so valuable as in the present organization."[23] Secretary Seddon in the end agreed with Northrop, and the detailed men were permitted to stay at work on the pine prairies.

With the coming of fall, demand for Florida cattle once again increased as it had in past years, but few of the commissary districts were able to produce the expected number of beeves for slaughter. The Fourth District contributed only 169 head during the first half of October. Major Summer's formal departure was partly to blame for this low yield, as was heightened enemy activity. Reports to the effect that large numbers of cattle from the Saint Marys River region were being illegally removed from the state made collections of beef in the north difficult. Such drainage of vital provisions could not continue if the needs of the military were to be met through another lean winter. Shrinking rebel-controlled territory plus increased demand strained the commissary system even further in what remained of the Confederacy.[24]

Chief Commissary White answered a query as to the number of head he anticipated delivering by the end of October with caution. With luck, he wrote, three to five hundred head per week might be realized, possibly one thousand before trail conditions deteriorated with the coming of winter and forced a halt to cattle drives. Major Guerin complained that his troops in South Carolina already were hungry and that they only occasionally were issued any sort of meat. Friction between social classes plagued Charleston, as poorer citizens grumbled that they suffered short rations while the remaining elite in the besieged city enjoyed meals including beef and even a little pork. To stave off social unrest, Guerin placed his minimum requirement at three thousand head a month, and he requested that cattle begin the trip via Savannah as soon as possible.[25]

Major White interpreted this petition from Guerin as an attempt to directly order him to supply the needed provisions. He angrily replied that he took his orders from the commissary-general in Richmond and that "no general [referring to Beauregard] can command me and I will obey no orders except from those to whom I report." The figure of three thousand head per month could never be met at that time; all the cattle White had collected waited in Georgia for Guerin's drovers. Realizing that White's amity was essential for obtaining Florida beef, the South Carolinian quickly apologized by clarifying his statements as to who gave orders to Florida's chief commissary. In a letter he explained that his true intention was to merely convey a request and not give an order. But his responsibilities forced him to inquire as to the number of cows Charleston might expect to receive from the peninsula in the near future. Mollified, White estimated that three to five hundred was the best that he could provide under the circumstances.[26]

Commissary-General Northrop also lashed back at his own critics, claiming that others caused food shortages, not he or his subordinates. He charged that since the past summer Generals Robert E. Lee and Beauregard had maintained agents in Florida who competed with Commissary Department representatives there. The fact that he had little solid evidence to prove his allegations did little to deter Northrop from continuing such attacks. Only his own energetic leadership, Northrop modestly asserted, prolonged the movement of such supplies as were reaching the armies. The commissary-general singled out General Beauregard for his special wrath, partly because of ill feelings generated during the Guerin controversy. The hero of Fort Sumter, in Northrop's view, was nothing but an incompetent egomaniac whose blunders were ruining the South's chances for winning independence. The Commissary Department needed less hindrance from "charlatans" of his stripe if it were to meet the coming challenges.[27]

Such challenges proved formidable indeed to those responsible for feeding the rebel armies in late 1864. An internal report on the economic situation, dated 18 October 1864, painted a grim picture. At that point Georgia, Alabama, and Mississippi were the only states still providing any substantial subsistence for the Confederate forces still active east of the Mississippi River. Then the chief commissary of Georgia telegraphed to Richmond that he could not forward another pound of meat for any command. Alabama and Mississippi authorities were doing their utmost to aid Beauregard's army and the Army of Tennessee, now under the fiery John Bell Hood. South Carolina at that time was barely feeding the soldiers and numerous prisoners of war held in camps such as the one located at Florence. Bountiful Florida "is exhausted and can only respond to local demand," ran one evaluation. Northrop needed only to make a short trip from his Richmond office to see the effects of hunger on the health and spirits of the men doing the fighting.[28]

By necessity cattle gathering continued late into the fall of 1864, with about five hundred head leaving the state each week. One commissary officer thought that figure firm unless "interference of our Commissary-General, or some unanticipated course breaks into our operations." In some areas there still existed some cattle ready for export to other states. Alabama, hosting Hood's army at the end of October, was forced to face the problem of how to supply the daily rations for its guests. Many parties from that state ventured into the Florida panhandle searching for cattle, and one wealthy contractor arranged for cows to be driven northward across the Shoal River and from there into southern Alabama. Informants claimed that at least seventy-five hundred head grazed within Walton County, these having been previously gathered by Confederates for their use. Bridges across the Shoal were constructed to facilitate cattle crossings, and soldiers were detailed for the construction and herding. Cavalrymen, for example from the Eighth Mississippi Cavalry regiment, drove the creatures along wilderness paths to the stream and beyond through largely uninhabited west Florida counties.[29]

Many Georgians also rode into Florida seeking cattle at about the same time. Colonel Daniel F. Cocke, a state commissary agent, led one group collecting cattle, and he managed to irritate Floridians in the process. Cocke and his men herded beef from the Fourth and Fifth Commissary Districts, as the colonel found the climate there most agreeable. Cocke's command earned a reputation for being careless drovers who lost too many head along the trail and who delivered their charges in very poor shape. While White badly needed all the assistance he could get, Cocke became almost a liability. Florida district commanders claimed that he was "an incompetent as far as operations in Florida . . . [were] concerned."[30]

White finally moved against Colonel Cocke when he discovered that the Georgian had made personal investments in large numbers of cattle in south Florida in hopes of turning a profit on them in his home state. White angrily confronted Cocke about these dealings, stating that under the circumstances his actions were not only unethical but bordered on being illegal. He ordered Cocke to turn over the beef in question to the proper governmental authorities or suffer the consequences. White then expelled the colonel and his band from the vital cattle country and sent

them into the western First District. Cocke's men soon complained that
there were few cows in the district and that most of the region to which
they had been assigned lay well inside Union-controlled territory. The
disgruntled Georgians managed to scrape together only about 150 head,
a number they found most unsatisfactory. Major White had skillfully
saved the south Florida herds from these freebooters by shunting them
off to the panhandle.[31]

Colonel Cocke was correct, however, in his conclusion that beef was
getting harder and harder to find. Some observers reckoned that Florida's
reserves of cattle stood on the brink of exhaustion. White strongly dis-
agreed with such gloomy opinions, pointing to the droves that continued
to come up from the south. Almost seven hundred, for example, passed
through Madison in November and went on into Georgia without much
delay. White anticipated that there would be a heavy demand for beef
from Confederate troops concentrating to oppose Sherman's march to
the sea, not knowing how few soldiers stood in the red-headed Ohioan's
path. Sherman's triumphant arrival before Savannah on 10 December
severed the rail link to Charleston, and the great campaign as a whole
wreaked havoc with rebel logistics. White learned from officers in Georgia that the Union army's wake of destruction in their state made them
even more dependent than ever on Floridians for food and supplies. "We
shall need all the beef you can furnish us," pleaded one official, "provided
we can keep open our communications with Charleston."[32]

Cattle gathering in Florida continued in hopes of filling such requests
until 22 December, but only with marginal success. The beeves taken
from the range in near-starving condition yielded only small amounts of
substandard meat, generating bitter complaints from the various units
receiving it. In response White issued instructions to his herdsmen to take
better care of the cows in their charge and not push them so hard while
on the trail. He expected his last reserve, the Fifth District, to contribute
a few more head before the end of the year. "You have saved our army
from starving," said the chief commissary in praise of district commander James McKay. The Scot meanwhile took on the additional responsibility of being the Confederate Indian agent for south Florida,
somehow finding trade goods and presents sufficient to keep the remaining Seminoles neutral in the continuing struggle. The government allot-
ted eighty thousand dollars for the purchase of such items and considered
it worthwhile if peaceful relations were maintained.[33]

December 1864, yet another hungry month for the embattled rebel
armies, passed with little to cheer the people on the home front. On 16
December the Army of Tennessee went down to a devastating defeat
before Nashville that all but eliminated it as an effective military force.

Meanwhile, Lee's "miserables" shivered in the trenches and "bomb-proofs" around Petersburg and watched the Federals opposing them grow steadily stronger while they grew only weaker. Southerners grumbled over this state of affairs and demanded explanations from their leaders, which none could give. As usual, the caustic commissary-general bore the brunt of criticism. Rumors circulated around Richmond that large, untouched stocks existed down in Georgia and that a competent person placed in charge could harvest it for the cause. Northrop labeled as absurd the notion that sustenance for all existed anywhere in the constantly contracting area under government control. He blamed enemy activity and the lack of grain and proper forage for the current meat shortages. The premature slaughter of young cows, forced by circumstances, decreased productivity in the herds remaining in Confederate hands, in his view. Other sources must be found, even if cotton had to be traded across the lines in exchange for food from the Yankees.[34]

As in the past, too much was expected from the Florida peninsula when plans were being formulated to provision the faltering South and its gray warriors. One Confederate official estimated that as many as twenty-five thousand head of beef cattle could still be found there, which translated in theory into millions of pounds of meat for army rations. To counter such rosy pronouncements and fend off increasingly bitter congressional attacks, Commissary-General Northrop issued a report describing the true state of the Confederacy's beef supply. According to him, Florida had indeed given large numbers of cattle and might be able to contribute still more. While the state might possibly furnish a few thousand more head, hundreds of thousands were impossible. "These marvelous accounts," wrote Northrop, "are believed to be idle, as this bureau has received accurate information of the number."[35]

On 9 January 1865 the cattle-driving season for 1864 officially ended. Chief Commissary White decided to terminate movements of beef out of the state for the reason that General Sherman's army, moving into South Carolina, effectively blocked communications. Furthermore, lack of forage for the cows themselves curtailed most droving operations. Despite the apparent collapse of Confederate resistance in Georgia, some Florida officers thought that cattle would still be needed in the spring for government use. Others, more realistic, worried that the dream of independence might be fading away despite all the sacrifices of the last four years. A despairing Major White rhetorically asked Governor Milton, "What is to be the fate of our armies, now almost solidly dependent upon this state for meat. Heaven only knows."[36]

In addition to meat, Florida cows supplied leather, a material critical to the rebel war effort in many ways. Cowhides were processed into shoes or harnesses for horses and mules pulling wagons or artillery. Leather grew increasingly scarce, forcing government agents to collect skins from cattle slaughtered by the Commissary Department or by the various armies. Soldiers, desperate for footwear during the winter, resorted to taking hides from the butcher pens and fashioning crude moccasins for themselves. In September 1864 the Quartermaster Department acquired permission to collect hides and create finished leather on the largest scale possible.

Major F. W. Dillard, a quartermaster stationed in Columbus, Georgia, was responsible for an area that included Florida with regard to skin gathering. By that time Columbus had become the chief domestic source of shoes for the Confederate army, so a steady supply of leather was more than essential. War Department orders specified that hides be purchased in addition to other products resulting from slaughtering cattle owned by the government. In the event that Commissary Department officers refused to surrender the skins, the Quartermaster Department was to confiscate them. Commissary officials were also to seize any hides kept by ranchers after selling the meat from their cows to the army. Such an arrangement indicated why the bureaucracy of the Confederacy at times hurt more than helped its conduct of the war. To have one government agency impressing goods from another showcases an organizational flaw that plagued the rebel procurement system during the last years of the conflict.[37]

Most Floridians endeavored to comply with the law regarding cattle hides, but in the wilds of the interior many cowmen failed to surrender their skins to government authorities. One reason for this reluctance was that cowhides, like so many once-common commodities in the South, were by the end of 1864 a high-priced and sought-after item. Speculators in the region bought up as many hides as they could find at much greater prices than the government was willing to pay. Potential profit led ranchers to kill cows on the range for their hides alone, leaving the meat to spoil. Major White asked that the governor stop such waste by seizing skins in private hands and thus put the speculators out of business. Illict slaughtering that in any way hindered the effort of the commissaries to buy or impress beef could not be tolerated. The major had nothing but contempt for these cattle owners "who are able to furnish the amount of beef they contract to deliver and still have a sufficiency left to furnish their families and negroes with leather."[38]

In January 1865 a significant realignment of Confederate military forces in Florida altered the state's ability to provide beef for the Confederacy. Munnerlyn's cattle battalion, commonly known as the Cow Cavalry, was transferred from Chief Commissary White's control and attached to state troops then being raised. As a result the Commissary Department in Florida now had to apply to state commanders for men from the battalion to be assigned to cattle collecting or to protect civilians so engaged. White naturally disliked this new chain of command, but he had little choice but to accept it. He instructed his district officers to compile lists of names of experienced wranglers and forward them to Tallahassee. These men would be needed soon, for White wished to resume herding operations as early as April. He hoped that by then the grasses in the upper section of the state could subsist beef on the move. He warned Captain McKay that the bulk of the year's cows for the government must come from his district, as other sections of the peninsula were depleted of cattle. "I do not anticipate when the demands may be made," he wrote, "nor their strength."[39]

Major White solicited Commissary-General Northrop's assistance in retaining the Cow Cavalry under his command, since the new system of control was less efficient than the old. He explained that these experienced cattle guards must remain at their special assignment. Without the contribution of these experts, Florida could never furnish the fifteen thousand head requested by the Confederate government. White decried the general lack of understanding of the importance of the beef supply for continuing the war. The annual number of cattle delivered, the major argued, exceeded in value to the Confederacy all other Florida products, excluding salt. "Experience has proven that our operations will be crippled," White pleaded, "and embarrassed during the whole season afterward for the lack of them." Northrop, who was under heavy pressure to step down from his post and was soon to be replaced, chose not to again involve himself in affairs in remote Florida. Thus, the orders remained unchanged, and White lost control of the special unit of armed drovers.[40]

Hunger arrived in Florida in February 1865, when troops stationed there failed to receive adequate rations for the first time. Beef brought in from the ranges as a last resort was so lean that many soldiers, even famished ones, refused to eat it. Troops complained that such rations as these would ordinarily be marked "condemned" and scrapped. Even units in supposedly cattle-rich south Florida groused about the quality of their daily meals. Their requests for such substitutes as salted beef, pork, or bacon went unanswered, for none was available. In order to maintain morale in the battalions defending east Florida, pickled beef, known as "salt horse," was issued to their cooks. An unknown amount of beef on the hoof still wandered in Walton and Holmes Counties, but the proximity of Federal outposts made any possible collection of them very risky. Agents from neighboring Alabama, seeking beef for the remnants of the once-formidable Army of Tennessee, requested permission to cross the state border once again to try their luck. Any meat they uncovered was pickled and sent northward to meet the still-great need among Confederate soldiers. Such commissary personnel working in the Florida panhandle in 1865 faced not only Union troops but numerous bands of rebel deserters rampaging through the countryside.[41]

Another struggle reached a climax in February on the political front in Richmond. With the clamoring in and out of Congress for change reaching a crescendo, Jefferson Davis named Kentuckian John C. Breckinridge as the new Secretary of War and nominated Robert E. Lee to become general-in-chief of all the Confederate armies. Both men quickly moved to ease the crippling food shortages, which were causing droves of soldiers to desert. For his part, Commissary-General Northrop could only offer unconvincing and sophistic excuses and evasions. After a final stormy session with President Davis and Breckinridge, his fate was sealed. Northrop's special relationship with Davis could no longer shield him from the blame and ultimate responsibility for the failures of his department. When Lee joined with those calling for his dismissal, Davis finally removed Northrop as commissary-general on 6 February. General Isaac M. Saint John soon afterward assumed the duties of the chief supply officer of the Confederacy.[42]

Saint John, formerly in charge of the Nitre and Mining Bureau, was highly respected by most government officials. More energetic and innovative than Northrop, he replaced the existing system of central depots with a series of local establishments to which farmers could deliver their produce directly. While the overall situation actually did not improve significantly, soldiers and civilians were hopeful that basic rations would soon be more plentiful now that the unpopular Northrop was gone. However, the fundamental problems of a failing railroad network, the pressure of the Union naval blockade, Sherman's invasion of the lower South with its slashing of supply lines, and the chaos caused by the lack of a stable currency all remained to be overcome. One is left to wonder how long the popularity of General Saint John as commissary-general would have lasted had his tenure extended beyond six weeks. His predecessor did not escape abuse even by leaving office. A clerk who saw Northrop on a Richmond street recorded that he "looks down, dark, and dissatisfied. Lee's army *eats* without him."[43]

In March 1865 the end was fast approaching for the Confederate States of America. Grant was slowly winning his battle of attrition around Petersburg, while the unstoppable Sherman and his "bummers" pressed on into the Carolinas. President Davis, unaccountably optimistic, told the rebel Congress on 13 March that the nation still possessed men and supplies "sufficient to obtain success." In order to continue the struggle, he conceded, productive areas and vital lines of communication must somehow be protected. Florida itself was finally connected with Georgia by the completion of the trunk line between the towns of Live Oak, Florida, and Lawton in Georgia. Plans existed—but not the resources in laborers and materials—to build a second connector from Quincy to the banks of the Chattahoochee River. Neither rail line, of course, had any real effect on the final outcome of the war. [44]

By the spring of 1865 even distant Florida felt the disintegration of the Confederate government; it was like the aftershocks of an earthquake. Purchasing by the Commissary Department all but ceased because of a lack of funds. White informed his superiors in Richmond that at least two million dollars must be forwarded without delay if the army was to have cattle from his state. The major also desired help in stopping Georgians from entering Florida to make unauthorized purchases of farm products. East Florida, now a poor cattle country, produced scarcely enough meat to satisfy local needs. Major White made it clear that Georgians or any-one else in need of supplies could draw them from well-stocked ware-houses like those in Tallahassee and that private parties gathering provender would not be tolerated. There was little food available for rural residents as it was. All the beeves gathered in the Fourth Commissary District during the month of March went to feed the soldiers of the Cow Cavalry, and probably their families as well. Also, an attempt by rebel officials to suspend the issue of fresh beef until the cattle gained weight by grazing on spring grasses failed miserably. [45]

The herding of cattle for the government resumed in April, but few cows made the journey to the depots. By that time many cattle owners presumed the war to be lost and were reluctant to sell their cattle for virtually worthless Confederate scrip. Supply officers had been forced to confiscate the cattle they obtained, in the process further alienating the demoralized civilian population. But White and his men remained determined to do their duty until the end. In a report to the new commissary-general, White explained the nature and history of the cattle trade and asked for instructions as to whether he should have the ready beeves driven or slaughtered on the spot and their flesh salted. He urged construction of the proposed line from Quincy to the Chattahoochee to link that town with Columbus via steamboats still running up the river. If such a new route were opened, beef cattle could be moved west of the Suwannee to some point on the Apalachicola River and there killed by military butchers. The salted meat could then be transported by boat to Columbus for possible transshipment to Macon. "We still have in Florida an immense number of stock cattle," White overoptimistically informed Richmond in the midst of its evacuation by the rebel government, "from which a continuing supply of 10–15 thousand may be drawn by the government."[46]

Gathering of such cattle for the Army of Northern Virginia, then rumored to be seeking to join General Johnston's command and fight on, progressed until after the surrender at Appomattox Court House. Major White, still unaware of events in Virginia, estimated that Florida range beef would be fit as army rations sometime in May. On 14 April he wrote to Saint John in regard to Lee's army that "from our forward position, in respect to beef from which they are cut off, we are expected to contribute a larger amount—in proportion to our supplies than others." White continued to collect provisions even after the government for which he labored was scattered to the winds. Nothing from Florida managed to reach Lee's forces before they ceased to exist as an army and entered the realm of legend.[47]

Even after Lee's surrender the war continued in other parts of the Confederacy as yet unoccupied. In an attempt to combat the ruinous flood of rumors, General Sam Jones, senior Confederate officer in Florida, issued a circular dated 28 April dealing with the meaning of the defeat in Virginia for the rest of the Confederate army. Inasmuch as the army Lee capitulated at Appomattox was scarcely two-thirds the size of the one lost with the fall of Vicksburg, in Jones's opinion the war was not yet lost. He urged the troops under his command "to stand firm and true and present a bold and defiant front to our enemies. Such a course will strengthen our government and aid in securing an honorable peace." Many weary soldiers, however, slipped away from the ranks and went home despite Jones's pleadings.[48]

Those men remaining with the units considered further resistance to be useless. Rather than face defeat, Governor Milton took his own life with a shotgun blast at his Marianna plantation home. Union forces occupied Tampa on 27 May and sent commissioners into the countryside to accept the surrenders of all remaining Confederate troops. On 5 June Munnerlyn's cattle battalion gave up its arms to the Federal army's Second Florida Cavalry. All other organized bodies of soldiers south of Brooksville followed suit in Tampa three days later. The paroled ex-rebels returned to their homes, often to find them reduced to shells, and began once again striving to earn a living in a region with a shattered economy.[49]

The Confederacy received at the very least fifty thousand head of Florida cattle during its brief existence. Stringy and unappetizing as the grass-fed beef was, the venison-like meat often served as the only protein in the rations of Confederate soldiers fighting in the lower South. Toward the end of the war such meat helped sustain men who were at times close to starvation. Florida beef aided in subsisting the Army of Tennessee during the hard winters of 1863, 1864, and 1865. Florida cattle also nourished the defenders of Charleston, as well as indirectly helping the Army of Northern Virginia by freeing other foodstuffs for its use. Union prisoners of war owed more than one meal to the exertions of the Commissary Department's Florida branch, but such efforts never came close to averting the human tragedy that was Andersonville prison.

Despite the amounts of beef Florida provided for the Confederate government, the expectations placed on the state by those in charge of its logistical planning could never be met. Poorly informed Confederate leaders tended to exaggerate the number of cattle in Florida and made unrealistic demands upon the peninsula. Even senior rebel officers with experience in Florida, including Commissary-General Northrop and Robert E. Lee, failed to take into account the problems involved with rounding up and driving range cattle. Supply officers in the state endured a constant bombardment of impractical requests for more and more cattle to feed troops serving all over the lower half of the Confederate States. In the end Florida beef only prolonged the conflict and did not alter its outcome.

7 Union Forces in Florida

John Hay of Illinois fell in love with the peninsula of Florida almost at first sight. The former law student, poet, and presidential secretary-turned-soldier enjoyed the opportunity to tour Union-held portions of the state early in 1864 while seeking support from native Unionists for the reconstruction of Florida along the lines of Lincoln's "ten percent" plan. While on this sensitive political mission, young Major Hay waxed poetic in letters to relatives and to his partner in the White House, John G. Nicolay, over the natural beauty he encountered. He wrote to his grandfather that he had never seen a more handsome country and that the soil was about as rich as the prairie loam in his home state. "All sorts of fruit and grain grow," he observed, "with very little cultivation, and fish and game of every kind abound." To his friend Nicolay he described tropical sunsets unlike any in the northern latitudes; to him the setting sun in Florida descended "over the pines like ashes of roses, and . . . [hung] for an instant on the horizon like a bubble of blood." Hay, enthralled by the landscape and hopeful of future profit, purchased seven tracts of land before his Florida sojourn came to an end.[1]

Thousands of such uniformed visitors passed through Florida throughout the war years, and their activities influenced the state's economic contributions to the Confederacy in many ways. Both Union soldiers and civilian leaders attempted to bring Florida back into the Union by encouraging local Unionists and by such methods as colonizing the peninsula with Yankees or freedmen. But the main thrust of Federal policy beginning in 1862 involved the interdiction and destruction of supplies destined for the rebel armies. During the second half of the conflict, Union officers were well aware of Florida's increasing importance as a source of beef, pork, corn, and salt, and they utilized the military forces at their disposal to injure the Confederate war-making capacity by striking at Florida's economy. But, with the exception of the abortive Olustee campaign of 1864, Florida remained largely a Union military sideshow, not rating the commitment of large numbers of troops that other theaters of war received. Nonetheless, Florida figured in logistic plans for the Federals' own units, located at the end of a long and complicated supply line. Union regiments were often encouraged to search the countryside for provisions to augment their regular rations.

As the Union land and naval forces established bases in coastal towns in early 1862, the concept of returning Florida to its old allegiance surfaced in the North. Eli Thayer of Massachusetts, educator, businessman, and free-soil zealot during the bloody antebellum years in Kansas, grasped the possibilities in the southern state at about the same time. His New England Immigrant Aid Company lobbied Congress for permission to raise a volunteer force of some twenty thousand men to eject Confederate sympathizers and then settle there as loyalists on free homesteads. The resulting solid block of Unionist support would help to convert the peninsula once more into a faithful member of the United States. The Committee of Military Affairs of the House of Representatives in Washington investigated Thayer's scheme and concluded that it might offer a means to strike the rebellion a telling blow and fulfill a Republican campaign promise to distribute free farmland to anyone wanting it. The state's strategic location and abundant pine forests were also viable justifications for implementing Thayer's plan of colonization. Even more persuasive to the committeemen was the suggestion that the growing numbers of escaped slaves entering Union lines could be settled in remote sections of the Florida peninsula.[2]

Interest in establishing a loyalist colony in Florida lasted well into 1863. Thayer himself publicized the design in speeches in New York's Cooper Institute, where he called for a wave of settlers to venture southward to the land of flowers. The Confiscation Acts approved by Congress earlier in the war, in his view, provided the legal means for acquiring land for such homesteaders. Under Thayer's plan, Florida planters were liable to forfeit all of their lands over 160 acres to faithful citizens. Fortunately for such agriculturalists, the momentum of the drive to implement such a colonization of Florida died when it reached the War Department. Secretary Edwin M. Stanton had neither the time nor the interest to support the project. Questions about the practicality of the Thayer proposal arose in departmental circles, and it was eventually pigeonholed.[3]

Floridians siding with the Confederate cause took such ideas seriously, for they confirmed long-held beliefs as to the ultimate intentions of

abolitionists like Thayer. Governor Milton for one entertained no doubts
that the Lincoln administration would use his state as a home for liber-
ated slaves if given the chance. Newspapers throughout the South attributed Northern interest in resettling Florida with blacks to a base
hunger for cotton. Obviously immigrants, regardless of race, could raise
considerable crops of cotton under the protection of the army and navy
of the United States, thereby opening a source of supply for New England textile mills and foreign markets. Only pressing needs for troops
on other fronts and cotton flowing northward from the Mississippi River
valley stopped an operation that might have turned Florida into an important outpost for Union forces.[4]

A wave of immigrants was not required to establish commercial ties
between blue-clad soldiers and sailors and natives of Florida, however.
Local trade continued within those areas under Union control, much to
the displeasure of Confederate officials. While in command at Pensacola
in 1861, General Braxton Bragg struggled to break up illicit trade among
unpatriotic Floridians and the enemy garrison at Fort Pickens. Some of
these civilians furnished the Federal troops on Santa Rosa Island with
fresh provisions carried there by small boats. Bragg banned all contact
between Pensacola and Walton County after learning that a few of the
residents of that area had been supplying the blockading Federal fleet
with vegetables and fresh beef. County citizens protested Bragg's restrictions during a meeting held on 21 June, and they chose a committee to
negotiate with the general about reopening this essential commerce. The
presence of Union forces eager to buy provisions, in this case, superseded
loyalty to the Confederacy and helped undermine support for the rebel
war effort.[5]

Further down the Gulf coast, illegal commercial contacts continued
despite efforts by Confederate authorities to suppress them. Numerous
sailing vessels of all types moved between Federal-controlled Key West
and the coast southwest of Tampa Bay. Late in 1861, officials there char-
tered a steamer, James McKay's *Scottish Chief,* and went after the fishermen and traders who were providing the Federals with food and
information. Armed with a single six-pound cannon, the *Chief* moved
down the coast, capturing some twenty-four small boats and their crews.
This effectively curtailed the traffic with Key West, but communications
between the island and the mainland continued throughout the war.
Parties of Union woodcutters from the Keys traded with small bands of
Seminoles remaining in the Miami River area, and such exchanges had
ominous connotations for Confederate hopes of keeping the Native
Americans out of the ongoing struggle.[6]

Commercial meetings between Federals and Floridians went on for the duration of the war as Union supply officers attempted to feed their soldiers. The quality of his rations always remained a primary interest to both Billy Yank and his Southern counterpart Johnny Reb. Beef was a key element in the diets of both Confederate and Union soldiers stationed in Florida during the Civil War. Despite the relative abundance of provisions enjoyed by Union troops, food shortages were a fact of life and did occur in almost every unit at one time or another. This was especially true in Florida, for men serving there were at the end of a long, complicated supply line subject to interruptions by enemy action or mismanagement by their own quartermasters. The presence of beef cattle within easy reach offered a solution to ration problems. Union commanders, well aware of the beef then flowing out of the state to the rebel armies, moved to interdict this trade and provision their own regiments at the same time. Thus, Federal operations aimed at seizing cattle herds not only damaged the Confederates' ability to continue fighting, but also helped to maintain their own forces on the peninsula. In addition, the army provided a ready market for cattle owned, or rustled, by anyone willing to sell. The purchase of such beeves supported the Unionist cause in the state with the power of the greenback as well as the bayonet.[7]

The area of northeast Florida between Saint Augustine and Fernandina proved an excellent base from which Union troops could wage a type of economic warfare on the Florida cattle business. Intelligence about the activities of Confederate commissary officers engaged in collecting and driving the bovines northward was not difficult for Federal commanders to gather, and its significance was not lost on them. General William Birney, for instance, launched raids up the Saint Johns River in May 1864 to stop cattle-driving operations by the rebels. Birney's men captured a commissary agent and the four hundred head of cattle he was herding to the waiting Confederate forces. The Union leader believed it well within his power to appropriate those droves being collected on the headwaters of the broad river, and with luck even those grazing in Brevard County to the south. Possibly as many as twenty thousand beef cattle, in Birney's view, could "belong to us if we choose to take them."[8]

Such raiding continued during the eventful summer of 1864, aimed at gathering cattle for Federal consumption while applying pressure on the rebels at all points in accordance with Lincoln's and Lieutenant General Ulysses S. Grant's strategy for winning the war. The Union Chief Commissary of Subsistence at Hilton Head, South Carolina, urged that such operations be continued in order to furnish troops camped at Fernandina and Saint Augustine with fresh meat. Cattle from the interior, driven to Fernandina, could be easily carried southward to the old city on naval transports to avoid Confederate cavalry attacks. What such a voyage did to the quality of the beef bound for the butcher's block is unknown, but certainly the taste suffered somewhat. Troops in the Saint Johns area received orders to drive in and slaughter any cows found in their neighborhoods and to use them either as their own rations or to feed "contrabands" or white Unionist refugees under their care. Armed with reports that the greater part of the beef in Florida roamed among the pines east of the Saint Johns, information that incidentally turned out to be erroneous, Yankee infantry and cavalry fanned out into the countryside searching for meals on the hoof.[9]

Captain Albert W. Peck of the Seventeenth Connecticut Infantry, stationed at Saint Augustine, worked out a system of his own for securing fresh beef for the men in his company. He would occasionally send out two soldiers on a horse-drawn cart into the nearby woods. There they hunted and with their rifles shot two or three cows, dressed the carcasses, and returned to camp with the meat and hides. If the owners of these slaughtered cattle were able to prove their loyalty to the Union they could apply at headquarters in Jacksonville for reimbursement for their lost animals. In such instances the government paid from four to six cents per pound for the beef, and four cents for cowhides. When cattle eventually grew scarce near their encampment, men from the Seventeenth Connecticut crossed to the other side of the Saint Johns to search for meat for their company cooks. Confederate pickets, upset by these incursions, posted a notice warning against cow hunting on the west side of the river. Captain Peck recalled later that his soldiers did not risk venturing across the Saint Johns to forage after this incident.[10]

Assembling cattle outside the safety of their fortified positions sometimes turned out to be a difficult and hazardous mission for Union troops. One party found themselves lost while trying to return to Saint Augustine with their booty and were forced to ask directions at a lonely cabin by the trail. The woman living there cheerfully pointed the bluecoats not toward the town but back into a swamp, where the Federal's four-legged prisoners all escaped. The soldiers might not have followed these faulty instructions if they had realized that they were talking to the mother of three Confederate soldiers. Other cattle gatherers were even less fortunate. A force of rebel cavalry ambushed some Union troops near Green Cove Springs on 23 October 1864 while they were returning with "a large drove of fine cattle to enrich their commissary stores with what they called rebel beef."[11]

Union soldiers often enjoyed the aid of loyalist sympathizers while engaged in military operations in Florida. Acting as guides, or herding the beef themselves, these Floridians often made the difference between success and failure in the field. Many of them were former cattlemen whose beef had gone to the Confederate army by impressment, an act ending any enthusiasm they may have harbored for the rebel cause. A Union officer in Saint Augustine, Lieutenant J. H. Linsley, remarked that the one genuine Union man he met during his tour in Florida had lost one son and five hundred head of cattle to the Confederates. As a rule, Federal foraging parties avoided seizing beef belonging to proven Unionists. However, they might take two to three calves to test their fidelity, and their flavor.[12]

Union soldiers based at Pensacola also competed with the rebels for use of the state's beef cattle reserves. Present in force since the first days of the war, United States military units operated from Forts Pickens and Barrancas to damage the Confederate economy while simultaneously improving their own food. A steamer, captured by the Union navy late in 1862, provided a quick and secure method for transporting seized cattle from Santa Rosa and Walton Counties back to the Federal positions around Pensacola Bay. As the herds close to such sites were depleted, the garrisons were forced to conduct raids deeper and deeper into the Florida panhandle during 1864. Confederate troops in the area responsible for opposing such thrusts were prevented from undertaking more worthwhile campaigns against their enemies. Union attacks kept such units very busy. "Being entirely without fresh beef," wrote Union Brigadier General Alexander Asboth on 27 January 1864, "I started day before yesterday a party of infantry and cavalry" in search of the needed meat and rebel troops.[13]

Asboth, a Hungarian-born volunteer, collected abandoned cattle in the immediate area of Pensacola Bay to keep them out of Confederate hands. He invited refugees and Florida Unionists to drive their cattle to the coast opposite Santa Rosa Island. There United States government agents paid six cents per pound for such animals. Representatives of the Union navy also purchased beef for issuance to crews of vessels on blockade duty. Supply officers from both services, in line with long tradition, competed vigorously and at times acrimoniously with each other to procure the grass-fed beef from the Florida ranges. At one point General Asboth warned Admiral David G. Farragut that if such conflicts did not cease, Union soldiers and sailors might end up fighting each other instead of the rebels.[14]

Federal attempts to raid effectively from Pensacola into the interior were hampered by a shortage of mounted units. Clearly, foot soldiers could not drive semiwild cattle from the wooded ranges to the shores of the Gulf of Mexico. Eventually, however, the organization of the Unionist First Florida Cavalry regiment late in 1863 gave the Federals the reach and mobility necessary to confiscate and drive hundreds of head. When a group of pro-Confederate planters slipped into Santa Rosa County with the intention of recovering their stock and taking them out of danger, Union horse soldiers rode to arrest them and seize their property. Such cavalry-led raids proved effective and doubly imperative when fresh meat ran short and government contractors failed to live up to their agreements. Union troops stripped the pastures of far western Florida of beef to such a degree that by the spring of 1865, civilians facing the prospect of starvation took food from the Federal authorities and thereby admitted that the Confederate government had failed to properly care for its people.[15]

Nowhere was the Union army's campaign against Florida beef herds conducted with as much vigor as in the southern half of the peninsula. Army leaders knew of the unsettled conditions in the near-wilderness and hoped to capitalize upon them. General Daniel P. Woodbury, one of the more vocal advocates of cutting Confederate supply lines in Florida, learned in 1863 that nearly eight hundred deserters or conscription evaders were lurking between Charlotte Harbor and Lake Okeechobee. The general thought that establishing a small base on the shores of the harbor might give these fugitives an opportunity to seek amnesty and enlist in the Federal forces. If sent against the cattle herds, they might disrupt the rebel beef trade in that part of the state. Woodbury estimated that the enemy was driving about two thousand cows each week to the Confederate armies. While Woodbury's estimate of the size of the weekly cattle trade was exaggerated tenfold, his conclusion that south Florida contained most of the Confederacy's remaining beef inventory was sound, and he was eager to curtail that supply even further.[16]

In December 1863 Union forces situated a base at old Fort Myers as an important first step in disrupting the economy of south Florida. Woodbury feared that Fort Myers was located too far south, but he used the Seminole War fort anyway as the best site available to him. His plan provided for two stages. First, his troops would raid inland to destroy saltworks and trading centers so far from the coast as to be beyond the reach of the navy. Woodbury then planned to take Tampa and begin pushing further to the north from that town to stop Confederate agents from gathering cattle in middle Florida and also to isolate the southern section from the rest of the Confederacy. General Nathaniel P. Banks of Massachusetts, the departmental commander, agreed that "a force should be sent there sufficiently large to scour the country," if the supply of beef in Florida was as important as Woodbury claimed. Despite Woodbury's death by yellow fever in 1864, the Federal high command was beginning to realize the value of Florida to the Confederate economy.[17]

Meanwhile, Union cavalry and infantry patrols ranged deep into cattle country seeking to secure these increasingly valuable animals before Confederate commissary officers located them. One such expedition in 1864 netted 350 head after a sweep near the old Seminole War–era post at Fort Thompson. Beef seized in these raids went by the dozen in boats down the Caloosahatchee River to Sanibel Island, where ships of the East Gulf Blockading Squadron put in for fresh provisions. So many head of cattle leaked through the Fort Myers "hole" that rebel forces launched an unsuccessful attack upon the Union bastion in February 1865. The assaulting column, composed of members of Munnerlyn's cattle battalion, failed to breach the fort's thick walls and had to retreat into the interior. Ironically, the Federals subsequently abandoned Fort Myers in March and left it as a shelter for rebel deserters and outlaws.[18]

As important as they were, the herds of beef cattle were not the only targets for Union troops waging war against Florida's economy. Some raiding parties gathered oranges as well as cattle. Particularly along the banks of the Saint Johns, citrus groves fell victim to the axes of Federal soldiers determined to deny their fruit to the enemy. While destroying trees, these men usually carried as many oranges as possible back to their bivouacs for consumption by their units. On one such expedition, enlisted men packed three hundred barrels with fruit for distribution within their regiment. A portion of this lot of citrus fruit was loaded aboard transport ships and taken to the lodgment at Hilton Head. Large quantities of citrus were shipped to army hospitals, especially the "sour" oranges thought by both Federal and Confederate doctors to be useful in treating malaria cases. One New York regimental commander heard a rumor that five hundred thousand such oranges awaited harvesting near New Smyrna and could be easily obtained for the government if a boat were sent down from Saint Augustine to retrieve them.[19]

Soldiers from the Seventeenth Connecticut Infantry acquired a taste for Florida citrus during their stay at Saint Augustine. Through the fall and winter months of 1864 details worked three and four times a week to pick oranges from a nearby grove whose owner permitted the bluecoats to help themselves. A fruit drink, probably braced with something stronger than orange juice, resulted from their labors. Like generations of tourists to follow, many Union soldiers sent Florida citrus fruit home to family and friends in the Northern states. Rolled in old newspapers and packed in boxes, the fruit was carried north to grace many tables in the dead of winter. This trade helped to revive the state's citrus industry during the postwar era.[20]

The countryside provided not only food for the occupying Union army, but also fuel and material with which to construct more durable shelters than canvas tents. Early in the conflict lumbermen who were willing to risk the wrath of secessionists by selling timber to the Federals became prosperous as a result. Union-held Key West, a practically tree-less island, was constantly short of wood. Loggers shipped in enough lumber and firewood, however, to meet military and civilian needs in the small community. Trees from the shores of Key Biscayne destined for Federal purchases fell to the woodsmen's axes, along with those on Florida's southwestern coast. One working party under contract to the authorities of the island ended up as prisoners of war as a result of cutting in the Fort Myers region in November 1861, but such events were unusual. The Confederates lacked enough men to patrol the vast area, so they could not prevent groups from Key West from landing and returning home with full cargoes of wood.[21]

Throughout the conflict Union forces roamed waterways all over north Florida, destroying saw mills and confiscating lumber and wood products. The navy searched for types of wood suitable for decks of warships, materials increasingly hard to obtain in the busy shipyards in the North. Hundreds of thousands of board feet of pine and countless barrels of resin and turpentine were acquired by the Yankees or were burned to deny their use to the rebels. Government agents preferred for timber to be taken intact, and they briskly competed for available forest products. In 1865 one such official received the authority to purchase one million board feet of lumber in Florida through the Federal-controlled port of Fernandina. President Lincoln personally issued orders to military personnel to provide transportation and "unmolested passage for purpose of getting said products through the lines."[22]

The greater Pensacola region, with its huge prewar lumbering industry, attracted the attention of Union officers. In August 1862 cavalrymen raided in the general vicinity of the village of Bagdad, once a lively industrial area. They loaded captured wood on boats for the return to the Federal enclave, and any left behind was put to the torch. An officer supervising such work sadly noted that the war had devastated once thriving business concerns such as the mills his men gleefully wrecked. "The valuable saw mills once so numerous in this section of the country," he wrote, "have been burned as have millions of feet of yellow pine and oak." As in the case of beef around Pensacola, soldier squared off against sailor over the useful timber. The army operated its own saw mill in the town and routinely exported lumber and logs to New Orleans for use by the government. Naval officers stationed at the Pensacola yard grew upset at the loss of wood they felt rightly belonged to them. They retaliated against the army by claiming cargoes of timber and refusing to issue passes for army units to use local waters for the conveyance of logs back to their bases. Only the end of hostilities cooled this internal quarrel.[23]

Although interservice rivalry flared over control of lumber and cattle, the Union army and navy more often than not cooperated in operations designed to inhibit Florida's capacity to contribute economically to the Confederacy. The state's many rivers provided not only avenues for them to attack plantations and farms in the interior, but also a means of speedy retreat should the rebels choose to fight. Beginning in 1862 gunboats plied the waters of the Saint Johns and helped to depopulate the river basin with their forays. Both sailors and soldiers plundered abandoned houses between Jacksonville and Enterprise on Lake Monroe. Some of the first African-American regiments raised for Federal service participated in missions here and along the Saint Marys River in early 1863. Crops of all types suffered damage because of their labors, and many agriculturalists left their lands near the rivers and headed inland. In this manner Confederates were deprived of otherwise productive farm land. Civilian morale also declined as people were economically ruined by the Union army's presence, which encountered only feeble responses by their own government. Such successes in east Florida inspired Federal officers to consider making even more daring moves aimed at preventing agricultural produce from reaching Confederates in South Carolina and Georgia.[24]

Almost from the start of the war, naval units on the Gulf coast conducted their own campaign of economic destruction in addition to carrying out their blockading duties. Operations to destroy saltworks located along the shores, as previously noted, occupied much of the sailors' and marines' time. However, nothing interested them so much as cotton. Neither officers nor enlisted men needed reminding how much prize money a single bale would bring. Raids up such rivers as the Suwannee provided plentiful opportunities to seize cotton, despite the real danger of being ambushed from the river banks by Confederate troops. Acting Ensign Christopher Craven of the gunboat USS *Sagamore* led such an expedition up the Suwannee in April 1864 and returned heavily laden with spoils. Craven's report catches the spirit of amphibious missions along the Florida coast:

> At dark I stood up to Old Clay landing (some 4 miles), which was formerly a rebel post. There were signs of a battery having been mounted. I landed in person and examined the place. Finding nothing worth capturing I stood up with boats. . . . Two miles further I passed some 10 bales of cotton which had been thrown in by refugees of my party, who landed below. One half mile further up I met the refugees floating down on bales of cotton. They told me the rebel agent at the landing had gone for assistance. I took them in the boats and started for the landing with the intention of burning the cotton. I arrived at that place [situated some 35 or

40 miles from the mouth of the river] at about 1:30 A.M. on the 23 instant. Finding no one there I stationed pickets and rafted 100 bales of cotton belonging to the rebel government, which I found stored in houses. The men being very much fatigued and daylight near at hand, I set fire to from 200 to 300 bales cotton, which was stored in four houses, one of which was a steam cotton gin and press. I spared one empty storehouse as I understood from the refugees it belonged to a sound Union man. I then manned the boats, took the raft in tow, and proceeded down the river.[25]

Craven's party and their valuable cotton bales safely returned to the coast and the waiting *Sagamore*. The gunboat's captain happily requested that a shallow-draft vessel transport all the captured fiber, mostly of the costly sea-island variety, back to his home port at Key West.

Union naval forces south of Tampa Bay concentrated not on cotton, but on sugar. Boatloads of sailors regularly cruised the Manatee River in search of hogsheads of sugar or molasses and the machinery used to process it. They burned well-known plantations to prevent future shipments to the rebel armies. In August 1864 a group from the Union warships *Stonewall* and *James L. Davis* ascended the Manatee some three miles in search of a sugar mill rumored to belong to "Jefferson Davis of Richmond" and therefore a most tempting target. Regardless of the mistake about its ownership, the blue-clad sailors pitched into the mill, systematically smashing presses and boilers and destroying all barrels stored there. An artillery shell with a crude time-delay fuse detonated in the mill building completed their work of eradication. As smoke from the burning mill rose, the crew reembarked for the trip downriver. Such missions devastated the remaining sugar growers in southwestern Florida and denied them a chance to regain a measure of prosperity derived from war-time demand for their crop. The Union military's policy of waging economic warfare in Florida bore fruit in a region far removed from the battlefields but of great importance nevertheless.[26]

The United States Navy chose its economic objectives with care, and the results of its endeavors were felt beyond the borders of Florida. Upon learning in October 1864 that a large fishery was located on Marsh's Island on the north bank of the Ochlockonee River to the west of Saint Marks, officers planned to attack it. Boats from the USS *Stars and Stripes,* containing some thirty men, headed for the island on the night of 19 October. Surprising the Confederate soldiers on guard duty, the sailors wrecked a large and valuable fishing sieve and two boats used in the work. They also burned every building on the site. The commander of the *Stars and Stripes* informed his superiors, after all hands had returned with sixteen prisoners, that the mission had been successful. His men broke up "one of the most important and reliable fisheries on the coast, furnishing large supplies not only to the interior districts of this State, but also to the commissariat of the rebel army." While the fishery, like saltworks similarly treated, arose quickly from the ashes to continue harvesting the sea for the South, these interruptions weakened an already strained Confederate logistics system. Such disruptions diminished the Confederate States' ability to provide its armies and people with food.[27]

While the navy struck at coastal areas and moved up and down the rivers in 1864, the Union army in Florida was pushing raids deeper into the hinterland. Between April 1862 and February 1864, conducting attacks against economic targets was the principal assignment of Union regiments in the state, which were otherwise occupied garrisoning towns such as Pensacola, Fernandina, and Saint Augustine. Such activities increased when the war progressed beyond the point where combatants respected private property, and when Union leaders began to realize the importance of the state's resources to their enemy. To be sure, fluctuating troop levels and a shortage of cavalry placed limits on the scope of these raids, as did the presence of rebel forces waiting to ambush unwary columns. Nevertheless, Union army personnel played a key part in reducing the material aid Florida was able to give the Confederate army. Military sweeps through the countryside at harvesttime were particularly painful for rebel supply officers.[28]

The Florida panhandle was a productive area for Federal attackers. In September 1864 a large-scale patrol from Pensacola to Marianna in Jackson County netted two hundred horses, seventeen wagons, over four hundred head of cattle, and close to six hundred "contrabands." Pleased with results such as these, senior officers ordered as many of these assaults as possible to be launched. Accordingly, less than a month after the raid on Marianna, another mounted column struck Milton in Santa Rosa County, destroying 85,000 feet of stockpiled lumber. Some 130 logs and 200 bushels of corn were also consumed by fires lit by troops of the Second Maine Cavalry. General Asboth desired that similar missions be sent from Pensacola as far inland as Columbus, Georgia, but he was denied permission to carry them out because of reports of heavy concentrations of Confederate troops in that area. The disappointed Hungarian subsequently satisfied his wish to hurt the rebel economy by striking out into west Florida, much to the distress of the inhabitants. Because of these raids one Jackson County resident was convinced that the enemy presence was so strong that he and his neighbors should be prepared to pay their taxes for 1864 to the Federals and not to Confederate officials.[29]

Like its naval counterpart, the Union army energetically searched the Florida countryside for cotton bales, which were worth hundreds of dollars each. In April 1863 Brigadier General Rufus Saxton reported to the War Department, after an expedition to eastern Florida by the First and Second South Carolina Infantry, that Union troops could secure large amounts of cotton there. Federal soldiers guarding captured cotton became a common sight in 1864 and 1865, while Treasury Department agents raced to acquire quantities for the government before private businessmen licensed to trade in cotton got them. The large sums of money to be earned from cotton tempted both officers and enlisted men serving in Florida to deal in it themselves. Indeed, Billy Yank shared with his rebel counterpart the ability to rationalize the combining of patriotic duty with personal profit.[30]

The economic warfare that the Federals were waging in Florida offered the chance to punish Confederate sympathizers as well as to seek personal monetary gain. Taking vengeance on civilians for starting the rebellion eventually became a common impulse as the conflict evolved into total war. Nothing pleased Union soldiers more than a chance to seize or destroy property of Confederate leaders. As formerly related, David L. Yulee's plantation and sugar mill on the Homosassa River were severely damaged in 1864 during such a visit. Subsequently, local newspapers reported that Yulee's slaves concealed valuables and livestock from the Yankees and that none deserted their master by leaving with the raiders. Since many blue-coated soldiers regarded rebel society as alien and evil, they felt it deserved nothing less than obliteration. Such concepts of their opponents made it acceptable to confiscate or destroy the means of survival even of civilians. Historian Reid Mitchell maintains that the idea of total war generally attributed to the likes of General William T. Sherman actually originated in the ranks. In his view the widespread devastation of property "expressed anger and contempt toward all Southern society."[31]

Implementing total war in Florida, Union troops invading central Florida engaged their foes in a bloody battle at Olustee fought on 20 February 1864. The origins of the Olustee campaign can be traced to Major General Quincy A. Gilmore, commander of the department that included eastern Florida. Frustrated by his lack of success in besieging Charleston, Gilmore marched into Florida to check the flow of supplies to the port city. The weakly defended peninsula appeared ripe for conquest by the Union army, with units idle in the swampy lowlands of coastal South Carolina. The general's plan was approved, but not without some misgivings in the War Department. Henry W. Halleck, general in chief of the Union army, did not expect useful results from such an expedition because it would require troops to hold captured areas of marginal significance when they might be employed to greater advantage elsewhere.

While Halleck (nicknamed "Old Brains") was underestimating Florida's value to the Confederate economy, Gilmore described some of the benefits to be derived from a major movement into the interior of the state. First, it would provide a convenient outlet for the easier export of cotton, lumber, and naval stores, all commodities the North badly needed. Second, cutting off an important source of commissary supplies might weaken Confederate armies in the lower South and assure the long-desired fall of Charleston. Third, large numbers of black recruits could be obtained for the army. Fourth, a Florida returned to the Union, like Louisiana, would provide political support for the Republicans during the upcoming 1864 presidential election. General Gilmore's main purpose, however, was preventing rebel supplies from reaching Charleston and the rest of South Carolina.[32]

Gilmore's campaign began with an amphibious attack on Jacksonville, delivered on 7 February, which quickly secured the port town. Gunboats and transports then moved up the Saint Johns River to seize Palatka and Picolata. The main body of Gilmore's force marched out of Jacksonville westward along the tracks of the Florida, Atlantic, and Gulf Railroad. The column, commanded by Brigadier General Truman A. Seymour, halted at the junction with the Florida Railroad at the hamlet of Baldwin. Along with cannons and railroad equipment, Seymour's men captured large amounts of tobacco, naval stores, and an estimated twenty-five thousand dollars worth of cotton. The Confederates retreated into the pine forests before the Union advance. Although meeting little resistance from the gray-clad enemy, the brigadier, a West Pointer and a veteran of the Mexican and Seminole wars, worried about supplying his men due to a shortage of rolling stock on the rail line he now controlled. Seymour informed his superior, General Gilmore, that foraging along his route of march might yield enough cattle for that purpose. At the end of the same dispatch to headquarters he added a jaunty remark, "If you want to see what Florida is good for come out to Baldwin." Seymour might have been less cheerful had he known that Confederate General Beauregard at that moment was rushing reinforcements to the rebel forces in Florida under General Joseph Finegan.[33]

On 10 February the Union invaders tramped twenty-three miles from Baldwin along the route of the railroad to the village of Sanderson. When the Federals arrived, the Confederate Quartermaster Department depot located there still contained masses of stores, despite desperate efforts to remove them to safety. Seymour's men found approximately three thousand bushels of corn and two thousand barrels of turpentine burning furiously, a blaze that the Unionists made no attempt to control. In the storehouse soldiers found quantities of salt, tents, saddles, and harnesses, in addition to rice and tobacco. While picking through the contents of the warehouse, some officers and a reporter for the *New York Herald* discovered that its commander, Major Joseph P. Baldwin, had left behind his personal papers. Among these documents was a confidential memorandum detailing the exact condition of Confederate supplies, which clearly revealed Florida's importance in feeding the rebel armies. The *Herald* correspondent assured his readers that the captured circular would "tell its own story better than any words of mine" could. He predicted that General Seymour's operations would soon return the state of Florida, with its immense stock of beef and pork, to the Union.[34]

The document uncovered in Sanderson indeed provided considerable useful information. Its author, none other than the state's chief commissary officer, Major Pleasant W. White, had composed the memorandum in November 1863 while he was trying to supply rations for Confederate troops in Georgia and South Carolina. Under pressure from commissary officers from these forces, White decided to issue a strongly worded declaration to the citizens of his state in the hour of crisis. The resulting paper, sent to various state leaders, gave accounts of food shortages by quoting excerpts from messages from out-of-state officials. White appealed to the patriotism of his fellow Floridians: "Support the soldiers or the South will be lost. If Southerners value their cattle and hogs, their corn and their money more than their cause, their army must fail. To give bountifully is the test of patriotism at home. . . . These brave men are suffering for lack of food. Not only are men from Florida in this condition but the whole army of the South is in this condition. Our honor as a people demands that we do our duty to them. They must be fed."[35] The major concluded his circular with a plea that all farms and plantations be converted entirely to food production. Insufficient food, he declared, could well lose the war for the Confederacy. Major White's bulletin was meant for state leaders, and not the general populace, because the sensitive facts it contained about the true condition of the Confederate armies might further demoralize the public. James McKay, shocked by admissions in the document, declined to release it to anyone in Tampa or South Florida. Unfortunately, its secrets, like most military confidences, were not kept long. Copies of the paper were found nailed to posts and trees and displayed at crossroads in many parts of the state as though it were a common handbill. It did not prove difficult for Union intelligence officers to acquire the White Circular and pass the information it disclosed to such generals as Gilmore and Seymour before operations began. In fact, Confederate officers became noticeably uneasy when Federals mentioned the circular and its contents during meetings under flags of truce. There can be little doubt that this extraordinary report influenced Union leaders in their decision to move deep into northern Florida in 1864.[36]

The White Circular became common knowledge to the residents of the North as well as to its military men. When the *New York Herald* reprinted it verbatim without comment on 20 February 1864, the rival paper *New York Tribune* editorialized that same day that General Gilmore's advance from Jacksonville was both wise and timely. Praising the invasion for cutting off the supply of Florida cattle, the *Tribune* commented on "how hopeless, then must be the conditions of the armies and the peoples of those Rebel States with their only source of food completely cut off." To the editors of the *Tribune*, unaware that its contents were already known, the knowledge gained through the circular would alone make the campaign worthwhile. The revelations of Major White's memorandum forecast the beginning of the end of the rebellion, or so it seemed. Eventually, most major newspapers alluded to the circular as far away as New Orleans.[37]

Ironically, the same day that the New York newspapers praised operations in far-off Florida, Union troops there were locked in bloody combat with a Confederate force of roughly equal strength. Ignoring orders to retreat and concentrate his brigades at the strategic junction at Baldwin, General Seymour led his 5,500 men and sixteen artillery pieces west toward Lake City. He planned to burn the railroad bridge across the Suwannee River and generally pillage the countryside. An ambitious officer hungering for distinction that so far in the war had evaded him, Seymour failed to grasp what the White Circular actually revealed. Because Florida was indeed absolutely essential to the defense of the states of Georgia and South Carolina, the Confederate leadership could not allow Seymour to interrupt their flow of supplies for a prolonged period without a struggle. Thus, all available troops in those states and middle Florida were sent to bolster Finegan's command on order of General Beauregard, who believed it to be necessary "in view of the importance of the resources of the section." When these reinforcements made Finegan's little army close in numbers to that of the advancing Federals, he prepared to meet them at Olustee Station. Finegan further requested more cavalry raids into Alachua and Marion Counties, and he urged that cattle herding be stopped until the attackers had been driven back.[38]

Participants in both blue and gray commented on the country through which they marched. A Confederate soldier informed readers of the Macon *Daily Telegraph* that the land around Olustee was "plain poor, piney woods, no undergrowth . . . the ground covered with wiregrass, but abounds in cattle." Lieutenant Charles M. Duren of the famed Fifty-Fourth Massachusetts Infantry regiment agreed on the nature of the re-

General Joseph Finegan. (Photograph courtesy of Florida State Archives)

gion. His men, despite having captured mountains of stores during the campaign, had to depend solely on their own commissaries for rations. Their attempts at foraging netted little food during the westward march because the area had been swept clean by enemy supply agents. "The Whites who are living here are wretchedly poor," wrote Duren. "They are women and children—hardly enough to cover their backs—and food I can not tell you what they live on."[39]

Any sympathy for civilians among the Union soldiers evaporated when the Federals came to grips with Finegan's Confederates at Olustee on 20 February. Despite hard fighting by most regiments, some of Seymour's units failed to perform well during the day-long clash, mainly because of inexperience and poor leadership by many of their officers. By 6:00 P.M. the weary Union troops, running low on ammunition and in danger of being flanked by the rebels, broke off the engagement. Two black regiments, the Fifty-Fourth Massachusetts and the First North Carolina, conducted a skillful rear-guard action that prevented the retreat to the east from becoming a rout. Wrecking the railroad as they went and destroying supplies they could not take with them, the defeated column abandoned Sanderson and Baldwin to seek shelter in Jacksonville. The badly mauled Confederates failed to effectively exploit their victory, however. Finegan contented himself with salvaging arms and ammunition from the battlefield. A clear Confederate triumph, the collision at Olustee cost the Union army 1,861 casualties; the rebels counted losses numbering 946.[40]

News of the success in Florida was welcomed across the unoccupied sections of the South, for it was one of few bright spots in the overall gloomy picture during 1864. Beauregard received praise for engineering yet another Manassas, although he had little tactical control over the battle. Battered Charleston sent hearty congratulations to "little sister" Florida for repelling the Federal invasion and protecting Confederate supply lines. Beauregard knew that the enemy thrust was aimed at him as much as at the Florida peninsula. The White Circular had clearly exposed that Charleston was utterly dependent on Florida for rations, and he believed that document was the catalyst for the entire Union action. Even though they were essential to protect the state's food supplies, Beauregard withdrew the reinforcements sent to north Florida for this action to meet new Yankee threats elsewhere. For a short time Seymour's advance did restrict the flow of cattle, bacon, and sugar to South Carolina, but supplies soon moved northward again at nearly the same volume until hindered later in the year by Sherman's march through Georgia.[41]

Confederate newspaper editors speculated on the motivations behind the Union incursion into northern Florida for a time after the battle of Olustee. Some of them concurred with Beauregard that frustrations among senior officers of the enemy army over repeated failures to capture Charleston had prompted the invasion. Federal deserters, according to some press accounts, told astounding tales of their mission to devastate the Florida hinterland. Supposedly, they were issued half rations and

ordered to forage for the rest. Many Southerners held that the purpose of
the Florida expedition was nothing other than a scheme to plunder northern counties of cotton and lumber. Florida Unionists were not only
accused of advocating such a plan, but also of acting as guides for
Seymour's regiments. Pro-Union Floridians and Federal veterans of
Olustee became subjects of ridicule and scorn after Union forces were
repulsed and fled back to the coast. That considerable numbers of
African-American troops were engaged at Olustee only increased the
animosity expressed in a variety of rebel newspapers. The Macon *Daily
Telegraph* described the luckless Yanks as marching "forty miles over the
most barren land of the South, frightening the salamanders and the
gophers, and getting a terrible thrashing."[42]

Some criticism of the Confederate military's lack of response during
the Olustee campaign appeared on local editorial pages as well as derision
of the enemy soldiers involved. The Charleston *Daily Courier* urged that
more rebel troops be assigned to the defense of Florida because the
Unionists now clearly knew the value of the state as the "garden farm of
the Confederacy." In addition there were editorials suggesting that cooperation between the army and civilians be improved so as to prevent
destruction of provisions and other movables by providing adequate
warnings of enemy activities. Since the Federal high command was following a policy of ravaging crops in order to decrease food supplies in the
South, "it is time our Generals would establish a good understanding
with producers and holders of provisions, and give timely notice for
removal." The Mobile *Daily Advertiser and Register* expressed the hope
that the bluecoats would avoid Florida after their resounding repulse. If
so, agriculturalists and rebel officials could furnish subsistence for the
Confederate army and the people of the South with a minimum of
hindrance.[43]

While Confederates may have been slightly dissatisfied with some aspects of their army's role in the 1864 Florida campaign, their complaints
were nothing compared with the criticism voiced in the North. General
Seymour was charged not only with disobeying orders but with being
incompetent at Olustee. While never court-martialed, he was relieved of
his Florida command and transferred to the Army of the Potomac. His
superior, Gilmore, eager to let the matter end quickly, did not push for
punishment for his former subordinate. However, newspapers, for example the *New York Post*, described Seymour as possessing "an aptitude
for walking into traps, and falling in with the enemy's plans," and suggested that he be dismissed from the service. Others blamed President
Lincoln himself for trying to reconstruct Florida in time for the fall
presidential election. Reproaching Seymour, asserted the editor of the

New York Herald, was nothing but "an ill-judged attempt to screen Old Abe at the expense of a gallant soldier." Antiadministration journals predicted that Lincoln would lose more votes in Northern counties than he ever expected to secure in the entire state of Florida when the general populace learned the true extent of the Federal "massacre." Soon, however, the rush of events diverted public attention to other battlefields and other issues as the armies of Grant, Sherman, and General George H. Thomas carried out the campaigns that in little more than a year brought the war to an end. Consequently, the Florida theater never again received as much notice or generated as much controversy as after the battle of Olustee.[44]

Despite the almost barren results of the Olustee campaign in terms of military gain or political advantage for the North, it did heighten awareness in the offices of the War Department in Washington of the material support Florida provided the rebellion. The wide exposure of the White Circular also inspired some Union leaders to suggest that military operations there be continued regardless of the setback at Olustee. Many realized that the size of the forces Beauregard sent into the state to check Seymour demonstrated that the Confederates placed a very high value on the peninsula as a source of foodstuffs. Such evidence of rebel dependence on Florida ranges and their large cattle herds, many believed, warranted dispatching at least a few regiments to curtail this trade. The *New York Times* observed that the Confederate States' tenacious defense of Florida must be attributed to its wealth in beef cattle. "We trust that, despite the ill-luck that has met the opening of the Florida campaign," ran a post-Olustee editorial of 28 February, "the work may still be kept up, if results should promise to be really as important as surmised." Not all Northerners agreed with the position of the *Times* in regard to Florida's value. A Union veteran of the fight at Olustee, for example, wrote, "The whole of Florida is not worth half the suffering and anguish this battle has caused."[45]

Throughout the remainder of the war Floridians feared a renewal of attacks on the scale of Seymour's invasion, believing that the Lincoln administration would "have the state if it cost 50,000" casualties. Yet such assaults never came. Instead, Union leaders during the rest of 1864 continued to gradually reduce their troop strength in Florida to a level sufficient only to garrison areas already under control. Confederate officers expected the Yankees to engage in large-scale raids along the upper Saint Johns River and into Marion, Sumter, and Alachua Counties in search of supplies and recruits for black regiments, but few such attacks were ever launched. Between Olustee and the collapse of rebel resistance, Union soldiers conducted only small thrusts into the interior or reacted to strikes aimed at them by the Confederates. These minor engagements led to losses on both sides in addition to the destruction of agricultural products destined for the rebel government. Federal officers grew concerned that this type of warfare would in the long run be detrimental to discipline and the fighting efficiency of their men. Nevertheless, the Unionists continued trying to interdict shipments of food bound for Confederate armies. After burning a railroad bridge at Baldwin in July 1864, General Birney reported that the rebels had stopped moving blockade-run items over the route at least temporarily. The general remained convinced that even with the limited forces available to him, "the abundant supply of corn and cattle from the southern and middle counties of Florida . . . is within our grasp."[46]

Continuous Union raiding accomplished more than simply damaging Confederate logistics in Florida. It hurt the morale of the civilian population by ruining their farms, wrecking their homes, and forcing many farm families to become refugees. These unfortunate victims of civil war had but three options: they could move deeper into the interior of the Florida peninsula, retreat to safer havens in Alabama or Georgia, or go east of the Saint Johns or west to Pensacola and pass through the Federal lines. The Gainesville *Cotton States* urged such people not to leave their fields or tamely submit to the hated enemy. "Floridians in the field or at home," ran one editorial, "are worthy of the cause of freedom, which they espouse with much zeal." But Union raiders dampened the spirits and patriotism of many pro-Confederates in late 1864 and early 1865. Atlanta, Savannah, Thomasville, Columbus, Charleston, and Montgomery all harbored Florida exiles during the last two years of war, over-taxing the already strained supplies of housing and edibles. By compelling citizens to flee, Federal troops heaped an additional burden on the rest of the lower South and indirectly contributed to eventual Confederate defeat.[47]

The victory on 6 March 1865 over a Union land force that advanced up the Saint Marks River at the battle of Natural Bridge brought some encouragement for Floridians because it saved Tallahassee from occupation by the Yankees. However, the conclusion of the long and bloody struggle was obviously close at hand. Even before the surrenders of Lee and Johnston, Union troops confidently began the task of rebuilding the state's economy. In January 1865 General Sherman, fresh from his triumphant Georgia campaign, authorized Federal officers to have foodstuffs such as beef, pork, mutton, fish, and vegetables for sale in the markets of such occupied cities as Fernandina and Jacksonville. Cotton was not on the list of permitted imports, but undoubtedly more than one bale made the journey from field to port via the United States Army. In February commanders at Pensacola requested permission to allow the reopening of regular steamship service between that city and New

Orleans. Probably these activities helped to speed defeatism by clearly demonstrating that normal life could be restored quickly by simply capitulating to the victorious Union forces. The fall of Tallahassee without a shot on 20 May 1865 ended the brief existence of the Confederate state of Florida and made such adjustments a reality for its people.[48]

Upon beginning their duties as an army of occupation in the summer of 1865, Union soldiers in the peninsula state also underwent profound changes. The battle-hardened troops had to adopt new attitudes toward the civilian population now that the Civil War was finally over. The commanding officer of the Union Second Florida Cavalry, for example, received orders to impress upon his men that foraging or any acts of vengeance would no longer be allowed and that violators of this edict faced sure punishment. Instead of raiding plantations and disrupting agricultural production as heretofore, Federal soldiers must now maintain order in the region while masters and their former slaves worked out new economic and social relationships and got on with the business of reconstructing Florida.[49]

In the remote Florida theater of operations, Union forces gave good if not glamorous service to their country by decreasing the state's economic value to the Confederacy. While handicapped by limited numbers in an area considered by senior officers to be of secondary importance, they prevented cattle, pork, corn, sugar, and other farm produce from reaching the Confederate government. Their raids cut lines of communication and transportation and helped reduce deliveries of goods brought through the blockade.[50] By living off the Florida countryside whenever possible, Federal troops consumed what might have been given to the rebels and at the same time eased the labor of their own supply establishment. They dispatched captured lumber and cotton northward to be used in their own war industries. The morale of Floridians suffered from their activities, depressing Confederate soldiers, who had to worry about their families.

Though the Union army and navy failed to completely isolate Florida from the rest of the Confederate South, this fact should not detract from their very real achievements against the rebel economy. No one can be certain what the effect of a large-scale invasion of the peninsula after the fall of Vicksburg and the severance of the trans-Mississippi region might have been on the South's ability to feed itself. But it is reasonable to conclude that completely removing Florida as a source of supply could very well have to some degree hastened the final defeat of the Confederacy.

8 Florida and the Confederate Economy

The Civil War profoundly altered the social and economic structure of every state of the Union, especially those opting to cast their lots with the Confederacy. When the Federal naval blockade isolated them from their usual sources of manufactured goods, Confederates quickly realized that their independence could only be won by mobilizing all of their indigenous human and material resources. Assembling large armies to protect their borders, however, removed about a half-million men from farms and plantations, thus seriously reducing the productivity of agriculture in the South, as well as depriving factories and railroads of many of their skilled workers.

During the 1850s commercial agriculture had provided the slave states, particularly those of the lower South, with a strong economic base that permitted Southerners to purchase food and factory-made items with the profits derived from cotton, sugar, rice, and tobacco crops. With the outbreak of sectional war, however, this concentration upon cultivating staple crops rather than foodstuffs became a source of weakness for the budding rebel economy. Ultimately, the inability of the seceded states to produce and distribute enough food to sustain both their military forces and their civilian population was a major cause of eventual Confederate defeat.

Although the Confederate and state governments proved in the end unable to persuade or compel farmers and planters to completely abandon their customary staple crops and devote their lands and labor entirely to growing food, enough corn, pork, and beef were produced to allow the Confederacy to wage war for four years. Florida made an economic contribution to the rebel war effort that was out of proportion to the number of its inhabitants. Unfortunately, many Confederate leaders grossly exaggerated Florida's agricultural potential. Throughout the conflict overly optimistic accounts of crop yields and estimates of numbers of animals ready for slaughter continued to appear in print all across the lower South. Titles like "granary of the Confederacy" and "garden farm of the Confederacy" appearing in the press reflected a general ignorance of Florida's real worth as a food producer.

Not until the final days of the war did rebel leaders realize that the peninsula state could not supply enough edibles to sustain the armies in Tennessee, Georgia, Alabama, and South Carolina. Overreliance on shipments of provisions from Florida weakened the government's attempts to construct a comprehensive logistical system for the Confederate field armies. As a result governmental inability to consistently provide adequate rations sapped the morale of the common Confederate soldier. As one commissary official sadly confessed in late 1863, even "the best appointed army must yield to hunger."[1]

During the war years the nature of agriculture in Florida was altered radically. Cultivation of traditional staples like cotton and tobacco declined under civic and official pressure to produce subsistence crops, although they were never entirely forsaken. "'What shall we eat' is a question of vast moment," ran an editorial in the Charleston *Daily Courier* in 1863. Indeed, the question as to whether the Confederate South could become self-sufficient in terms of food while the area upon which it drew shrank weighed heavily on the minds of leaders at all levels.[2]

As Union forces overran large sections of the Confederate States, Florida became increasingly important as a source of rations for the rebel armies. Corn, alcohol, sugar, citrus, and pork left the state in considerable amounts, especially between 1863 and 1865. Beef cattle, second only to salt as a contribution to the Confederate economy, fed soldiers from Chattanooga to Charleston. Fish from the state's seacoasts nourished both soldiers and slaves laboring on the home front. Yet Florida's fertile agriculture could not continue to generate ever more food with declining numbers of workers at a time when civilian and military demands were rising. Shortages became greater as order after order arrived in the state via government agents as well as private individuals for commodities from the farm and the range.[3]

The Union naval blockade also damaged Florida's economy and weakened its ability to support the Confederate cause. Trade between the peninsula and such large markets as Charleston, New Orleans, and the Cuban ports slowed to a trickle as a result of the growing Federal sea power off the Gulf and Atlantic coasts. Blockade running quickly replaced regularly scheduled shipping as Florida's commercial link to much of the outside world. Without overstating the value of such traffic to the Confederate economy, it can be safely asserted that Florida served as a

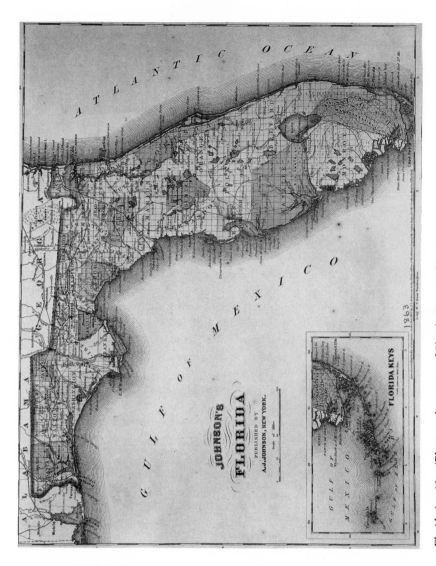

Florida in 1863. (Photograph courtesy of Florida State Archives)

notable port of entry for critical goods coming into the South from abroad.

Conversely, such local products as cotton and naval stores filled the holds of outward-bound vessels to exchange for war materials and consumer products. While the passage of such imports through the state was hampered by poor overland transportation and mismanagement such as that evidenced in the *Kate* affair, Florida did serve as a considerable conduit for the tools of war. If the peninsula had not remained a viable destination for smugglers, the Union navy would have been freed from the burden of patrolling some thirteen hundred miles of hostile coastline and thereby allowed to concentrate its ships and men against the South's remaining ports.

One of the revolutionary changes wrought on the South by the war was the drive to create an industrial base to manufacture what the blockade runners could not deliver. Those resources existing in rebel-held territory had to be utilized to their fullest extent in order to meet military requirements. In this regard Florida furnished its share of the sinews of modern war by providing quantities of lead, nitre, scrap metal, and iron rails. But the state's largest manufacturing effort involved the production of salt. In purely monetary terms this was the most valuable contribution to the war economy. Sites large and small on both coasts extracted from seawater thousands of bushels of salt, not only for domestic use but for export to Georgia and Alabama as well. Despite concerted Union attacks aimed at depriving the Confederates of a mineral essential to their economic and social order, and despite a shortage of materials needed to construct salt plants, Florida provided large amounts of a strategic substance indispensable to the Southern war effort.

Florida's capacity to contribute materially to that effort was retarded as the social divisions in the state worsened with each passing year. This divisiveness may have been a key factor in limiting Florida's productiveness as a supply source for the South. At times devotion to the Confederacy suffered when citizens were faced with the potential profits of not doing business with its government. Planters continued raising cotton, farmers concealed grain, and ranchers sometimes refused to surrender any of their cattle to waiting commissaries. Indeed, the state government itself often chose states' rights over the greater Confederate need, as in its stance on the issue of impressment. The Union forces operating on and around the Florida peninsula knew how large a part saltworks, blockade runners, and the state's agriculture played in making the region a supply reservoir for the Confederate government. Almost from the start they waged a modern type of economic warfare to damage or destroy the area's worth to the rest of the rebel states. Naval raids on saltworks tried to diminish the mineral's production and shipment to the rest of the lower South, albeit with limited success. Army units moved through the countryside to halt the work of Confederate commissary agents and obliterate as much of the country's agricultural capacity as possible. These soldiers themselves subsisted on the cattle and citrus fruit they seized, easing the load on the far-flung Union logistical organization.

Alerted by the 1863 White Circular to Florida's role in the feeding of the Confederate Army of Tennessee and the defenders of Charleston, the Federals launched the ill-fated Olustee campaign to interdict exports of foodstuffs. Union defeat there slowed but did not stop missions meant to block Confederates from procuring rations from Florida until the summer of 1865. Although such operations did reduce agricultural productivity, the bluecoats failed to eradicate the rebel supply-gathering network. The end of the war found that system in Florida relatively intact and still functioning despite the general collapse across the South.

Florida was a key component of the Confederate economy and a factor in its supply planning. This was especially true during the 1863–1865 period, when the state became a major source of beef, pork, corn, and salt. Southern leaders depended, at times too much, on the region to feed soldiers and civilians throughout the lower Confederate states. The lack of a pragmatic appraisal of Florida's agricultural resources impeded any move to create a national supply plan for the war-time South. Also, the failure to defend adequately an area so important to the success of the cause may well have speeded its eventual defeat.

As an economic member of the Confederacy, Florida deserved recognition as a state as vital to the country as practically any other. To fully understand what occurred economically, socially, and militarily in the lower South and beyond during the Civil War, the material contributions of Florida must be considered. Dismissing the state as a backwater of the larger conflict and relatively insignificant to the overall Confederate war effort is an error that historians must strive to correct.

Appendix

White Circular

Office of Chief Commissary
Quincy, Fla.
November 2, 1863

It has been a subject of anxious consideration how I could, without injury to our cause, expose to the people throughout the State the present perilous condition of our army. To do this through the public press would point out our sources of danger to our enemies. To see each one in person, or even a sufficient number to effect the object contemplated, is impossible; yet the necessity of general and immediate action is imperative to save our army, with it our cause, from disaster. The issues of this contest are now transferred to the people at home. If they fail to do their duty and sustain the army in its present position it must fall back. If the enemy break through our present line, the wave of desolation may roll even to the shores of the Gulf and the Atlantic. In discipline, valor, and the skill of its leaders our army has proved more than a match for the enemy. But the best-appointed army cannot maintain its position without support at home. The people should never suffer it be said that they valued their cattle and hogs, their corn and money, more than their liberties and honor, and that they had to be compelled to support an army they sent to battle in their defense. We hope it will not become necessary to resort to impressments among a people fighting for their existence and in defense of their homes and country and institutions. We prefer to appeal to them by every motive of duty and honor, by the love they bear their wives and daughters, by the memory of the heroic dead and the future glory and independence of their country, to come to its rescue in this darkest hour of its peril.

A country which can afford to send forth in its defense the flower of its youth and the best of its manhood can afford, and is in honor bound, to sustain them at any cost and sacrifice of money and property. They have sacrificed home and ease and suffered untold hardships, and with their lives are now defending everything we hold most sacred.

Florida has done nobly in this contest. Her sons have achieved the highest character of their state and won imperishable honors for themselves. These brave men are now suffering for want of food. Not only the men from Florida, but the whole army of the South are in this condition. Our honor as a people demands that we do our duty to them. They must be fed. The following extracts from official letters in my possession do but partly represent the present condition of the armies of Generals Bragg and Beauregard, and their gloomy prospects for future supplies:

Maj. J. F. Cummings, who supplies General Bragg's army, writes: "It is absolutely and vitally important that all cattle that can possibly be brought here shall be brought as promptly as possible."

And again, on 5th of October, he says: "I cannot too strongly urge upon you the necessity—yes, the urgent necessity of sending forward cattle promptly. It appears that all other resources are exhausted, and that we are now dependent upon your State for beef for the very large army of General Bragg. I know you will leave no stone unturned, and I must say all is now dependent on your exertions, so far as beef is concerned. In regard to bacon, the stock is about exhausted, hence beef is our only hope. I know the prospect is very discouraging, and it only remains with those of us having charge of this most important work to do all we can to exhaust our resources, and when we have done this, our country cannot complain of us. If we fail to do all that can be done, and our cause shall fail, upon us will rest the responsibility; therefore let us employ every means at our command."

Again, on the 6th, he says: "Major Allen can explain to you the great and absolute necessity for prompt action in the matter. I assure you that nearly all now depends on you."

And on the 19th of October he says: "Captain Townsend, assistant commissary of subsistence, having a leave of absence for thirty days from the Army of Tennessee, I have prevailed on him to see you and explain to you my straightened condition and the imminent danger of our army suffering for want of beef."

And on the 20th of October, he wrote: "The army is to-day on half rations of beef and I fear within a few days will have nothing but bread to eat. This is truly a dark hour with us, and I cannot see what is to be done. All that is left for us to do is to do all we can, and then we will have a clear conscience, no matter what the world may say."

Mr. Locke, chief commissary of Georgia, wrote: "I pray to you major, to put every agency in motion that you can to send cattle without a moment's delay toward the Georgia borders. The troops in Charleston are in great extremity. We look alone to you for cattle; those in Georgia are exhausted."

Major Guerin, chief commissary of South Carolina, wrote: "We are almost entirely dependent on Florida, and it is of the first importance at this time that the troops should be subsisted."

Again he says: "As it is, our situation is full of danger from the want of meat, and extraordinary efforts are required to prevent disaster."

And on the 9th of October, he says: "We have now 40,000 troops and laborers to subsist. The supply of bacon on hand in the city is 20,000 pounds, and the cattle furnished by this State is not one-tenth of what is required. My anxieties and apprehensions, as you may suppose, are greatly excited."

Major Millen, of Savannah, on the 10th of October says: "I assure you major, that the stock of bacon and beef for the armies of the Confederate States is now exhausted, and we must depend entirely upon what we may gather weekly. Starvation stares the army in the face; the handwriting is on the wall."

On the 26th of October, he says: "From the best information I have, the resources of food (meat) of both the Tennessee and Virginia armies are exhausted. This remark now applies with equal force to South Carolina and Georgia, and the army must henceforth depend upon the energy of purchasing commissaries through their daily or weekly collections. I have exhausted the beef-cattle and am obliged to kill stock cattle."

From these you perceive that there is too much cause for the deep solicitude manifested by the writers. They should excite the fears and apprehensions of every lover of his country. Truly the responsibility upon us is great, when we are expected to feed these vast armies whether the producers will sell to us or not. The slightest reflection would teach any one that it is impossible to provide for such armies by impressments alone. The people must cheerfully yield their supplies or make up their minds to surrender their cause. It is their cause. It is not the cause of the Government. The Government is theirs. The army, the Government, you and I, and every one, and everything we have are staked upon this contest. To fail is total and irretrievable ruin, universal confiscation of everything, and abject and ignominious submission and slavery to the most despicable and infamous race on earth. Whoever has any other thought but to fight on, at any cost of life and property, until we achieve independence or all perish in the struggle, deserves to be the slave of the enemy. But under the guidance of Providence our cause is safe in the hands of our army, provided we do our duty at home.

But Providence will not help a people who will not help themselves. Our enemies have no hope of conquering us by arms. Their only hope is that we will be untrue to ourselves, and in the blind pursuit of gain lose sight of our country, and thus suffer our army, and with it our cause to perish. How stands the case? You know the resources of Tennessee are lost to us; the hog cholera and other causes have cut short the prospect in Georgia and other States. It is ascertained that the last year's crop of bacon is about exhausted, and it is certain that the crop of this year will be much shorter than that of last year. Now two large armies look almost solely to Florida to supply one entire article of subsistence. The entire surplus of this year's bacon throughout the Confederacy, even when husbanded with the utmost economy, will be inadequate to the demands of the Government. This makes it the duty of every man to economize as much as possible—to sell not a pound to any one else while there is any danger of our army suffering, and to pledge at schedule rates his entire surplus bacon, beef, sugar, and sirup, to the Government. I solemnly believe our cause is hopeless unless our people can be brought to this point.

I have thought it my duty to address this confidential circular to the principal men in various sections of the State, and invoke their aid and co-operation with the purchasing commissaries and Government agents in their districts in inaugurating and putting into operation some system by which our armies can be more promptly supplied, and all our resources which are necessary secured to the Government. The appeals to me are more and more urgent every day; the pressure upon our State is very great. Should she now respond to the call made upon her resources as she has upon the bloodiest battle-fields of the war, the measure of her glory will be full. But if we withhold our supplies we cripple our army and render it impossible for them to advance after achieving the most signal victories. The people at home must put themselves upon a war footing. This they have never yet done. They must sow and plant and gather for the Government. Then, and not till then, will the bright rays of peace break through the clouds of war which now overhang us.

P. W. White
Major and Chief Commissary

P.S. You are specially requested not to allow this circular to go out of your possession, but to read it to such persons as you know to be true and prudent, and able to begin the work contemplated immediately.

Notes

The following abbreviations have been used in the notes:

DU   William R. Perkins Library, Duke University
FHQ   *Florida Historical Quarterly*
FSA   Florida State Archives, Tallahassee, Fla.
GPO   Government Printing Office
JSH   *Journal of Southern History*
NA   National Archives, Washington, D.C.
O.R.   *War of the Rebellion; A Compilation of the Official Records of the Union and Confederate Armies.* 128 vols. (Washington, D.C.: Government Printing Office, 1880–1901)
O.R.N.   *Official Records of the Union and Confederate Navies in the War of the Rebellion.* 26 vols. (Washington, D.C.: Government Printing Office, 1901)
PKY   P. K. Yonge Library of Florida History, University of Florida, Gainesville, Fla.
RG   Record Group
UG   University of Georgia Libraries, Athens, Ga.

1. Florida's Economy in the 1850s

1. *Southern Cultivator* 18 (August 1860): 233.
2. *American Agriculturalist* 10 (May 1851): 148.
3. *Southern Cultivator* 18 (August 1860): 233–34.
4. *De Bow's Review* 11 (October 1851): 410.
5. Ibid. 18 (March 1855): 338.
6. Ibid. 21 (March 1858): 618, 8 (January 1850): 157; *American Agriculturalist* 10 (May 1851): 148; Edwin L. Williams, Jr., "Negro Slavery in Florida, Part II," *FHQ* 28 (January 1950): 182–83. The six leading agricultural counties by farms over 100 acres in 1860 were Leon (215), Jackson (186), Gadsden (180), Marion (174), Jefferson (167), and Madison (152). For a further enumeration see U.S. Bureau of Census,

Agriculture of the United States in 1860: Compiled from the Original Returns of the Eighth Census (Washington, D.C.: GPO, 1864), 195, 222 (hereinafter cited as *Agriculture of the United States*).

7. Charlton W. Tebeau, *A History of Florida* (Coral Gables, Fla.: University of Miami Press, 1980), 182; Julia F. Smith, *Slavery and Plantation Growth in Antebellum Florida* (Gainesville: University of Florida Press, 1973), 89, 94; Larry Rivers, "Dignity and Importance: Slavery in Jefferson County Florida 1827–1860," *FHQ* 61 (April 1983): 404–30. The six leading slaveholding counties in 1860 were Leon (9,089), Jefferson (6,374), Gadsden (5,409), Marion (5,314), Jackson (4,903), and Alachua (4,457) (figures are from *Agriculture of the United States, 225*).

8. Edwin L. Williams, Jr., "Florida in the Union, 1845–1861" (Ph.D. diss., University of North Carolina, 1951), 248; John E. Johns, *Florida During the Civil War* (Gainesville: University of Florida Press, 1963), 140. For additional statistics see U.S. Congress, *Eighth Census, 1860, Agriculture and Industry, Florida*.

9. Tallahassee *Floridian and Journal*, 12 June 1858, p. 2.

10. Ibid., 8 August 1857, p. 2; *American Agriculturalist* 10 (May 1851): 148; Ulrich B. Phillips, *Life and Labor in the Old South* (Boston: Little, Brown, 1929), 273.

11. *De Bow's Review* 11 (October 1851): 410; *American Agriculturalist* 10 (May 1851): 149; Gavin Wright, *The Political Economy of the Cotton South* (New York: Norton, 1978), 17.

12. *De Bow's Review* 24 (January 1858): 77, 14 (March 1853): 509; *Southern Cultivator* 18 (August 1860): 234; Jerrell H. Shofner and William Warren Rogers, "Sea Island Cotton in Antebellum Florida," *FHQ* 40 (April 1962): 373.

13. Charleston *Daily Courier*, 27, 28 September 1858, p. 1.

14. *De Bow's Review* 11 (November 1851): 501; Weymouth T. Jordan, *Rebels in the Making: Planter's Conventions and Southern Propaganda* (Tuscaloosa, Ala.: Confederate Publishing, 1958): 35, 98, 206.

15. Saint Augustine *Ancient City*, 12 January 1850, p. 2; *De Bow's Review* 8 (April 1850): 492; J. Carlyle Sitterson, "Antebellum Sugar Culture in the South Atlantic States," *JSH* 3 (May 1937): 186–87; J. Carlyle Sitterson, *Sugar Country: The Cane Sugar Industry in the South, 1753–1950* (Lexington: University of Kentucky Press, 1953).

16. Saint Augustine *Ancient City*, 2 February 1850, p. 2; Herbert J. Doherty, Jr., *Richard Keith Call: Southern Unionist* (Gainesville: University of Florida Press, 1961), 138; Smith, *Slavery and Plantation Growth*, 130–32.

17. *De Bow's Review* 10 (April 1851): 410, 30 (June 1861): 644; John S. Otto, "Florida's Cattle-Raising Frontier: Manatee and Brevard Counties (1860)," *FHQ* 64 (July 1985): 51.

18. Michael S. Schene, "Sugar Along the Manatee: Major Robert Gamble Jr. and the Development of Gamble Plantation," *Tequesta* 51 (1981): 69–81.

19. Jacksonville *Florida News*, 14 February 1857, p. 2; James C. Ballagh, ed., *The South in the Building of the Nation*, 12 vols. (Richmond: Southern Historical Publishing Society, 1909), 5:194–95, 188.

20. David A. Avant, Jr., ed., *J. Randall Stanley's History of Gadsden County*

(Tallahassee: L'Avant Studios, 1985), 59; *American Agriculturalist* 10 (August 1851): 234; *De Bow's Review* 18 (March 1855): 39.

21. U.S. Commissioner of Agriculture, *Report of the Commissioner of Agriculture for the Year 1862* (Washington, D.C.: GPO, 1863), 61, 569; Donald L. Kemmerer, "The Pre-Civil War South's Leading Crop, Corn," *Agricultural History* 23 (October 1949): 236–39.

22. *De Bow's Review* 30 (June 1861): 643, 11 (October 1851): 410–11; Jacksonville *Florida News*, 8 July 1857, p. 2.

23. Macon *Daily Telegraph*, 19 September 1860, p. 1; Saint Augustine *Examiner*, 25 August 1860, p. 2; Diane Lindstrom, "Southern Dependence upon Interregional Grain Supplies: A Review of the Trade Flows," *Agricultural History* 44 (January 1970): 113.

24. *De Bow's Review* 10 (April 1851): 407.

25. *Southern Cultivator* 18 (April 1860): 128.

26. *De Bow's Review* 11 (October 1851): 410, 10 (April 1851): 406–7; Smith, *Slavery and Plantation Growth*, 227.

27. *De Bow's Review* 11 (October 1851): 412; Saint Augustine *Ancient City*, 9 August, p. 2, 26 July 1851, p. 2; Fernandina *East Floridian*, 29 October 1859, p. 2; also see *Southern Cultivator* 18 (October 1860): 324.

28. *De Bow's Review* 11 (October 1851): 412.

29. *De Bow's Review* 10 (April 1851): 408; Charleston *Daily Courier*, 26 September 1860, p. 1.

30. Sam B. Hilliard, *Hog Meat and Hoecake: Food Supply in the Old South 1840–1860* (Carbondale: Southern Illinois University Press, 1972), 44–45; Forrest McDonald and Grady McWhiney, "The Antebellum Southern Herdsman: A Reinterpretation," *JSH* 51 (May 1975): 147–66. See also Eugene D. Genovese, *The Political Economy of Slavery: Studies in the Economy and Society of the Slave South* (New York: Knopf, 1965; reprint, New York: Vintage, 1967), 106–18 (page citations are to the reprint edition).

31. George H. Dacy, *Four Centuries of Florida Ranching* (Saint Louis: Britt Printing, 1940), 20, 23; W. Theodore Mealor, Jr., and Merle C. Prunty, "Open-Range Cattle Ranching in South Florida," *Annals of the Association of American Geographers* 66 (September 1976): 361.

32. James R. Simpson and Aubry Bordelon, "The Production-Marketing Connection in Florida's Beef Industry: A Historical Perspective," *Florida Cattleman and Livestock Journal* 48 (February 1984): 51; John S. Otto, "Hillsborough County (1850): A Community in the South Florida Flatwoods," *FHQ* 62 (October 1983): 180–93.

33. John S. Otto, "Florida's Cattle-Ranching Frontier: Hillsborough County (1860)," *FHQ* 63 (July 1984): 78; Simpson and Bordelon, "The Production-Marketing Connection," 51; Dorothy Dodd, "Florida in the Civil War, 1861–1865," in *Florida Handbook 1961–1962*, ed. Allen Morris (Tallahassee: Peninsular Publishing, 1961), 295.

34. *Southern Cultivator* 18 (September 1860): 270.

35. Otto, "Florida's Cattle-Ranching Frontier: Hillsborough County," 77; Rodney E. Dillon, Jr., "South Florida in 1860," *FHQ* 60 (April 1982): 441, 449.

36. Charleston *Daily Courier,* 28 June 1856, p. 2; Forrest McDonald and Grady McWhiney, "The South from Self-Sufficiency to Peonage: An Interpretation," *American Historical Review* 85 (December 1980): 1107.

37. Charleston *Daily Courier,* 15 March, p. 2, 20 April, p. 1, 11 May 1860, p. 1.

38. Saint Augustine *Examiner,* reprinted in Charleston *Daily Courier,* 15 August 1859, p. 2.

39. *De Bow's Review* 10 (April 1851): 411.

40. Tampa *Florida Peninsular,* 28 July 1860, p. 2; Otto, "Florida's Cattle-Ranching Frontier: Hillsborough County," 76–77; John S. Otto, "Open-Range Cattle Herding in Southern Florida," *FHQ* 65 (January 1987): 317–34.

41. *De Bow's Review* 29 (May 1860): 60.

42. *Southern Cultivator* 18 (September 1860): 270.

43. *De Bow's Review* 30 (May–June 1861): 645.

44. Jacksonville *Florida News,* 31 January 1857, p. 2.

45. Catherine C. Hopley, *Life in the South: From the Commencement of the War by a Blockaded British Subject,* 2 vols. (London: Chapman and Hall, 1863), 2:250–52; John S. Otto, "The Migration of the Southern Plain Folk: An Interdisciplinary Synthesis," *JSH* 51 (May 1985): 200.

46. Total number of cattle in the South in 1860 by state: Texas (2,761,736), Georgia (631,707), Virginia (615,882), Alabama (454,543), North Carolina (416,676), Mississippi (416,660), Tennessee (413,000), and South Carolina (320,209) (figures taken from *Agriculture of the United States,* 154).

47. Tebeau, *History of Florida,* 195; John A. Eisterhold, "Lumber and Trade in Pensacola and West Florida 1800–1860," *FHQ* 51 (January 1973): 267. For descriptions of the lumbering business in Florida see *De Bow's Review* 14 (March 1853): 322, 27 (July 1859): 105.

48. Eisterhold, "Lumber and Trade in Pensacola," 280; U.S. Congress, *Commerce and Navigation,* Senate Executive Document no. 6, 36th Congress, 2d sess., 1859, 211; Cedar Keys *Telegraph,* 24 March 1860, p. 2.

49. *De Bow's Review* 10 (April 1851): 411–12.

50. Ibid. 20 (March 1856): 518; *Southern Cultivator* 12 (May 1854): 160. For general overviews of the Southern naval stores industry see Percival Perry, "The Naval Stores Industry in the Antebellum South, 1789–1861" (Ph.D. diss., Duke University, 1947); Percival Perry, "The Naval Stores Industry in the Old South," *JSH* 34 (November 1968): 509–26.

51. *De Bow's Review* 11 (October 1851): 411; Ballagh, ed., *South in the Building of the Nation,* 5:270.

52. G. M. West, *St. Andrews, Florida . . .* (Panama City, Fla.: Panama City Publishing, 1922), 51; William Warren Rogers, *Outposts on the Gulf: Saint George Island and Apalachicola from Early Exploration to World War II* (Pensacola: University of West Florida Press, 1986), 120.

53. *De Bow's Review* 30 (June 1861): 645; Dillon, "South Florida in 1860," 441; Ballagh, ed., *South in the Building of the Nation,* 5:270.

54. *Southern Cultivator* 18 (October 1860): 324; Williams, "Florida in the Union," 187; Rembert W. Patrick, *Florida Under Five Flags* (Gainesville: University of Florida Press, 1945), 57. See also Julia F. Smith, "Slavetrading in Ante-

bellum Florida," *FHQ* 50 (January 1972): 255, 261; Donald R. Hadd, "The Secession Movement in Florida 1850–1861" (M.A. thesis, Florida State University, 1960), 11.

55. *American Agriculturalist* 10 (May 1851): 148. For more on slave diet see Kenneth M. Stampp, *The Peculiar Institution: Slavery in the Antebellum South* (New York: Knopf, 1956; reprint, New York: Vintage, 1985), 282 (page citation is to the reprint edition).

56. Tallahassee *Floridian and Journal*, 17 January 1857, p. 2; *De Bow's Review* 11 (October 1851): 411; Lula D. K. Appleyard, "Plantation Life in Middle Florida 1821–1845" (M.A. thesis, Florida State College for Women, 1940), 105. See also Lynn Willoughby, "Apalachicola Aweigh: Shipping and Seamen at Florida's Premier Cotton Port," *FHQ* 69 (October 1990): 185.

57. Ocala *Florida Home Companion*, 23 December 1857, p. 2; Donald Markwalder, "The Ante-Bellum South as a Market for Food—Myth or Reality?" *Georgia Historical Quarterly* 54 (Fall 1970): 408–18. See also Genovese, *Political Economy*, 113–15.

58. U.S. Congress, *Commerce and Navigation*, 1859, 99; *De Bow's Review* 14 (March 1853): 335; James W. Cortada, "Florida's Relations with Cuba During the Civil War," *FHQ* 59 (July 1980): 45.

59. Ocala *Florida Mirror*, 19 August 1853, p. 2; U.S. Congress, *Commerce and Navigation*, Senate Executive Document no. 55, 32d Congress, 1st sess., 1852, 70; Edward A. Mueller, "East Coast Florida Steamboating 1831–1861," *FHQ* 40 (January 1962): 241–60.

60. Harry P. Owens, "Apalachicola Before 1861" (Ph.D. diss., Florida State University, 1966), 260; *Southern Cultivator* 18 (November 1860): 336; Willoughby, "Apalachicola Aweigh," 194.

61. *Southern Cultivator* 18 (November 1860): 336.

62. Tallahassee *Floridian and Journal*, 7 February 1857, p. 2; Robert C. Black III, *The Railroads of the Confederacy* (Chapel Hill: University of North Carolina Press, 1952), 37, 42–43.

63. *De Bow's Review* 25 (November 1858): 589; Charleston *Daily Courier*, 7 March 1860, p. 2; Black, *Railroads of the Confederacy*, 51.

64. Samuel Proctor, ed., *Florida a Hundred Years Ago* (Tallahassee: Florida State Library, 1960–1965), December 1960, 1; Johns, *Florida During the Civil War*, 134.

65. Columbus *Daily Enquirer*, 27 September 1858, p. 2; Johns, *Florida During the Civil War*, 124–25. The reference to South Carolinians working in Key West is found in the Charleston *Daily Courier*, 12 December 1859, p. 2.

66. *De Bow's Review* 10 (April 1851): 407; Charleston *Daily Courier*, 25 December 1856, p. 2. Salt prices are compared in the Newport *Wakulla Times*, 23 June 1858, p. 2, 9 February 1859, p. 3.

67. *American Agriculturalist* 10 (May 1851): 147; Arthur C. Cole, *The Irrepressible Conflict 1850–1865* (New York: Macmillan, 1934; reprint, Chicago: Quadrangle, 1971), 203 (page citation is to the reprint edition).

68. Charleston *Daily Courier*, 17 April 1860, p. 1; *De Bow's Review* 10 (April 1851): 405.

69. Thomas Graham, *The Awakening of Saint Augustine: The Anderson Family*

and the Oldest City 1821–1924 (Saint Augustine, Fla.: Saint Augustine Historical Society, 1978), 90; Charleston *Daily Courier,* 5 January 1861, p. 1.

70. The thesis of duality is advanced by Morton Rothstein in "The Antebellum South as a Dual Economy: A Tentative Hypothesis," *Agricultural History* 41 (October 1967): 373–82.

2. Secession, War, and the Blockade

1. Charleston *Daily Courier,* 19 November 1860, p. 2; Tampa *Florida Peninsular,* 24 November 1860, p. 2; Saint Augustine *Examiner,* 24 November 1860, p. 2; see also Bruce Catton, *The Coming Fury* (New York: Doubleday, 1961; reprint, New York: Pocket Books, 1974), 108 (page citation is to reprint edition); and more recently James M. McPherson, *The Battle Cry of Freedom: The Civil War Era* (New York: Oxford University Press, 1988), 237.

2. David M. Potter, *The Impending Crisis 1848–1861,* completed and edited by Don E. Fehrenbacher (New York: Harper and Row, 1976), 496; Drew G. Faust, *The Creation of Confederate Nationalism: Ideology and Identity in the Civil War South* (Baton Rouge: Louisiana State University Press, 1988), 34; John E. Johns, *Florida During the Civil War* (Gainesville: University of Florida Press, 1963), 20.

3. Johns, *Florida During the Civil War,* 18–20.

4. *West Florida Enterprise,* reprinted in Montgomery *Weekly Post,* 19 December 1860, p. 1; Charleston *Daily Courier,* 23 November, p. 2, 4 December 1860, p. 2. For South Carolina's influence on other states' seceding see Charles E. Cauthen, *South Carolina Goes to War 1860–1865* (Chapel Hill: University of North Carolina Press, 1950); William L. Barney, *The Secessionist Impulse: Alabama and Mississippi in 1860* (Princeton, N.J.: Princeton University Press, 1974).

5. The quotation is taken from James Oakes, *The Ruling Race: A History of American Slaveholders* (New York: Random House, 1982), 227. For Florida secession see Dorothy Dodd, "The Secession Movement in Florida, 1850–1861, Part II," *FHQ* 12 (October 1933): 45–66; Jon L. Urbach, "An Appraisal of the Florida Secession Movement, 1859–1861" (M.A. thesis, Florida State University, 1972); Johns, *Florida During the Civil War,* 14, 22.

6. James M. McPherson, *Ordeal by Fire: The Civil War and Reconstruction* (New York: Knopf, 1982), 129.

7. Atlanta *Southern Confederacy,* 27 April 1861, p. 2; Malcolm C. McMillan, *The Disintegration of a Confederate State: Three Governors and Alabama's Wartime Home Front 1861–1865* (Macon, Ga.: Mercer University Press, 1986), 17, 37; Johns, *Florida During the Civil War,* 47.

8. Office of the Comptroller, Territorial and State Military Expenditures, 1839–1869, FSA, RG 350, ser. 4, boxes 1, 3, folders 1, 3 (hereinafter cited as Military Expenditures).

9. *Southern Cultivator* 19 (April–June 1861): 122, 192.

10. Macon *Daily Telegraph,* 11 February 1861, p. 1; *Journal of the Proceedings of the Convention of the People of Florida . . . 1861* (Tallahassee: Tallahassee *Floridian and Journal,* 1861; reprint, Jacksonville, Fla.: W. B. Drew, 1928), 41 (page citation is to the reprint edition).

11. Larry Schweikart, *Banking in the American South from the Age of Jackson to Reconstruction* (Baton Rouge: Louisiana State University Press, 1987), 267, 292; John C. Schwab, *The Confederate States of America 1861–1865: A Financial and Industrial History of the South During the Civil War* (New York: Scribner's, 1901), 130, 306; Eugene M. Lerner, "The Monetary and Fiscal Programs of the Confederate Government," *Journal of Political Economy* 62 (October 1954): 522. In September 1861 the Mobile *Daily Advertiser and Register* reported that the Confederate Congress had passed a bill to reimburse Florida for some three hundred thousand dollars of military expenses. "The reimbursement to her in advance of the other Confederate States was urged," ran the account, "from the fact that her State Treasury was empty, and that she had no present means to carry on her military operations" (10 September 1861, p. 1).

12. Macon *Daily Telegraph*, 13 May 1864, p. 2; Edward A. Pollard, *The Lost Cause* (New York: J. S. Morrow, 1868), 425; Richard C. Todd, *Confederate Finance* (Athens: University of Georgia Press, 1954), 27. See also Douglas B. Ball, *Financial Failure and Confederate Defeat* (Urbana: University of Illinois Press, 1991), 171, 241.

13. Charleston *Daily Courier*, 20 May 1863, p. 1; John Milton to General Assembly, 13 December 1862, Office of the Governor, Correspondence of the Governors, 1857–1888, FSA, RG 101, ser. 577, box 1, folder 4; Johns, *Florida During the Civil War*, 109.

14. McPherson, *Ordeal by Fire*, 199–200; Todd, *Confederate Finance*, 157. See also David Y. Thomas, "Florida Finance in the Civil War," *Yale Review* 16 (November 1907): 311–18.

15. *O.R.*, ser. 1, 6:300; Milton to Stephen R. Mallory, 2 November 1861, Correspondence of the Governors, ser. 577, box 1, folder 4. In 1857 the Ocala *Florida Home Companion* stated that "Florida . . . [was] the most exposed state in the Union to foreign attack" (30 December 1857, p. 2).

16. Milton to Jefferson Davis, 18 October, 19 November 1861, John Milton Papers, Collection of the Florida Historical Society, Tampa, Fla.; Lynda L. Crist, ed., *The Papers of Jefferson Davis: Volume 7, 1861* (Baton Rouge: Louisiana State University Press, 1992), 364; Daisy Parker, "John Milton, Governor of Florida, a Loyal Confederate," *FHQ* 20 (April 1942): 357; William L. Gammon, "Governor John Milton of Florida, Confederate States of America" (M.A. thesis, University of Florida, 1948), 230. For Florida defenses see George C. Brittle, "In Defense of Florida: The Organized Florida Militia from 1821–1920" (Ph.D. diss., Florida State University, 1965); Gilbert S. Guinn, "Coastal Defense of the Confederate Atlantic Seaboard States, 1861–1862" (Ph.D. diss., University of South Carolina, 1973).

17. *Journal of the Proceedings of the House of Representatives of the General Assembly of the State of Florida* (Tallahassee: *Florida Sentinel*, 1860–1865), 11th sess., 28 (hereinafter cited as *Journal . . . House*).

18. *O.R.*, ser. 1, 1:448; Maxine Turner, *Navy Gray: A Story of the Confederate Navy on the Chattahoochee and Apalachicola Rivers* (Tuscaloosa: University of Alabama Press, 1988), 28, 33.

19. *O.R.*, ser. 1, 6:826–28; Robert E. Lee to Milton, 24 February 1862, Lee to James H. Trapier, 19 February 1862, in *The Wartime Papers of R. E. Lee*, ed.

Clifford Dowdey and Louis H. Manarian (New York: Bramball House, 1961), 116–17, 120. A Florida soldier thought "that Florida will be invaded from the fact that all the seaport towns will be left open for the enemy to come in without a struggle" (see Franklin A. Dotz, "The Civil War Letters of Augustus Henry Mathers, Assistant Surgeon, 4th Florida Regiment, C.S.A.," *FHQ* 36 [October 1957]: 123).

20. A. Robert Sellew, "High Prices in the Confederacy," *South Atlantic Quarterly* 24 (April 1925): 154–55; Francis B. C. Bradlee, *Blockade Running During the Civil War and the Effect of Land and Water Transportation on the Confederacy* (Salem, Mass.: Essex Institute, 1925), 21.

21. *O.R.,* ser. 1, 35, part 2:606; Stephen R. Wise, *Lifeline of the Confederacy: Blockade Running During the Civil War* (Columbia: University of South Carolina Press, 1988), 8–9, 18–19; Hamilton Cochran, *Blockade Runners of the Confederacy* (Indianapolis: Bobbs-Merrill, 1958), 16; Stanley L. Itkin, "Operations of the East Gulf Blockade Squadron in the Blockade of Florida 1862–1865" (M.A. thesis, Florida State University, 1962), 11. Shelby Foote described the Confederate coast as a "3,000-mile coastal portion, belly and crotch of the continent, bisected by the phallic droop of the Florida peninsula, [that] was doubled . . . by intricate mazes of sandalons, lagoons, and outlying islands" (see Foote, *The Civil War: A Narrative,* 3 vols. [New York: Random House, 1958–1974], 1:113).

22. Marcus W. Price, "Ships That Tested the Blockade of the Georgia and East Florida Ports, 1861–1865," *American Neptune* 15 (April 1955): 98–99; Cochran, *Blockade Runners,* 156.

23. *O.R.N.,* ser. 1, 5:778; Norman Browson to Henry Summer, 6 August 1861, Henry Summer Papers, Southern Historical Collection, University of North Carolina–Chapel Hill.

24. Charleston *Daily Courier,* 5 September 1861, p. 2; Johns, *Florida During the Civil War,* 69.

25. Macon *Daily Telegraph,* 28 June 1862, p. 3.

26. William W. Davis, *The Civil War and Reconstruction in Florida* (New York: Columbia University Press, 1913), 198n; Branch Cabell and A. J. Hanna, *The St. Johns: A Parade of Diversities* (New York: Farrar and Rinehart, 1943), 212; Michael G. Schene, "A History of Volusia County, Florida" (Ph.D. diss., Florida State University, 1976), 198.

27. *O.R.,* ser. 1, 6:370; Abraham C. Myers to E. C. Simkins, 6 January 1862, Correspondence of the Governors, ser. 32, vol. 6, folder 3; Wise, *Lifeline of the Confederacy,* 59.

28. Madison S. Perry to Milton, 22 March 1862, Correspondence of the Governors, ser. 32, vol. 6, folder 2; *O.R.,* ser. 1, 53:227; Schene, "History of Volusia County," 200; Wise, *Lifeline of the Confederacy,* 60.

29. Milton to Governor Thomas Moore, 1 April 1862, Richard F Floyd to Milton, 4 April 1862, Correspondence of the Governors, ser. 32, vol. 6, folder 2; Atlanta *Southern Confederacy,* 29 March 1862, p. 2; Johns, *Florida During the Civil War,* 73.

30. *O.R.,* ser. 1, 53:231, 239, 241; Alonzo B. Noyes to Milton, 22 April 1862, Correspondence of the Governors, ser. 32, vol. 6, folder 2. Jacob Summerlin of

Hillsborough County allegedly purchased one thousand dollars' worth of arms and ammunition from the New Smyrna cargo.

31. *O.R.*, ser. 1, 53:250, 14:494.

32. Charleston *Daily Courier*, 10 August 1863, p. 2; Price, "Ships That Tested the Blockade," 121; William M. Robinson, Jr., *Justice in Gray: A History of the Judicial System of the Confederate States of America* (Cambridge: Harvard University Press, 1941), 307–8. For U.S. Navy operations off southeast Florida see *O.R.N.*, ser. 1, 17:286, 292, 346, 369, 435.

33. Turner, *Navy Gray*, 31, 33; Todd, *Confederate Finance*, 124.

34. W. S. Walker to Milton, March 1862, Correspondence of the Governors, ser. 32, vol. 6, folder 2; Catherine C. Hopley, *Life in the South: From the Commencement of the War by a Blockaded British Subject*, 2 vols. (London: Chapman and Hall, 1863), 2:288–90; Wise, *Lifeline of the Confederacy*, 79.

35. *O.R.N.*, ser. 1, 17:240, 381; Edward F. Keuchel, *A History of Columbia County, Florida* (Tallahassee: Sentry, 1981), 99–100; Edward A. Mueller, "Suwannee River Steamboating," *FHQ* 45 (January 1967): 277; Dotz, "Civil War Letters," 105. See also Cyperian T. Jenkins to Milton, 13 June 1862, Correspondence of the Governors, ser. 32, vol. 6, folder 3.

36. James W. Cortada, "Florida's Relations with Cuba During the Civil War," *FHQ* 59 (July 1980): 46, 51; Wise, *Lifeline of the Confederacy*, 169.

37. *O.R.N.*, ser. 1, 17:829; Macon *Daily Telegraph*, 17 February 1865, p. 1.

38. Atlanta *Southern Confederacy*, 27 May 1862, p. 2; Columbus *Daily Enquirer*, 12 March 1864, p. 2; H. L. Hart to J. R. Adams, 11 September 1862, J. R. Adams Papers, Florida Collection, FSA. For the importation of medical supplies see J. E. A. Davidson to Surgeon General's Office, 23 December 1862, J. E. A. Davidson Papers, PKY, folder 2; W. H. Prioleau to Simkins, n.d., Confederate States Army, Medical Department, Letters Sent, Medical Purveyor's Office, Savannah, Ga. . . . 1862, RG 109, chap. 7, vol. 572, p. 221, NA. See also Kathryn A. Hanna, "Incidents of the Confederate Blockade," *JSH* 11 (May 1945): 214–29.

39. *Journal . . . House*, 12th sess., 22; *O.R.N.*, ser. 1, 17:324, 340, 359, 363–64; (?) Adams to J. R. Adams, 25 July 1862, Adams Papers.

40. *O.R.N.*, ser. 1, 17:86, 67; Jerrell H. Shofner, *History of Jefferson County* (Tallahassee: Sentry, 1976), 254.

41. Mary B. Chesnut, *A Diary from Dixie*, ed. Ben Ames Williams (Boston: Houghton Mifflin, 1950), 1; George W. Gift to Ellen Shackleford, 23 May 1863, Ellen S. Gift Papers, Southern Historical Collection, University of North Carolina–Chapel Hill, folder 2; Itkin, "Operations of East Gulf Blockade Squadron," 194; Bradlee, *Blockade Running*, 113.

42. *O.R.*, ser. 1, 1:1173; *O.R.N.*, ser. 1, 16:855–57.

43. Joseph Finegan to Milton, April 1863, Correspondence of the Governors, ser. 32, vol. 6, folder 5; R. R. Reid to Adams, 30 June 1863, Adams Papers.

44. Historians, for example E. Merton Coulter, Charles P. Roland, and Bern Anderson, have argued that the Union naval blockade was one of the ultimate causes of Confederate defeat. Anderson wrote that "without the relentless pressure of Union sea power . . . economic disintegration could not have been achieved" (Bern Anderson, *By Sea and by River: The Naval History of the Civil War*

[New York: Knopf, 1962], 232). Another school originated by Frank L. Owsley and augmented by Marcus W. Price and Frank E. Vandiver discounts the effects of the blockade and calls it ineffective. The most recent work in this school is Stephen R. Wise's *Lifeline of the Confederacy: Blockade Running During the Civil War* (Columbia: University of South Carolina Press, 1988). William N. Still, Jr., has also advocated this argument in "A Naval Sieve: The Union Blockade in the Civil War," *Naval War College Review* 36 (May/June 1982): 38–45; and in *Why the South Lost the Civil War*, by Richard E. Beringer, Herman Hattaway, Archer Jones, and William N. Still, Jr. (Athens: University of Georgia Press, 1986).

45. Charleston *Daily Courier*, 12 June 1863, p. 2, 26 July 1864, p. 1. For leather goods see William B. Teasdale to Adams, 7 October 1863, Adams Papers; Susan Bradford Eppes, *Through Some Eventful Years* (Chicago: Joseph S. Branch, 1926; reprint, Gainesville: University of Florida Press, 1968), 162 (page citation is to the reprint edition); Lester J. Cappon, "Government and Private Industry in the Southern Confederacy," *Humanistic Studies in Honor of John Calvin Metcalf* (Charlottesville: University of Virginia Press, 1941), 168. For Florida wartime lumber activity see Military Expenditures, ser. 43, box 1, folder 9; New Orleans *Picayune*, 12 May 1861, p. 5.

46. *O.R.*, ser. 1, 3:167–68, 499, 7:500; Dorothy Dodd, "The Manufacture of Cotton in Florida Before and During the Civil War," *FHQ* 13 (July 1934): 13–15; Johns, *Florida During the Civil War*, 125–26. For the centralizing effect of Confederate supply agencies see Frank E. Vandiver, *Their Tattered Flags: The Epic of the Confederacy* (New York: Harper's Magazine Press, 1970), 242.

47. Report, Department of the Gulf, 5 October 1862, U.S. War Department, *Letters Sent by the Department of Florida and Successor Commands, April 1861-January 1869* (NA, 1980), reel 1.

48. Macon *Daily Telegraph*, 2 June 1862, p. 4; Isaac M. Saint John to George W. Randolph, 30 June 1862, Confederate States of America, War Department, Nitre and Mining Bureau, Correspondence and Reports, 1862–1865, RG 109, box 1, folder 1, NA (hereinafter cited as Nitre and Mining Bureau Correspondence); Special Order no. 86, Confederate States of America, War Department, Adjutant and Inspector-General's Office, Letters and Papers, 1861–1865, Manuscript Department, DU. The best work on Confederate munitions is Frank E. Vandiver's *Ploughshares into Swords: Josiah Gorgas and Confederate Ordnance* (Austin: University of Texas Press, 1952).

49. Nitre and Mining Bureau Correspondence, box 1, folder 1; Nathaniel A. Pratt to Charles F. Stubbs, 1 April 1865, Confederate States of America, War Department, Nitre and Mining Bureau, District of South Carolina, Georgia, Florida, and Alabama . . . Letter-book, 31 October 1864–14 April 1865, Special Collections Division, UG; Milton to D. P. Holland, 11 October 1862, Correspondence of the Governors, ser. 32, vol. 6, folder 4. See also Samuel Proctor, ed., *Florida a Hundred Years Ago* (Tallahassee: Florida State Library, 1960–1965), July 1962, 2, 4; E. Merton Coulter, *The Confederate States of America* (Baton Rouge: Louisiana State University Press, 1950), 206.

50. James H. Warner to W. W. Ansell, 3 March 1863, Warner to (?) Loper, 30 December 1863, James H. Warner Papers, James W. Woodruff, Jr., Confederate

Naval Museum, Columbus, Ga., box 1; Turner, *Navy Gray*, 165–68; Fernandina *Peninsula*, 27 August 1863, p. 2; Finegan to Milton, 12 May 1863, Milton to Finegan, 21 May 1863, Correspondence of the Governors, ser. 32, vol. 6, folder 5; *O.R.*, ser. 1, 47, part 2:983. See also Robert L. Clarke, "The Florida Railroad Company in the Civil War," *JSH* 19 (May 1953): 180–92.

3. Salt Production in Confederate Florida

1. U.S. Department of the Interior, Bureau of Mines, *Mineral Resources of the United States* (Washington, D.C.: GPO, 1883), 539; U.S. Department of the Interior, U.S. Geological Survey, *Salt Resources of the United States* (Washington, D.C.: GPO, 1919), 1. See also Dale W. Kaufmann, *Sodium Chloride* (London: Chapman and Hall, 1960), 9–11.

2. Macon *Daily Telegraph*, 17 August 1861, p. 1; *De Bow's Review* 21 (October–November 1861): 443; Ella Lonn, *Salt as a Factor in the Confederacy* (University: University of Alabama Press, 1965), 35, 43. A surgeon in the Fourth Florida Regiment stationed near Sea Horse Key on the Gulf coast wrote, "It is impossible to get Salt here at anything like a fair price. There has been as high as ten dollars bid for salt here, and when it is Sold, there is no telling what it will bring" (see Franklin A. Dotz, "The Civil War Letters of August Henry Mathers, Assistant Surgeon, 4th Florida Regiment, C.S.A.," *FHQ* 36 [October 1957]: 100).

3. Victor S. Clark, *History of Manufacturing in the United States*, 2 vols. (New York: McGraw, 1929), 2:50–51; "Memoirs," Joshua H. Frier Papers, FSA, p. 2 (hereinafter cited as Frier "Memoirs"). For a description of salt reclamation from smokehouses see Herman Ulmer, Jr., ed., "The Correspondence of Will and Ju Stockton 1845–1869," Florida Collection, FSA.

4. Samuel Proctor, ed., *Florida a Hundred Years Ago* (Tallahassee: Florida State Library, 1960–1965), June 1962, 3; John E. Johns, *Florida During the Civil War* (Gainesville: University of Florida Press, 1963), 128.

5. Frier "Memoirs," p. 12; Stanley L. Itkin, "Operations of the East Gulf Blockade Squadron in the Blockade of Florida" (M.A. thesis, Florida State University, 1962), 95–96; Maxine Turner, *Navy Gray: A Story of the Confederate Navy on the Chattahoochee and Apalachicola Rivers* (Tuscaloosa: University of Alabama Press, 1988), 114.

6. Macon *Daily Telegraph*, 31 July, p. 2, 1 September 1862, p. 4.

7. *Acts and Resolutions Adopted by the General Assembly of Florida, 1862* (Tallahassee: Florida Sentinel, 1861–1865), 12th sess., 68; Lonn, *Salt as a Factor*, 80, 137. See also Herman Hattaway and Archer Jones, *How the North Won: A Military History of the Civil War* (Urbana: University of Illinois Press, 1983), 290–91.

8. Macon *Daily Telegraph*, 12 May 1862, p. 2. This article also appeared in the Columbus *Daily Enquirer*, 8 May 1862, p. 2, and in the Atlanta *Southern Confederacy*, 15 May 1862, p. 2.

9. *O.R.*, ser. 4, 1:1147; Atlanta *Southern Confederacy*, 25 March 1862, p. 2.

10. Atlanta *Southern Confederacy*, 13 May 1862, p. 2. For further press reaction

to the salt famine see the Columbus *Daily Enquirer,* 9 October 1862, p. 2; Macon *Daily Telegraph,* 5 March, p. 1, 12 April, p. 2, 14 July 1862, p. 4.

11. Macon *Daily Telegraph,* 23 April 1862, p. 2; Atlanta *Southern Confederacy,* 1 June 1862, p. 3. For the role of Georgia businessmen in the Confederate war effort see Mary A. DeCredico, *Patriotism for Profit: Georgia's Urban Entrepreneurs and the Confederate War Effort* (Chapel Hill: University of North Carolina Press, 1990), 45–46.

12. Columbus *Daily Enquirer,* 19 June, p. 2, 24 June 1862, p. 2.

13. Charleston *Daily Courier,* 18 November 1862, p. 1; James F Bozeman to John Milton, 6 September 1862, Office of the Governor, Correspondence of the Governors, 1857–1888, FSA, RG 101, ser. 32, vol. 6, folder 4.

14. George W. Scott to Rebekah Scott, 18 March 1864, George W. Scott Papers, FSA; Augusta *Daily Chronicle and Sentinel,* 11 March 1864, p. 1; Atlanta *Southern Confederacy,* 30 September 1862, p. 2; William W. Davis, *The Civil War and Reconstruction in Florida* (New York: Columbia University Press, 1913), 203. See also H. L. Hart to J. R. Adams, 9 November 1862, J. R. Adams Papers, Florida Collection, FSA.

15. *O.R.,* ser. 4, 1:1010. For more on the effect of salt shortages on Alabama see Malcolm C. McMillan, *The Disintegration of a Confederate State: Three Governors and Alabama's Wartime Home Front 1861–1865* (Macon, Ga.: Mercer University Press, 1986), 20.

16. Milton to John G. Shorter, 9 April 1862, Shorter to Milton, 8 April 1862, Correspondence of the Governors, ser. 32, vol. 6, folder 2.

17. *O.R.,* ser. 1, 14:716; Lonn, *Salt as a Factor,* 177.

18. Tallahassee *Floridian and Journal,* 18 December 1862, as printed in Macon *Daily Telegraph,* 19 December 1862, p. 4, and in Columbus *Daily Enquirer,* 19 December 1862, p. 2.

19. Marion B. Lucas, "Civil War Career of Colonel George Washington Scott," *FHQ* 58 (October 1972): 132; Lonn, *Salt as a Factor,* 178. For a postwar description of Saint Andrews Bay area see U.S. Department of Agriculture, *Tide Marshes of the United States* (Washington, D.C.: GPO, 1885), 178.

20. D. W. Everett to Milton, 10 December 1862, Correspondence of the Governors, ser. 32, vol. 6, folder 4.

21. *O.R.N.,* ser. 1, 17:594; Catherine C. Hopley, *Life in the South: From the Commencement of the War by a Blockaded British Subject,* 2 vols. (London: Chapman and Hall, 1863), 2:308.

22. *O.R.N.,* ser. 1, 17:316, 593–96; G. M. West, *St. Andrews, Florida . . .* (Panama City, Fla.: Panama City Publishing, 1922), 59.

23. *O.R.N.,* ser. 1, 17:719.

24. Ibid., 17:707.

25. Ibid., 17:323, 121, 310.

26. Ibid., 17:350, 619.

27. Atlanta *Southern Confederacy,* 9 November 1862, p. 2; Charleston *Daily Courier,* 31 October 1862, p. 4.

28. Susan Bradford Eppes, *Through Some Eventful Years* (Chicago: Joseph S.

Branch, 1926; reprint, Gainesville: University of Florida Press, 1968), 207; Macon *Daily Telegraph,* 28 November, p. 1, 9 December 1862, p. 3.

29. James Barrow to Daniel C. Barrow, 11, 3 December 1863, Daniel C. Barrow Papers, Special Collections Division, UG, box 3, folder 27.

30. William B. Braswell to Daniel C. Barrow, 15 January 1864, W. E. David to Daniel C. Barrow, 8 January 1864, Barrow Papers, box 3, folder 29. The Macon *Daily Telegraph* reported that the "coast in the immediate vicinity of the Salt Works is becoming mirey and almost impossible for teams passing to and from them" (16 June 1864, p. 2).

31. Braswell to Captain John A. Cobb, 28 February 1864, Cobb to Daniel C. Barrow, 5 March 1864, Braswell to Barrow, 24 April 1864, all in Barrow Papers, box 3, folder 29.

32. Pope Barrow to Eather (?), 26 March 1865, Barrow Papers, box 3, folder 30.

33. Kathryn T. Abbey, "Documents Relating to El Destino and Chemonie Plantations, Middle Florida, 1828–1868, Part III," *FHQ* 8 (July 1929): 42; Ethelred Philips to James J. Philips, 21 December 1863, James J. Philips Papers, Southern Historical Collection, University of North Carolina–Chapel Hill, folder 1; Lonn, *Salt as a Factor,* 19.

34. Ethelred Philips to James J. Philips, 21 December 1863, 26 June 1862, Philips Papers, folder 1.

35. Baker Daniel to Daniel C. Barrow, 6 October 1864, Barrow Papers, box 3, folder 29; Columbus *Daily Enquirer,* 18 September 1862, p. 2.

36. *O.R.N.,* ser. 1, 17:468, 648–49, 651; Charleston *Daily Courier,* 25 June 1863, p. 2, 11 March 1864, p. 1; Augusta *Daily Chronicle and Sentinel,* 23 July 1863, p. 1. See also F. A. Rhodes, "Salt Making on the Apalachee Bay," *Tallahassee Historical Society Annual* 12 (1935): 17–20.

37. Macon *Daily Telegraph,* 9 June, p. 1, 5 June 1863, p. 2; Charleston *Daily Courier,* 12 June 1863, p. 2.

38. Thaddeus W. H. Hentz Diary, Thaddeus W. H. Hentz Papers, PKY, p. 9; James Barrow to Daniel C. Barrow, 11 August 1863, Barrow Papers, box 3, folder 27.

39. *O.R.N.,* ser. 1, 17:650, 712; *O.R.,* ser. 1, 14:753; William T. Cash, "Taylor County History and Civil War Deserters," *FHQ* 27 (July 1948): 46.

40. *O.R.N.,* ser. 1, 17:317–18. Further references to salt raids can be found in the David Levy Yulee Papers, PKY, reel 149-C.

41. M. F. Dickinson and S. W. Edwardson, "The Salt Works of Salt Island, Florida: A Site Survey and Historical Perspective," *Florida Anthropologist* 37 (June 1984): 63–64, 73.

42. *O.R.N.,* ser. 1, 17:715, 741; Gainesville *Cotton States,* 10 March, p. 1, 16 April 1864, p. 1. For a postwar description of the Rocky Point works see R. E. C. Stearns, "Rambles in Florida," *American Naturalist* 3 (November 1869): 455–58. See also David J. Coles, "Unpretending Service: The *James L. Davis,* the *Tahoma,* and the East Gulf Blockading Squadron," *FHQ* 71 (July 1992): 41–62.

43. *O.R.N.,* ser. 1, 17:775–76, 780.

44. James M. Hunter to Milton, 27 April 1862, Correspondence of the Governors, ser. 32, vol. 6, folder 4; Charleston *Daily Courier,* 17 February 1862, p. 2; Ianthe B. Hebel, *Southern Country Folks at War: Volusia County, Florida During the Civil War 1861–1865* (Daytona Beach, Fla.: n.p., 1960), 5 (copy in Florida Collection, R. N. Strozier Library, Florida State University, Tallahassee).

45. *O.R.N.,* ser. 1, 17:398, 437; *O.R.,* ser. 1, 14:190.

46. Mobile *Daily Advertiser and Register,* 2 November 1862, p. 2; Johns, *Florida During the Civil War,* 100; John C. Schwab, *The Confederate States of America 1861–1865: A Financial and Industrial History of the South During the Civil War* (New York: Scribner's, 1901), 230; Paul D. Escott, *After Secession: Jefferson Davis and the Failure of Confederate Nationalism* (Baton Rouge: Louisiana State University Press, 1978), 122.

47. Milton to Jefferson Davis, 11 November 1862, Correspondence of the Governors, ser. 32, vol. 6, folder 4; Johns, *Florida During the Civil War,* 129.

48. Quincy *Semi-Weekly Dispatch,* 11 October 1862, p. 2; Proctor, ed., *Florida a Hundred Years Ago,* November 1962, 1.

49. Cobb to Daniel C. Barrow, 23 December 1861, Barrow Papers, box 3, folder 27.

50. Macon *Daily Telegraph,* 6 December 1862, p. 2.

51. Braswell to Daniel C. Barrow, 6 March 1864, Barrow Papers, box 3, folder 29; W. W. Davis, *Civil War and Reconstruction in Florida,* 205.

52. McMillan, *Disintegration of a Confederate State,* 96; Ella Lonn, "The Extent and Importance of Federal Naval Raids on Salt-Making in Florida, 1862–1865," *FHQ* 10 (April 1932): 181.

53. Everett to Milton, 10 December 1862, Correspondence of the Governors, ser. 32, vol. 6, folder 4; *O.R.,* ser. 1, 52, part 2:373. It took 1¼ bushels of salt to preserve a five-hundred-pound cow. See Jeffrey N. Lash, *Destroyer of the Iron Horse: General Joseph E. Johnston and Confederate Rail Transport, 1861–1865* (Kent, Ohio: Kent State University Press, 1991), 126.

54. Braswell to Cobb, 25 February 1864, Braswell to Daniel C. Barrow, 6 March 1864, Barrow Papers, box 3, folder 29; *O.R.,* ser. 1, 14:753–54.

55. *O.R.N.,* ser. 1, 17:652; Milton to James A. Seddon, 5 January 1863, Correspondence of the Governors, ser. 32, vol. 6, folder 4; Lonn, *Salt as a Factor,* 61, 127. For more on Florida and conscription see Albert B. Moore, *Conscription and Conflict in the Confederacy* (New York: Macmillan, 1924), 235.

56. Frier "Memoirs," 13.

57. William Miller to J. S. Preston, 22 October 1864, W. G. Poole to J. J. Daniel, 22, 24 April 1865, W. G. Poole Papers, FSA.

58. Braswell to Daniel C. Barrow, 25 January 1865, J. W. Williams to Daniel C. Barrow, 9 January 1865, W. C. Hanham to Daniel C. Barrow, 9 April 1865, all in Barrow Papers, box 3, folder 30.

59. *O.R.N.,* ser. 1, 17:812, 834; W. W. Davis, *Civil War and Reconstruction in Florida,* 210.

60. Lonn, *Salt as a Factor,* 208; Johns, *Florida During the Civil War,* 134; Rembert W. Patrick, *Florida Under Five Flags* (Gainesville: University of Florida Press, 1945), 67.

1. William B. Hesseltine, ed., *The Tragic Conflict: The Civil War and Reconstruction* (New York: Braziller, 1962), 327–29; New Orleans *Picayune,* 24 May 1861, p. 1; Saint Augustine *Examiner,* 18 May 1861, p. 2. See also Charles W. Ramsdell, *Behind the Lines in the Southern Confederacy* (Baton Rouge: Louisiana State University Press, 1944), 34; and Raimondo Luraghi, *The Rise and Fall of the Plantation South* (New York: New Viewpoints, 1978), 110.

2. Atlanta *Southern Confederacy,* 27 April 1861, p. 2; *Southern Cultivator* 19 (October 1861): 269; John E. Johns, *Florida During the Civil War* (Gainesville: University of Florida Press, 1963), 142. See also Douglas B. Ball, *Financial Failure and Confederate Defeat* (Urbana: University of Illinois Press, 1991), 86, 94.

3. Gainesville *Cotton States,* 16 April 1864, p. 2; Mobile *Daily Advertiser and Register,* 8 December 1863, p. 1; Johns, *Florida During the Civil War,* 143, 145; James L. Roark, *Masters Without Slaves: Southern Planters in the Civil War and Reconstruction* (New York: Norton, 1977), 45. In March 1865 the Florida attorney general ruled that a planter with lands in different counties could grow the maximum amount of cotton or tobacco in proportion to slaves on each holding (see Augusta *Daily Chronicle and Sentinel,* 30 March 1865, p. 1).

4. Paul W. Gates, *Agriculture and the Civil War* (New York: Knopf, 1965), 14, 19. Captain Winston Stephens of the Second Florida Cavalry instructed his wife to pick as much cotton as possible in November 1862 as he was "going to try to sell it down on Indian river as they are offering 50 cts for it at that place" (see Ellen E. Hodges and Stephen Kerber, eds., "'Rogues and Black Hearted Scamps': Civil War Letters of Winston and Octavia Stephens, 1862–1863," *FHQ* 57 (July 1978): 75.

5. Charleston *Daily Courier,* 11 November 1863, p. 1, 7 April 1864, p. 1.

6. *O.R.,* ser. 4, 3:167; U.S. Congress, *Cotton Sold to the Confederate States,* Senate Executive Document no. 987, 62d Congress, 3d sess., 1913, 61, 151, 163, 205, 210; Surgeon General's Office to J. E. A. Davidson, 28 January 1864, J. E. A. Davidson Papers, PKY, folder 2; R. R. Reid to J. R. Adams, 2 March 1863, J. R. Adams Papers, Florida Collection, FSA.

7. U.S. Treasury Department, "Personal Cotton Books of Gazaway B. Lamar," RG 366, NA; *O.R.,* ser. 4, 2:487; Edwin B. Coddington, "The Activities of a Confederate Business Man: Gazaway B. Lamar," *JSH* 9 (February–November 1943): 18–19.

8. Samuel Proctor, ed., *Florida a Hundred Years Ago* (Tallahassee: Florida State Library, 1960–1965), May 1963, 4; New Orleans *Picayune,* 27 December 1861, p. 2; Charleston *Daily Courier,* 14 November 1861, p. 3, 3 September 1862, p. 3; David A. Avant, Jr., ed., *J. Randall Stanley's History of Gadsden County* (Tallahassee: L'Avant Studios, 1985), 61, 107.

9. H. L. Hart to Adams, 23 July 1863, Adams Papers; "Estimate of Tobacco Rations," 30 September 1864, Raphael J. Moses to Pleasant W. White, n.d., Pleasant W. White Papers, Collection of the Florida Historical Society, Tampa, Fla.

10. John Milton to Judah P. Benjamin, 21 November 1861, Office of the Governor, Correspondence of the Governors, 1857–1888, FSA, RG 101, ser. 557,

box 1, folder 4; Macon *Daily Telegraph,* 9 July 1861, p. 2, 6 June 1861, p. 2; Milton to Jefferson Davis, 9 December 1861, John Milton Papers, Collection of the Florida Historical Society, Tampa, Fla.; *O.R.,* ser. 1, 1:467. One bushel of shelled corn weighed fifty-six pounds and one of corn on the ear seventy pounds.

11. Macon *Daily Telegraph,* 18 January 1862, p. 2.

12. Charleston *Daily Courier,* 29 July 1862, p. 1; Columbia *Daily Enquirer,* 19 July 1862, p. 2.

13. *O.R.,* ser. 1, 14:683, 703–4, 53:259; Clement Eaton, *A History of the Southern Confederacy* (New York: Macmillan, 1954), 242. In December 1862 a consignment of flour from North Carolina was sent to Florida for sale (see Zebulon Vance to Milton, 24 December 1862, Correspondence of the Governors, ser. 32, vol. 6, folder 4).

14. "To the Planters of Florida," 24 February 1863, "To the Citizens of Florida," 21 October 1863, Correspondence of the Governors, ser. 32, vol. 6, folders 4 and 5; Dunbar Rowland, ed., *Jefferson Davis, Constitutionalist: His Letters, Papers, and Speeches,* 9 vols. (Jackson: Mississippi Department of Archives and History, 1923), 6:21; Larkin B. Smith to Adams, 25 July 1863, Adams Papers; Charleston *Daily Courier,* 24 January, p. 1, 20 April 1863, p. 2; Emory M. Thomas, *The Confederate Nation 1861–1865* (New York: Harper and Row, 1979), 202–5.

15. *O.R.,* ser. 4, 3:47; Hart to Adams, 6 December 1863, Adams Papers; James McKay to White, 9 December 1863, White Papers, box 1.

16. Gainesville *Cotton States,* 10 March 1864, p. 2; *O.R.,* ser. 4, 3:15, 18, 47. Supply Officer Pleasant W. White wrote in 1864, "The corn crop in this state was much shorter than was expected and in my present opinion . . . none can be expected except from West Florida" (see Confederate States of America, War Department, *Compiled Service Records of Confederate General and Staff Officers and Nonregimental Enlisted Men* [NA, 1962], reel 265).

17. *Southern Cultivator,* 22 (February 1864): 39. For another glowing account of war-time Florida see Macon *Daily Telegraph,* 23 May 1863, p. 2.

18. Circular, 3 August 1864, Confederate States of America, War Department, Quartermaster General's Office, Manuscript Division, DU; *O.R.,* ser. 1, 33:1077; Joseph D. Locke to White, 29 June 1864, White Papers, box 1. For reports on 1864 corn prospects see Macon *Daily Telegraph,* 13 May 1864, p. 2; Gainesville *Cotton States,* 5 March, p. 2, 16 April, p. 2, 18 June 1864, p. 2.

19. William B. Teasdale to Adams, 2 July 1864, Adams Papers; *O.R.,* ser. 1, 35, part 2:431.

20. Andrew Hobb to Milton, 11 August 1862, Thomas L. Long to Paymaster W. J. Kelly, C.S.N., 23 December 1862, Correspondence of the Governors, ser. 32, vols. 32, 6, folders 3, 4; Mary S. Ringold, *The Role of State Legislatures in the Confederacy* (Athens: University of Georgia Press, 1966), 43. See also Jerrell H. Shofner, *Jackson County, Florida—A History* (Marianna, Fla.: Jackson County Heritage Association, 1985), 234.

21. Lake City *Columbian,* 30 December 1863, p. 1; Milton to Joseph Finegan, 5 January 1863, Milton to John C. Pelot, 5 January 1863, Milton to E. W. Johns, 26 February, 6 April 1863, Proclamation, 21 October 1863, all in Correspondence of the Governors, ser. 32, vol. 6, folders 4, 5.

22. Johns to Milton, 3 October 1862, Correspondence of the Governors, ser. 577, box 1, folder 5; Surgeon General's Office to Davidson, 15 April, 25 May, 31 August 1864, all in Davidson Papers, folder 1.

23. Surgeon General's Office to Davidson, 1 October 1862, 19 March, 22 August, 16 April, 3 November 1864, all in Davidson Papers, folders 1 and 2; Norman H. Franke, "Official and Industrial Aspects of Pharmacy in the Confederacy," *Georgia Historical Quarterly* 37 (September 1953): 185. Davidson, himself a physician, was formerly surgeon general of Florida. For more on Florida's relations with the Confederate medical establishment see Confederate States Army, Medical Department, Letters Sent, Medical Purveyor's Office, Savannah, Ga., 1862, RG 109, chap. 7, vol. 572, 27, NA (hereinafter cited as Medical Purveyor's Office).

24. Gainesville *Cotton States,* reprinted in Macon *Daily Telegraph,* 1 October 1861, p. 3; Charleston *Daily Courier,* 30 September 1861, p. 2. See also *Southern Cultivator* 19 (June 1861): 192.

25. W. H. Prioleau to Samuel P. Moore, 27, 28 October 1862, Medical Purveyor's Office, chap. 6, vol. 573, 28, vol. 523, 357; Thomas Y. Henry to Milton, 17 October 1863, Correspondence of the Governors, ser. 32, vol. 32, folder 5, Hart to Adams, 17 August 1862, Adams Papers; Charleston *Daily Courier,* 3 April 1862, p. 2.

26. Charleston *Daily Courier,* 24 March 1864, p. 2; Roderick S. Shaw to (?), 16 April 1864, James K. Shaw Papers, Florida Collection, FSA; R. E. Kilcrease to Miss (?) Sawyer, 20 January 1865, Daniel C. Barrow Papers, Special Collections Division, UG, box 3, folder 30.

27. Walter Prichard, "The Effects of the Civil War on the Louisiana Sugar Industry," *JSH* 5 (August 1939): 319, 332; Bell I. Wiley, *The Plain People of the Confederacy* (Baton Rouge: Louisiana State University Press, 1943), 37; Gates, *Agriculture and the Civil War,* 103.

28. Charleston *Daily Courier,* 26 July 1862, p. 2; Mobile *Daily Advertiser and Register,* 5 August 1862, p. 1; Office of the Comptroller, Territorial and State Military Expenditures, 1839–1869, RG 350, FSA, ser. 43, box 2, folder 1 (hereinafter cited as Military Expenditures); John C. Schwab, *The Confederate States of America 1861–1865: A Financial and Industrial History of the South During the Civil War* (New York: Scribner's, 1901), 177.

29. Thomas C. Bryan, *Confederate Georgia* (Athens: University of Georgia Press, 1953), 91; Lucius B. Northrop to White, 24 October 1863, White Papers, box 1; Reid to Adams, 7 December 1863, Adams Papers.

30. "Report of Purchases," Fourth District, December 1864, A. G. Summer to White, 5 May, 5 December 1864, White Papers, box 1; J. W. Eichelberger to James Stewart, 22 March 1864, Summer to E. Houston, 23 March 1864, A. G. Summer Papers, PKY. The Gainesville *Cotton States* of 16 April 1864 reported that according to government schedules sugar sold for from $1.10 to $1.20 per pound.

31. Charleston *Daily Courier,* 20 May 1864, p. 2; Antonia A. Canova to David L. Yulee, 25 July 1863, David Levy Yulee Papers, PKY, reel 149-C, box 23; William W. Davis, *The Civil War and Reconstruction in Florida* (New York: Columbia University Press, 1913), 93. All the pertinent documents in the Yulee sugar

case are contained in *Reports of Cases Argued in the Supreme Court of Florida at Terms Held in 1864–1867*, vol. 11 (Tallahassee: Dyke and Sparhawk, 1867), 2–62. For more on Canova see Hodges and Kerber eds., " 'Rogues and Black Hearted Scamps,' " 67.

32. J. D. Westcott to Teasdale, 11 January 1865, George S. Thompson Papers, Southern Historical Collection, University of North Carolina–Chapel Hill, box 2, folder 22; *O.R.,* ser. 1, 35, part 2:606; R. C. Williams to White, 4 May 1864, Northrop to White, 10, 15 October, 12 November 1864, all in White Papers, box 1.

33. Frank L. Owsley, *State Rights in the Confederacy* (Chicago: University of Chicago Press, 1925), 225; Ringold, *Role of State Legislatures,* 32; W. W. Davis, *Civil War and Reconstruction in Florida,* 190.

34. *O.R.,* ser. 4, 2:976; Owsley, *State Rights,* 243–44.

35. Proctor, ed., *Florida a Hundred Years Ago,* November 1963, 3.

36. Charleston *Daily Courier,* 28 February 1863, p. 2; *O.R.,* ser. 4, 3:560–61; Confederate States of America, War Department, *General Orders from the Adjutant and Inspector-General's Office, Confederate States Army, from January 1, 1864 to July 1, 1864* . . . (Columbia, S.C.: Evans and Cogswell, 1864), 53, 73–75.

37. *O.R.,* ser. 4, 2:916–17; E. Merton Coulter, *The Confederate States of America 1861–1865* (Baton Rouge: Louisiana State University Press, 1950), 247.

38. Macon *Daily Telegraph,* 3 September 1861, p. 2; *Acts and Resolutions Adopted by the General Assembly of Florida 1860–1861* (Tallahassee: *Florida Sentinel,* 1861–1865), 10th sess., 67–69. For more on the demand for Florida fish see Macon *Daily Telegraph,* 12 December 1861, p. 2, 9 December, p. 2, 17 December 1863, p. 2; and Charleston *Daily Courier,* 23 May 1863, p. 1.

39. William S. Dilworth to Milton, 19 April 1862, Correspondence of the Governors, ser. 32, vol. 6, folder 2; McKay to White, 9 November 1863, White Papers, box 1.

40. Northrop to White, 15 October 1864, White Papers, box 1; James M. Dancy, "Reminiscences of the Civil War," *FHQ* 37 (July 1958): 79.

41. *O.R.,* ser. 1, 46, part 2:1223, 35, part 2:606; W. G. Poole Papers, FSA. See also Kilcrease to Daniel Barrow, 20 January 1865, Barrow Papers, box 3, folder 30.

42. Augusta *Daily Chronicle and Sentinel,* 9 April 1864, p. 1; Kathryn T. Abbey, "Documents Relating to El Destino and Chemonie Plantations, Middle Florida, 1828–1868, Part I," *FHQ* 7 (January 1929): 192–93. For a breakdown of Florida's slave population in 1862 see *O.R.,* ser. 1, 53:260.

43. Frank L'Engle to Edward M. L'Engle, 5 November 1864, Edward M. L'Engle Papers, Southern Historical Collection, University of North Carolina–Chapel Hill, folder 7; Reid to Adams, 27 September 1863, Adams Papers; Military Expenditures, 27 March 1862, box 2, folder 3; "List of Commissary Department Employees," February 1864, "List of Employees," Second Commissary District, 11 February 1865, White Papers, box 1; Confederate States of America, War Department, Department of South Carolina, Georgia, and Florida, "Report of Persons Hired, February to May 1863," RG 109, box 45, NA.

44. "Memoirs," Joshua H. Frier Papers, FSA, 32, 50; William Miller to J. J. Daniel, 8 January 1865, Poole Papers.

45. Hart to Adams, 13, 17 August 1862, Adams Papers; Johns, *Florida During the Civil War,* 153.

46. Catherine C. Hopley, *Life in the South: From the Commencement of the War by a Blockaded British Subject,* 2 vols. (London: Chapman and Hall, 1863), 2:249–50. See also Susan Bradford Eppes, *The Negro of the Old South* (Chicago: Joseph S. Branch, 1925), 111.

47. Atlanta *Southern Confederacy,* 6 April 1862, p. 2; Coulter, *Confederate States of America,* 246. Records of state pork purchases are contained in Military Expenditures, box 1, folder 9, and box 2, folder 1. For laws governing pork see *Acts and Resolutions,* 11th sess., 8, 12th sess., 36.

48. Report, February 1863, Henry C. Guerin Papers, South Caroliniana Library, University of South Carolina, Columbia, S.C., folder 11; Atlanta *Southern Confederacy,* 28 April 1863, p. 2.

49. *O.R.,* ser. 4, 3:412; McKay to White, 27 August 1863, White Papers; Proctor, ed., *Florida a Hundred Years Ago,* April 1963, 2, 3.

50. White to James A. Seddon, 15 December 1863, White Papers, box 1.

51. R. R. Smith to Alonzo B. Noyes, 11 May 1864, Locke to White, 27 August 1864, S. L. Cobe to White, 29 August 1864, Westcott to White, 31 August 1864, all in White Papers, box 1; *O.R.,* ser. 1, 14:786. For the hog situation in the South in 1864 see *Southern Cultivator* 22 (January 1864): 14.

52. Albany *Patriot,* 3 June 1864, p. 2; Charles F. Stubbs to White, 10 January 1864, White Papers, box 1.

53. Westcott to White, 27 November 1864, T. E. Gibson to Westcott, 28 November 1864, Thompson Papers, box 2, folder 20; John L'Engle to Edward L'Engle, 23 March 1864, L'Engle Papers, folder 7; A. M. Allen to White, 30 March 1865, White Papers, box 1; Teasdale to Adams, 6 March 1865, Adams Papers; *O.R.,* ser. 1, 35, part 2:606. See also *Southern Cultivator* 23 (February 1865): 19; Herman Hattaway and Archer Jones, *How the North Won: A Military History of the Civil War* (Urbana: University of Illinois Press, 1983), 183.

54. *New York Tribune,* 29 February 1864, p. 1; Gainesville *Cotton States,* 16 April 1864, p. 1; Davis, *Civil War and Reconstruction in Florida,* 186. In April 1864 the supply depots in Gainesville contained four thousand pounds of bacon, fifteen thousand bushels of corn, seventy-five bushels of peas, and four hogsheads of sugar (see *O.R.,* ser. 1, 35, part 2:407).

55. *O.R.,* ser. 4, 2:576; Chandler C. Yonge to Seddon, 30 December 1864, Chandler C. Yonge Papers, PKY; Edward Hagerman, *The American Civil War and the Origins of Modern Warfare* (Bloomington: Indiana University Press, 1988); Richard D. Goff, *Confederate Supply* (Durham, N.C.: Duke University Press, 1969), 157.

56. Teasdale to Thompson, 3 January 1865, Thompson to Alexander R. Lawton, 4 April 1865, Thompson Papers, box 2, folders 22, 24. The supply figures are calculated from entries in an account book of Major William B. Teasdale, chief quartermaster at Lake City, located in the Adams Papers. The data for Tallahassee are from *O.R.,* ser. 1, 49, part 2:944.

57. Thomas, *Confederate Nation,* 200, 298; Eaton, *History of the Southern Confederacy,* 240; Hagerman, *American Civil War,* 129; Frank E. Vandiver, "Confed-

erate Plans for Procuring Subsistence Stores," *Tyler's Quarterly Historical and Genealogical Magazine* 27 (April 1946): 277.

5. Rebel Beef: 1861–1863

1. Antoine Henri Jomini, *The Art of War* (1834; Philadelphia: Lippincott, 1862), 129. For more on Confederate logistics see Frank E. Vandiver, *Rebel Brass: The Confederate Command System* (Baton Rouge: Louisiana State University Press, 1956), 79.

2. Vandiver, *Rebel Brass,* 90; Paul W. Gates, *Agriculture and the Civil War* (New York: Knopf, 1965), 12, 122.

3. Office of the Comptroller, Territorial and State Military Expenditures, 1839–1869, FSA, RG 350, ser. 43, box 1, folder 9.

4. Charleston *Daily Courier,* 13 May 1861, p. 2; Mary E. Massey, *Ersatz in the Confederacy* (Columbia: University of South Carolina Press, 1952), 61; Charles P. Roland, *The Confederacy* (Chicago: University of Chicago Press, 1960), 70.

5. Richard D. Goff, *Confederate Supply* (Durham, N.C.: Duke University Press, 1969), 36; *O.R.,* ser. 4, 1:873–75; Louise Frisbie, "The First Summerlin," *Pioneers* (n.d.), Collection of the Polk County Historical Society, Bartow, Fla., part 4, 1–2.

6. Frisbie, "The First Summerlin," 4; George H. Dacy, *Four Centuries of Florida Ranching* (Saint Louis: Britt Printing, 1940), 52; Charleston *Daily Courier,* 10 October 1861, p. 2.

7. Frisbie, "The First Summerlin," 2.

8. Dacy, *Four Centuries of Florida Ranching,* 52.

9. Ibid., 51.

10. *Records of Marks and Brands for Hillsborough County,* vol. 1, Hillsborough County Historical Commission, Tampa, Fla.; Varnie Sloan, "Daniel Sloan 1811–1888," *South Florida Pioneers,* no. 3 (January 1975): 2; Kyle S. VanLandingham, "John L. Skipper 1826–1907," *South Florida Pioneers,* no. 12 (April 1977): 24–25.

11. William S. Dilworth to John Milton, 19 April 1862, in Office of the Governor, Correspondence of the Governors, 1857–1888, FSA, RG 101, ser. 32, vol. 6, folder 2; John F. Tenney, *Slavery, Secession, and Success: Memories of a Florida Pioneer* (New York: Peter Smith, 1934), 24; Harold Lamson, "Comments on Florida in the Confederacy," Swisher Library, Jacksonville University, Jacksonville, Fla. (1957).

12. *O.R.,* ser. 1, 17, part 2:628, 15:108; Samuel Proctor, ed., *Florida a Hundred Years Ago* (Tallahassee: Florida State Library, 1960–1965), June 1962, 2.

13. *O.R.N.,* ser. 1, 6:308.

14. *O.R.,* ser. 4, 2:159.

15. Ibid., 2:193.

16. Robert G. H. Kean, *Inside the Confederate Government: The Diary of Robert Garlick Hill Kean, Head of the Bureau of War,* ed. Edward Younger (New York: Oxford University Press, 1957), 32; Edward A. Pollard, *The Lost Cause* (New York: J. S. Morrow, 1868), 483.

17. Dacy, *Four Centuries of Florida Ranching*, 55.

18. Joe G. Warner, *Biscuits and 'Taters: A History of Cattle Ranching in Manatee County* (Bradenton, Fla.: Great American, 1980), 10.

19. James W. Cortada, "Florida's Relations with Cuba During the Civil War," *FHQ* 59 (July 1980): 46, 51.

20. *O.R.N.*, ser. 1, 17:381.

21. *O.R.*, ser. 1, 23, part 2:680, 689; Thomas L. Connelly, *Autumn of Glory: The Army of Tennessee, 1862–1865* (Baton Rouge: Louisiana State University Press, 1971), 17.

22. *O.R.*, ser. 1, 23, part 2:658, 702; Joseph E. Johnston, *Narrative of Military Operations During the Late War Between the States* (New York: D. Appleton, 1874; reprint, Bloomington: Indiana University Press, 1959), 351.

23. A. G. Summer to Pleasant W. White, 13 March 1863, Pleasant W. White Papers, Collection of the Florida Historical Society, Tampa, Fla., box 1; Charleston *Daily Courier*, 21 January 1863, p. 1.

24. *O.R.*, ser. 1, 35, part 1:525; Thomas R. Hay, "Lucius B. Northrop: Commissary-General of the Confederacy," *Civil War History* 9 (March 1963): 7.

25. Vandiver, *Rebel Brass*, 109.

26. *O.R.*, ser. 1, 23, part 2:759–60; Willard E. Wright, ed., "Some Letters of Lucius Bellinger Northrop, 1860–1865," *Virginia Magazine of History and Biography* 68 (October 1960): 471–74.

27. White to Samuel Cooper, July 1863, White Papers, box 2. See also Robert A. Taylor, "A Problem of Supply: Pleasant White and Florida's Cow Cavalry," in *Divided We Fall: Essays on Confederate Nation-Building*, ed. John M. Belohlavek and Lewis N. Wynne (Saint Leo, Fla.: Saint Leo College Press, 1991), 177.

28. Gates, *Agriculture and the Civil War*, 73–74.

29. *O.R.*, ser. 4, 2:574; Richard M. McMurry, *Two Great Rebel Armies: An Essay in Confederate Military History* (Chapel Hill: University of North Carolina Press, 1989), 71. For a different view of McKay's motivations see Canter Brown, Jr., "Tampa's James McKay and the Frustration of Confederate Cattle-Supply Operations in South Florida," *FHQ* 70 (April 1992): 425–26.

30. *O.R.*, ser. 4, 2:18–19; White to Summer, 13 August 1863, White Papers, box 2.

31. Summer to White, 13 July 1863, White to Summer, 22 July 1863, White Papers, boxes 1, 2.

32. Joseph D. Locke to White, n.d., White Papers, box 1; John B. Jones, *A Rebel War Clerk's Diary at the Confederate States Capital*, ed. Earl Schenck Miers (New York: A. S. Barnes, 1961), 246.

33. White to Seth B. French, 4, 5 August 1863, White Papers, box 2. Again for a different interpretation of McKay's actions see Brown, "Tampa's James McKay," 426–29.

34. White to French, 7, 14 August 1863, White Papers, box 2.

35. White to John F. Cummings, 25 August 1863, White Papers, box 2.

36. White to Summer, 25 August 1863, White Papers, box 2.

37. Milton to Thomas F. Green, 25 August 1863, John Milton Papers, Collection of the Florida Historical Society, Tampa, Fla.

38. James McKay to Alonzo B. Noyes, 27 August 1863, White to Summer, 27

August 1863, White to Locke, 31 August 1863, all in White Papers, boxes 1, 2.

39. *O.R.,* ser. 1, 30, part 4:552; White to Lucius B. Northrop, 29 August 1863, White to Locke, 2 September 1863, White to Summer, 2 September 1863, all in White Papers, box 1.

40. White to Summer, 2 September 1863, White to John J. Walker, 5 October 1863, White Papers, box 2.

41. Summer to White, 2 September 1863, White Papers, box 1.

42. Summer to White, 9 September 1863, Charles F. Stubbs to White, 14 November 1863, White Papers, box 1.

43. M. B. Millen to White, 14 September 1863, McKay to White, 27 September 1863, White Papers, box 1.

44. McKay to White, 30 September 1863, White to Locke, 5 September 1863, White Papers, box 1.

45. "Report on Commissary Stores," Fourth District, September 1863, White Papers, box 1.

46. White to Joseph P. Baldwin, 2 October 1863, White to McKay, 2 October 1863, White Papers, box 2; John E. Johns, *Florida During the Civil War* (Gainesville: University of Florida Press, 1963), 191.

47. Johns, *Florida During the Civil War,* 191.

48. White to Northrop, 5 October 1863, White to Locke, 5 October 1863, White Papers, box 2.

49. White to Northrop, 6 October 1863, White Papers, box 2. See also Robert A. Taylor, "Unforgotten Threat: Florida Seminoles in the Civil War," *FHQ* 69 (January 1991): 300–14.

50. *O.R.,* ser. 1, 30, part 4:714–15; Jones, *A Rebel War Clerk,* 288; Connelly, *Autumn of Glory,* 114; Stanley F. Horn, *The Army of Tennessee: A Military History* (Indianapolis: Bobbs-Merrill, 1941; reprint, Norman: University of Oklahoma Press, 1953), 282.

51. Henry C. Guerin to White, 9, 10 October 1863, Cummings to White, 6, 19, 20 October 1863, all in White Papers, box 1.

52. White to Stubbs, 23 October 1863, White to Baldwin, 31 October 1863, White Papers, box 2; *O.R.,* ser. 1, 30, part 4:717. Beauregard, according to Northrop, was not "satisfied that full energy and foresight are employed by officers and agents of the Subsistence Department for developing the food resources of South Carolina, Georgia, and Florida, which he has reason to believe are far more abundant than is indicated by the results" accomplished by Guerin and White (see Northrop to Cooper, 7 December 1863, Henry C. Guerin Papers, South Caroliniana Library, University of South Carolina, Columbia, S.C., folder 10).

53. McKay to White, 6, 9 November 1863, White to McKay, 17 November 1863, White Papers, boxes 1, 2.

54. "Report on Commissary Stores," Fourth District, November 1863, "Return of Supplies at Sanderson," 15 November 1863, White Papers, box 1.

55. *O.R.,* ser. 1, 28, part 2:462; J. D. Westcott to White, 1 December 1863, Stubbs to White, 18 December 1863, Noyes to White, 23 December 1863, all in White Papers, box 1.

56. White to French, 23 December 1863, White to Noyes, 27 December 1863, White to Isaac Widgeon, 18 December 1863, White to Summer, 16 December 1863, all in White Papers, box 2.

57. Johnston, *Narrative of Military Operations*, 263, 266. See also Jeffrey N. Lash, *Destroyer of the Iron Horse: General Joseph E. Johnston and Confederate Rail Transport, 1861–1865* (Kent, Ohio: Kent State University Press, 1991), 104–7.

58. White to Stubbs, 30 October 1863, White Papers, box 2.

59. White to Joseph Finegan, 11 December 1863, White to James Seddon, 15 December 1863, White Papers, box 2.

60. "Report of Beef Cattle," Fourth District, December 1863, White to Northrop, 4 February 1864, White Papers, boxes 1, 2. For summaries of the cattle situation by the end of 1863 see *O.R.*, ser. 4, 2:968; U.S. Commissioner of Agriculture, *Report of the Commissioner of Agriculture for the Year 1863* (Washington, D.C.: GPO, 1863), 264.

6. Cattle for the Confederacy: 1864–1865

1. Charlton W. Tebeau, *A History of Florida* (Coral Gables, Fla.: University of Miami Press, 1980), 232; *New York Times*, 3 October 1862, p. 1.

2. Gainesville *Cotton States*, reprinted in Charleston *Daily Courier*, 30 January 1864, p. 2; Pleasant W. White to Lucius B. Northrop, 3 March 1864, Pleasant W. White Papers, Collection of the Florida Historical Society, Tampa, Fla., box 2; Macon *Daily Telegraph*, 11 May 1864, p. 1. For the role of deserters see Ella Lonn, *Desertion During the Civil War* (New York: Century, 1928), 65.

3. *O.R.*, ser. 4, 3:46.

4. *O.R.*, ser. 1, 53:346, 35, part 2:331. Miller was a colonel until his promotion on 2 August 1864. He assumed command of Florida troops five weeks later.

5. John B. Jones, *A Rebel War Clerk's Diary at the Confederate States Capital*, ed. Earl Schenck Miers (New York: A. S. Barnes, 1961), 326; *O.R.*, ser. 1, 35, part 1:507; Allen Candler, ed., *The Confederate Records of the State of Georgia*, 6 vols. (Atlanta: Charles P. Byrd, State Printer, 1910), 3:461.

6. *O.R.*, ser. 1, 35, part 1:522; White to John F. Cummings, 6 January 1864, Daniel F. Cocke to White, 22 February 1864, White Papers, boxes 1, 2.

7. *O.R.*, ser. 1, 35, part 1:508, 520–21; White to Henry C. Guerin, 9 November 1863, White Papers, box 2.

8. *O.R.*, ser. 1, 33:1065; Dunbar Rowland, ed., *Jefferson Davis, Constitutionalist: His Letters, Papers, and Speeches*, 9 vols. (Jackson: Mississippi Department of Archives and History, 1923), 8:181–82.

9. White to Seth B. French, 15 January 1864, White Papers, box 2; John Milton to Northrop, 13 January 1865, John Milton Papers, Collection of the Florida Historical Society, Tampa, Fla. According to Commissary Department records, 51,240 pounds of fresh beef were on hand in Savannah from Florida sources on 31 January 1864. See Confederate States Army, Commissary of Subsistence, "Return of Provisions Received and Issued at Savannah, Ga. During the Months of August 1863 to December 1864," Special Collections Division, UG (here-

inafter cited as "Return of Provisions"). See also Jeffrey N. Lash, *Destroyer of the Iron Horse: General Joseph E. Johnston and Confederate Rail Transport, 1861–1865* (Kent, Ohio: Kent State University Press, 1991), 124.

10. White to Wilkinson Call, 2 February 1864, White to Northrop, 28 February 1864, White Papers, box 2.

11. Clipping in James K. Shaw Papers, Florida Collection, FSA. A lieutenant in the First Florida Infantry, on deserting, told his Union captors that "rations consist of Florida beef and corn. The beef is so poor that the men can not eat it." See *O.R.,* ser. 1, 35, part 2:13.

12. *O.R.,* ser. 1, 35, part 1:615; White to Isaac Widgeon, 8 February 1864, White to French, 9 February 1864, White Papers, box 2. See also "Return of Provisions," 18 March 1864, for records of the 111,968 pounds of Florida beef on hand on that date.

13. White to Joseph D. Locke, 12 March 1864, A. M. Allen to White, 15, 25 March 1864, White to Allen, 30 March 1864, White Papers, boxes 1, 2. The standard work on Andersonville is Ovid L. Futch's *History of Andersonville Prison* (Gainesville: University of Florida Press, 1968).

14. J. J. Dickison, "Florida," in *Confederate Military History,* ed. Clement A. Evans, 13 vols. (Atlanta: Blue and Grey Press, 1899), 11:90.

15. James McKay to White, 25 March 1864, White to Northrop, 25 February 1864, White to A. G. Summer, 10 March 1864, White Papers, boxes 1, 2. For the formation and campaigns of the cattle battalion see Robert A. Taylor, "Cow Cavalry: Munnerlyn's Battalion in Florida," *FHQ* 64 (October 1986): 196–214.

16. A. S. Muram to White, 1 April 1864, White to Locke, 4 April 1864, "Pay Roll," Third District, April 1864, White Papers, boxes 1, 2.

17. Jon L. Wakelyn, *Biographical Dictionary of the Confederacy* (Westport, Conn.: Greenwood, 1977), 377; "Return of Supplies," June 1864, White to W. S. Barth, 29 June 1864, Alonzo B. Noyes to White, 29 July 1864, White Papers, boxes 1, 2.

18. *O.R.,* ser. 2, 7:499; Allen to White, 1, 6 May, 29 June, 25 July 1864, Charles F. Stubbs to White, 9 August 1864, White Papers, boxes 1, 2.

19. Locke to White, 13 August 1864, Allen to White, 11 August, 23 September 1864, White Papers, box 1.

20. S. W. Moody to White, 1 September 1864, White Papers, box 1. Major Summer continued to protest his innocence, which he claimed was based on mistakes in his reports. By April 1865 he convinced Major White of this and White asked then commissary-general Saint John to request his reinstatement by order of President Davis (see White to Isaac M. Saint John, 24 April 1865, White Papers, box 2). See also Canter Brown, Jr., "Tampa's James McKay and the Frustration of Confederate Cattle-Supply Operations in South Florida," *FHQ* 70 (April 1992): 429–30.

21. White to Northrop, 11 October 1864, Northrop to White, 15 October 1864, White Papers, boxes 1, 2.

22. J. Patton Anderson to White, 15 July 1864, J. Patton Anderson Papers, PKY, box 64. For press reaction to Anderson's efforts see Macon *Daily Telegraph,* 24 May 1864, p. 2.

23. *O.R.,* ser. 4, 3:730–31.

24. "Report on Purchased Stores," October 1864, J. B. Bill to White, 12 October 1864, White Papers, box 1.

25. M. B. Millen to White, 31 October 1864, Guerin to White, 31 October 1864, White Papers, box 1.

26. White to Guerin, 2 November 1864, White Papers, box 2.

27. Douglas S. Freeman, *Lee's Lieutenants,* 3 vols. (New York: Scribner's, 1942–1944), 3:493.

28. Edward A. Pollard, *The Lost Cause* (New York: J. S. Morrow, 1868), 649; Frank E. Vandiver, "The Food Supply of the Confederate Armies, 1865," *Tyler's Quarterly Historical and Genealogical Magazine* 26 (October 1944): 80.

29. I. C. Clancy to Guerin, 23 November 1864, White Papers, box 1; *O.R.,* ser. 1, 35, part 1:443; General J. Bailey to Major James E. Clark, 22 October 1864, U.S. War Department, *Letters Sent by the Department of Florida and Successor Commands, April 1861–January 1869* (NA, 1980), reel 1.

30. Summer to White, 17 April 1864, McKay to White, 4 February 1864, Cocke to White, 16 December 1863, White to Cummings, 14 March 1864, White Papers, boxes 1, 2.

31. White to Cocke, 2 November 1864, Cocke to White, 29 November 1864, White Papers, boxes 1, 2. See also Mary A. DeCredico, *Patriotism for Profit: Georgia's Urban Entrepreneurs and the Confederate War Effort* (Chapel Hill: University of North Carolina Press, 1990), 71.

32. Millen to White, 1 December 1864, White to Stubbs, 29 November 1864, "Purchases," Fourth District, November 1864, Stubbs to White, 12 December 1864, White Papers, boxes 1, 2.

33. White to McKay, 10 December 1864, White to Stubbs, 27 December 1864, White Papers, box 2.

34. Northrop to James A. Seddon, 29 December 1864, in "Some Letters of Lucius Bellinger Northrop, 1860–1865," ed. Willard E. Wright, *Virginia Magazine of History and Biography* 68 (October 1960): 473; Josiah Gorgas, *The Civil War Diary of General Josiah Gorgas,* ed. Frank E. Vandiver (Tuscaloosa: University of Alabama Press, 1947), 157. See also Wiley Sword, *Embrace an Angry Wind: The Confederacy's Last Hurrah: Spring Hill, Franklin, and Nashville* (New York: HarperCollins, 1992), 393, 406.

35. Charles H. Wesley, *The Collapse of the Confederacy* (Washington, D.C.: Associated Publishers, 1937), 7; Southern Historical Society, *Southern Historical Society Papers,* 52 vols. (Richmond: Southern Historical Society, 1876–1959).

36. White to Milton, 9 December 1864, White Papers, box 2.

37. Charleston *Daily Courier,* 8 February 1865, p. 2; Lonn, *Desertion During the Civil War,* 8; DeCredico, *Patriotism for Profit,* 51, 60–61.

38. White to J. D. Westcott, 1 January 1865, McKay to White, 17 March 1864, White Papers, boxes 1, 2; *O.R.,* ser. 1, 28, part 2:461–62. For more on hides consult Georgia Department of Archives and History, "Annual Report of the Quartermaster of Georgia, 1863," Atlanta, Ga.

39. White to McKay, White to Summer, 14 January 1865, White to T. M. Dudley, 30 January 1865, White Papers, box 2.

40. White to Northrop, 10 February 1865, White Papers, box 2.

41. White to Westcott, 12 February 1865, Noyes to White, 25 February 1865, George Gillespie to White, 23 February 1865, White Papers, boxes 1, 2.

42. Gorgas, *Civil War Diary,* 165; Robert G. H. Kean, *Inside the Confederate Government: The Diary of Robert Garlick Hill Kean, Head of the Bureau of War,* ed. Edward Younger (New York: Oxford University Press, 1957), 200; Wilfred B. Yearns, *The Confederate Congress* (Athens: University of Georgia Press, 1960), 122. See also William C. Davis, *Jefferson Davis: The Man and His Hour* (New York: HarperCollins, 1991), 586.

43. Jones, *A Rebel War Clerk,* 508; Richard D. Goff, *Confederate Supply* (Durham, N.C.: Duke University Press, 1969), 235; Thomas R. Hay, "Lucius B. Northrop: Commissary-General of the Confederacy," *Civil War History* 9 (March 1963): 23.

44. *O.R.,* ser. 1, 47, part 2:1390; William Miller to Samuel Cooper, 2 January 1865, W. G. Poole Papers, FSA; Jerrell H. Shofner and William Warren Rogers, "Confederate Railroad Construction: The Live Oak to Lawton Connection," *FHQ* 43 (January 1965): 217–28.

45. White to Northrop, 20 March 1865, White to McKay, 23 March 1865, White Papers, box 2.

46. White to Saint John, 3 April 1865, White Papers, box 2.

47. White to Westcott, 4 April 1865, White Papers, box 2; E. B. Long, *The Civil War Day by Day: An Almanac 1861–1865* (Garden City, N.Y.: Doubleday, 1971), 666.

48. Circular, Headquarters, District of Florida, 28 April 1865, in Edward M. L'Engle Papers, Southern Historical Collection, University of North Carolina–Chapel Hill, folder 7.

49. Mary E. Dickison, *Dickison and His Men* (Louisville, Ky.: n.p. 1890; reprint, Gainesville: University of Florida Press, 1962), 212; *O.R.,* ser. 1, 41, part 2:984. For a good account of the end of the war in Florida see Francis C. M. Boggess, *A Veteran of Four Wars* (Arcadia, Fla.: Champion Press, 1900).

7. Union Forces in Florida

1. William R. Thayer, *The Life and Letters of John Hay,* 2 vols. (Boston: Houghton Mifflin, 1915), 1:154–55, 271.

2. *New York Times,* 13 January 1863, p. 2; Robert L. Clarke, "Northern Plans for the Economic Invasion of Florida 1862–1865," *FHQ* 28 (April 1950): 262–70.

3. Frank P. Moore, ed., *The Rebellion Record,* 12 vols. (New York: G. P. Putnam, 1861–1868; reprint, New York: Arno, 1977), 6:44; "Memoirs," Calvin L. Robinson Papers, Florida Collection, FSA, 56; Clarke, "Northern Plans," 263–64.

4. *O.R.,* ser. 1, 53:258; Columbus *Daily Enquirer,* 13 October 1862, p. 2. The item was also carried in the Macon *Daily Telegraph,* 9 October 1862, p. 2.

5. New Orleans *Picayune,* 17 July 1861, p. 1; Columbus *Daily Enquirer,* 22 February 1861, p. 2. Secretary of War George W. Randolph informed Major

General Samuel Jones, commander of the Department of Alabama and West Florida, that no general prohibition of the exportation of produce from the Confederacy existed, but that he was to stop any trading with the enemy. However, he "should also bear in mind that it is a good policy to exchange produce for arms and ammunition with anyone willing to make such exchanges" (see Randolph to Jones, 14 April 1862, Confederate States of America, War Department, Office of the Secretary of War, 1861–1865, Manuscript Department, DU).

6. Macon *Daily Telegraph,* 5 December 1861, p. 2; Henry Prossens to John Milton, 14 April 1863, John Milton Papers, Collection of the Florida Historical Society, Tampa, Fla. See also *O.R.N.,* ser. 1, 4:159.

7. James I. Robertson, Jr., *Soldiers Blue and Gray* (Columbia: University of South Carolina Press, 1988), 66, 71, 73; Bell I. Wiley, *The Life of Billy Yank: The Common Soldier in the Civil War* (Baton Rouge: Louisiana State University Press, 1952), 225, 231; Richard E. Beringer, Herman Hattaway, Archer Jones, and William N. Still, Jr., *Why the South Lost the Civil War* (Athens: University of Georgia Press, 1986), 15; *New York Tribune,* 5 May 1861, p. 3. A member of the Twenty-Fourth Massachusetts Infantry, stationed at Saint Augustine in 1863, recalled that "a good soldier never forgets his stomach, and as these men were in Florida to recuperate they were doing their best to accomplish the desired results" (see Alfred S. Roe, *The Twenty-Fourth Regiment, Massachusetts Volunteers 1861– 1865* [Worcester, Mass.: Twenty-Fourth Veteran Association, 1907], 243).

8. *O.R.,* ser. 1, 35, part 1:389; James H. Gordon, *A War Diary in the War of the Great Rebellion 1863–1865* (Boston: James R. Osgood, 1882).

9. *O.R.,* ser. 1, 35, part 2:27, 35, 195; Gordon, *A War Diary,* 227, 302; Roe, *Twenty-Fourth Regiment,* 240, 244. The Augusta *Daily Chronicle and Sentinel* thought "the plans of the enemy seem to be to steal all the cattle and provisions they can, and destroy the property of loyal citizens along the St. Johns" (29 May 1864, p. 1). For early Confederate reaction to such tactics see Ellen E. Hodges and Stephen Kerber, eds., "'Rogues and Black Hearted Scamps': Civil War Letters of Winston and Octavia Stephens, 1862–1863," *FHQ* 57 (July 1978): 71–72.

10. "Reminiscences," Albert W. Peck Papers, FSA, 43, 44 (hereinafter cited as Peck "Reminiscences"); Justus M. Silliman, *A New Canaan Private in the Civil War: Letters of Justus M. Silliman, 17th Connecticut Volunteers,* ed. Edward Marcus (New Canaan, Conn.: New Canaan Historical Society, 1984), 82. For more on the export of Florida hides see U.S. Treasury Department, Settler Book, 5th Special Agency, Saint Augustine, Fla., RG 366, vol. 286, NA.

11. J. J. Dickison, "Florida," in *Confederate Military History,* ed. Clement A. Evans, 13 vols. (Atlanta: Blue and Grey Press, 1899), 11:119; Alice Strickland, *Ormond on the Halifax: A Centennial History of Ormond Beach, Florida* (Holly Hill, Fla.: Southwest, 1980), 32.

12. Diary, 1 November 1863, J. H. Linsley Papers, PKY; Peck "Reminiscences," 51, 52; Gordon, *A War Diary,* 297.

13. *O.R.,* ser. 1, 35, part 1:274; U.S. War Department, *Letters Sent by the Department of Florida and Successor Commands, April 1861–January 1869* (NA, 1980), reel 1, 247–48.

14. Alexander Asboth to David G. Farragut, 8 June 1864, U.S. War Depart-

ment, *Letters Sent by the Department of Florida*, reel 1, 179. See also reel 1, 19, 248.

15. U.S. War Department, *Letters Sent by the Department of Florida*, reel 1, 111, 151, 155, 184, 230. See also *O.R.*, ser. 1, 49, part 2:307.

16. *O.R.*, ser. 1, 26, part 1:873.

17. Ibid., part 1:874, 35, part 2:16, 103, 461.

18. Ibid., 52, part 1:614; Rodney E. Dillon, Jr., "The Civil War in South Florida" (M.A. thesis, University of Florida, 1980), 294. A Union soldier wrote from Charlotte Harbor on 20 January 1864 that "a number of troops under Gen. Woodbury had arrived at Punta Rassa, their object being to cut off the large supply of beeves the rebels are taking from Fla., which are at the rate of 150 per week" (see New Orleans *Picayune*, 16 February 1864, p. 1).

19. *O.R.*, ser. 1, 35, part 1:38, 376; John E. Johns, *Florida During the Civil War* (Gainesville: University of Florida Press, 1963), 69. Not all troops were satisfied with the fruit available to them. Men of the Twenty-Fourth Massachusetts "expected lemons and limes to be sour, but they were disappointed to find oranges having the same characteristic" (see Roe, *Twenty-Fourth Regiment*, 237).

20. Peck "Reminiscences," 52.

21. New Orleans *Picayune*, 27 October 1861, p. 2.

22. Samuel Proctor, ed., *Florida a Hundred Years Ago* (Tallahassee: Florida State Library, 1960–1965), December 1964, 4; *O.R.*, ser. 1, 35, part 2:302; *O.R.N.*, ser. 1, 14:430. For more on Union lumber operations see Fernandina *Peninsula*, 25 February 1864, p. 2; Thomas B. Brooks Papers, FSA, folder 8.

23. Asboth to Farragut, 24 March 1864, U.S. War Department, *Letters Sent by the Department of Florida*, reel 1, 30; *O.R.*, ser. 1, 15:127.

24. *O.R.N.*, ser. 1, 14:366; *O.R.*, ser. 1, 14:195–98. See Thomas Wentworth Higginson, *Army Life in a Black Regiment* (Boston: James R. Osgood, 1870; reprint, Boston: Beacon, 1962), 62–96; Joseph T. Glatthaar, *Forged in Battle: The Civil War Alliance of Black Soldiers and White Officers* (New York: Free Press, 1990). Operations are also described by Johns in *Florida During the Civil War*, 67–70.

25. *O.R.N.*, ser. 1, 17:686–87. See also *O.R.N.*, ser. 1, 17:578, 671, 685, 718.

26. *O.R.N.*, ser. 1, 17:741, 491, 804. See also David J. Coles, "Unpretending Service: The *James L. Davis*, the *Tahoma*, and the East Gulf Blockading Squadron," *FHQ* 71 (July 1992): 53–54.

27. *O.R.N.*, ser. 1, 17:767–68.

28. Macon *Daily Telegraph*, 24 May 1864, p. 2; Charleston *Daily Courier*, 12 June 1863, p. 2; Johns, *Florida During the Civil War*, 71. A helpful guide to military operations is Allen W. Jones's "Military Events in Florida During the Civil War, 1861–1865," *FHQ* 39 (July 1960): 42–45.

29. Ethelred Philips to James J. Philips, 23 February 1864, James J. Philips Papers, Southern Historical Collection, University of North Carolina–Chapel Hill, folder 1; Asboth to Daniel Sickles, 10 August 1864, U.S. War Department, *Letters Sent by the Department of Florida*, reel 1, 324–25; *O.R.*, ser. 1, 35, part 1:444, 447–49, part 2:165. See also Mark F. Boyd, "The Battle of Marianna," *FHQ* 29 (April 1951): 225–42.

30. *O.R.*, ser. 3, 3:116; Gordon, *A War Diary*, 296.

31. Reid Mitchell, *Civil War Soldiers: Their Expectations and Their Experiences*

(New York: Viking, 1988), 138, 146; Arthur W. Thompson, "Confederate Finance: A Documentary Study of a Proposal of David L. Yulee," *FHQ* 30 (October 1951): 196; Gainesville *Cotton States*, 4 June 1864, p. 2. In the matter of slaves captured by Federal forces the *Richmond Enquirer* felt that "as a matter of retaliation in kind every Yankee captured in Florida should be handed over to suffering slave owners and to supply the place of a stolen negro." See Macon *Daily Telegraph*, 15 May 1863, p. 2. For details of Federal troops looting see Hodges and Kerber, eds., "'Rogues and Black Hearted Scamps,'" 69–70.

32. *O.R.*, ser. 1, 35, part 1:276, 279; Robert Selph Henry, *The Story of the Confederacy* (Indianapolis: Bobbs-Merrill, 1931), 335. For the Olustee campaign see Shelby Foote, *The Civil War: A Narrative*, 3 vols. (New York: Random House, 1958–1974), 2:898–906; Richard M. McMurry, "The President's Tenth and the Battle of Olustee," *Civil War Times Illustrated* 16 (January 1978): 12–24; David J. Coles, "'A Fight, A Licking, and a Footrace': The 1864 Florida Campaign and the Battle of Olustee" (M.A. thesis, Florida State University, 1985); William H. Nulty, *Confederate Florida: The Road to Olustee* (Tuscaloosa: University of Alabama Press, 1990).

33. *O.R.*, ser. 1, 53, 53:99, 35, part 1:293; Vaughn D. Bornet, "A Connecticut Yankee Fights at Olustee: Letters from the Front," *FHQ* 27 (January 1949): 244. Union forces had brought the railroad locomotive "Marion" and four cars for use on the captured rail lines, but they were not functional because of mechanical problems (see Lieutenant Edward K. Talcott to Major Thomas B. Brooks, 14 February 1864, Brooks Papers, folder 6).

34. *New York Herald*, 20 February 1864, p. 2; Pleasant W. White to Joseph D. Locke, 11 April 1864, Pleasant W. White Papers, Collection of the Florida Historical Society, Tampa, Fla., box 2. For the loss of government hides at Sanderson see Albany *Patriot*, 10 March 1864, p. 1.

35. *O.R.*, ser. 1, 35, part 2:394. For the full text of the White Circular see Appendix.

36. *O.R.*, ser. 1, 35, part 2:392.

37. *New York Tribune*, 20 February 1864, p. 6; *New York Herald*, 20 February, p. 5, 21 February 1864, p. 5; New Orleans *Picayune*, 3 March 1864, p. 1. A map on page 4 of the *New York Herald* of 10 February 1864 showed most of Florida as being under Union control.

38. *O.R.*, ser. 1, 35, part 1:325–26. See also Charleston *Daily Courier*, 11 February 1864, p. 1.

39. Charles M. Duren to his mother, 15 February 1864, Charles M. Duren Papers, PKY; Macon *Daily Telegraph*, 8 March 1864, p. 2.

40. *O.R.*, ser. 1, 35, part 1:302, 337, 298; McMurry, "President's Tenth," 20–21; Johns, *Florida During the Civil War*, 198–99.

41. *O.R.*, ser. 1, 35, part 1:322, 35, part 1:392, 53:346; Charleston *Daily Courier*, 24 February, p. 1, 10 March 1864, p. 1. For the effect of the Olustee campaign on supplying Charleston see White to Seth B. French, 11 March 1864, White Papers, box 2.

42. Macon *Daily Telegraph*, 25 February, p. 2, 26 February, p. 2, 11 May 1864, p. 2; *New York Herald*, 1 March 1864, p. 1. The Augusta *Daily Chronicle and*

Sentinel reported that when mounted infantrymen of the Fortieth Massachusetts occupied the town of Starke enroute to a raid on Gainesville during the Union attack on Florida, "they were almost famished besides and some of them declared that they had not tasted meat for four days and begged around among the people" (1 March 1864, p. 2).

43. Mobile *Daily Advertiser and Register,* 9 March 1864, p. 1; Charleston *Daily Courier,* 10 February, p. 1, 28 February 1864, p. 2. The Gainesville *Cotton States* thought "the insolent enemy seem[ed] to be impressed on account of a diabolical mistake and blunder of an official that our armies are dependent on Florida for supplies" (10 March 1864, p. 2).

44. *New York Herald,* 1 March 1864, p. 4; *New York Post,* reprinted in Charleston *Daily Courier,* 11 March 1864, p. 1. For a survey of Northern newspaper opinion see New Orleans *Picayune,* 16 March 1864, p. 1. See also William H. Nulty, "The Seymour Decision: An Appraisal of the Olustee Campaign," *FHQ* 65 (January 1987): 298–316.

45. *New York Tribune,* 29 February, p. 1, 17 February 1864, p. 4; *New York Times,* 28 February, p. 4, 1 March, p. 1, 18 March 1864, p. 4.

46. *O.R.,* ser. 1, 35, part 1:420, part 2:320, 492. See also Macon *Daily Telegraph,* 18 April 1864, p. 2.

47. Gainesville *Cotton States,* 28 May 1864, p. 2; Mary E. Massey, *Refugee Life in the Confederacy* (Baton Rouge: Louisiana State University Press, 1964), 81–85, 87. See also Charleston *Daily Courier,* 27 April 1863, p. 1.

48. *O.R.,* ser. 1, 49, part 1:63, 687, 707; Augusta *Daily Chronicle and Sentinel,* 2 February 1865, p. 2; Johns, *Florida During the Civil War,* 209.

49. *O.R.,* ser. 1, 49, part 2:1074, 1083–84. Colonel James H. Gordon summarized the Union military's mission in Florida as "to forecast Presidential action in utilizing the orange groves and the cotton lands, the lumber and hogs of this land of sun and flowers" (see Gordon, *A War Diary,* 297).

50. In all at least twenty-one "raids" or "expeditions" were conducted by Union troops in Florida from 1862 to 1865. For a breakdown of such activity see Jones, "Military Events in Florida," 42-45.

8. Florida and the Confederate Economy

1. Pleasant W. White to Lucius B. Northrop, 6 November 1863, Pleasant W. White Papers, Collection of the Florida Historical Society, Tampa, Fla., box 2; Richard M. McMurry, *Two Great Rebel Armies: An Essay in Confederate Military History* (Chapel Hill: University of North Carolina Press, 1989), 24. See also Frank E. Vandiver, "The Confederacy and the American Tradition," *JSH* 28 (August 1962): 286; Thomas L. Connelly, "The Cycle of Military and Economic Interests: A Theory of Confederate Defeat," *Alabama Historical Review* 30 (Fall/Winter 1968): 125; Douglas B. Ball, *Financial Failure and Confederate Defeat* (Urbana: University of Illinois Press, 1991), 1, 17, 253.

2. Charleston *Daily Courier,* 23 October 1863, p. 1.

3. E. Merton Coulter, "The Movement for Agricultural Reorganization in the

Cotton South During the Civil War," *North Carolina Historical Review* 4 (January 1927): 34; Frank E. Vandiver, "The Food Supply of the Confederate Armies, 1865," *Tyler's Quarterly Historical and Genealogical Magazine* 26 (October 1944): 86. See also Edwin B. Coddington, "A Social and Economic History of the Seaboard States of the Southern Confederacy" (Ph.D. diss., Clark University, 1939), 120–21.

Bibliography

Primary Sources

United States Documents

U.S. Bureau of Census. *Agriculture of the United States in 1860: Compiled from the Original Returns of the Eighth Census.* Washington, D.C.: Government Printing Office, 1864.

U.S. Commissioner of Agriculture. *Report of the Commissioner of Agriculture for the Year 1862.* Washington, D.C.: Government Printing Office, 1863.

————. *Report of the Commissioner of Agriculture for the Year 1863.* Washington, D.C.: Government Printing Office, 1864.

U.S. Congress. *Commerce and Navigation.* Senate Executive Document no. 6. 32d Congress, 2d sess., 1852.

————. *Commerce and Navigation.* Senate Executive Document no. 55. 32d Congress, 1st sess., 1852.

————. *Commerce and Navigation.* Senate Executive Document no. 6. 36th Congress, 2d sess., 1859.

————. *Cotton Sold to the Confederate States.* Senate Executive Document no. 987. 62d Congress, 3d sess., 1913.

————. *Eighth Census, 1860.* Washington, D.C.: Government Printing Office, 1864.

U.S. Department of Agriculture. *Tide Marshes of the United States.* Washington, D.C.: Government Printing Office, 1885.

U.S. Department of the Interior. Bureau of Mines. *Mineral Resources of the United States.* Washington, D.C.: Government Printing Office, 1883.

————. U.S. Geological Survey. *Salt Resources of the United States.* Washington, D.C.: Government Printing Office, 1919.

U.S. Treasury Department. "Personal Cotton Books of Gazaway B. Lamar." Record Group 366. National Archives, Washington, D.C.

————. Settler Book, 5th Special Agency, Saint Augustine, Fla. Record Group 366. National Archives, Washington, D.C.

U.S. War Department. *Letters Sent by the Department of Florida and Successor Commands, April 1861–January 1869.* National Archives, Washington, D.C., 1980.

——. *Official Records of the Union and Confederate Navies in the War of the Rebellion.* 26 vols. Washington, D.C., 1901.

——. *War of the Rebellion: A Compilation of the Official Records of the Union and Confederate Armies.* 128 vols. Washington, D.C.: Government Printing Office, 1880–1901.

Confederate States Documents

Confederate States Army. Commissary of Subsistence. "Return of Provisions Received and Issued at Savannah, Ga. During the Months of August 1863 to December 1864." Special Collections Division, University of Georgia Libraries, Athens, Ga.

——. Medical Department. Letters Sent, Medical Purveyor's Office, Savannah, Ga. . . . 1862. Record Group 109. National Archives, Washington, D.C.

Confederate States of America. War Department. Adjutant and Inspector-General's Office. Letters and Papers, 1861–1865. Manuscript Department, William R. Perkins Library, Duke University.

——. *Compiled Service Records of Confederate General and Staff Officers and Non-regimental Enlisted Men.* National Archives, Washington, D.C., 1962.

——. Department of South Carolina, Georgia, and Florida. "Report of Persons Hired, February to May 1863." Record Group 109. National Archives, Washington, D.C.

——. *General Orders from the Adjutant and Inspector-General's Office, Confederate States Army, from January 1, 1864 to July 1, 1864* . . . Columbia, S.C.: Evans and Cogswell, 1864.

——. Nitre and Mining Bureau. Correspondence and Reports, 1862–1865. Record Group 109. National Archives, Washington, D.C.

——. Nitre and Mining Bureau. District of South Carolina, Georgia, Florida, and Alabama . . . Letter-book, 31 October 1864–14 April 1865. Special Collections Division, University of Georgia Libraries, Athens, Ga.

——. Office of the Secretary of War, 1861–1865. Manuscript Division, William R. Perkins Library, Duke University.

——. Quartermaster General's Office. Manuscript Division, William R. Perkins Library, Duke University.

Georgia Department of Archives and History. "Annual Report of the Quartermaster of Georgia, 1863." Atlanta, Ga.

State and Local Documents

Acts and Resolutions Adopted by the General Assembly of Florida, 1860–1865. Tallahassee: *Florida Sentinel,* 1861–1865.

Journal of the Proceedings of the Convention of the People of Florida . . . 1861. Tallahassee: Tallahassee *Floridian and Journal,* 1861; reprint, Jacksonville, Fla.: W. B. Drew, 1928.

Journal of the Proceedings of the House of Representatives of the General Assembly of the State of Florida. Tallahassee: *Florida Sentinel,* 1860–1865.

Office of the Comptroller. Territorial and State Military Expenditures, 1839–1869. Record Group 350. Florida State Archives, Tallahassee, Fla.

Office of the Governor. Correspondence of the Governors, 1857–1888. Record Group 101. Florida State Archives, Tallahassee, Fla.

Records of Marks and Brands for Hillsborough County. Vol. 1. Hillsborough County Historical Commission, Tampa, Fla.

Reports of Cases Argued in the Supreme Court of Florida at Terms Held in 1864–1867. Vol. 11. Tallahassee: Dyke and Sparhawk, 1867.

Manuscripts

Adams, J. R. Papers. Florida Collection, Florida State Archives, Tallahassee, Fla.

Anderson, J. Patton. Papers. P. K. Yonge Library of Florida History, University of Florida, Gainesville, Fla.

Barrow, Daniel C. Papers. Special Collections Division, University of Georgia Libraries, Athens, Ga.

Brooks, Thomas B. Papers. Florida State Archives, Tallahassee, Fla.

Davidson, J. E. A. Papers. P. K. Yonge Library of Florida History, University of Florida, Gainesville, Fla.

Duren, Charles M. Papers. P. K. Yonge Library of Florida History, University of Florida, Gainesville, Fla.

Frier, Joshua H. Papers. Florida State Archives, Tallahassee, Fla.

Gift, Ellen S. Papers. Southern Historical Collection, University of North Carolina–Chapel Hill.

Guerin, Henry C. Papers. South Caroliniana Library, University of South Carolina, Columbia, S.C.

Hentz, Thaddeus W. H. Papers. P. K. Yonge Library of Florida History, University of Florida, Gainesville, Fla.

L'Engle, Edward M. Papers. Southern Historical Collection, University of North Carolina–Chapel Hill.

Linsley, J. H. Papers. P. K. Yonge Library of Florida History, University of Florida, Gainesville, Fla.

McKay, James. Papers. Collection of the Florida Historical Society, Tampa, Fla.

Milton, John. Papers. Collection of the Florida Historical Society, Tampa, Fla.

Peck, Albert W. Papers. Florida State Archives, Tallahassee, Fla.

Philips, James J. Papers. Southern Historical Collection, University of North Carolina–Chapel Hill.

Poole, W. G. Papers. Florida State Archives, Tallahassee, Fla.

Robinson, Calvin L. Papers. Florida Collection, Florida State Archives, Tallahassee, Fla.

Scott, George W. Papers. Florida State Archives, Tallahassee, Fla.

Shaw, James K. Papers. Florida Collection, Florida State Archives, Tallahassee, Fla.

Summer, A. G. Papers. P. K. Yonge Library of Florida History, University of Florida, Gainesville, Fla.

Summer, Henry. Papers. Southern Historical Collection, University of North Carolina–Chapel Hill.

Thompson, George S. Papers. Southern Historical Collection, University of North Carolina–Chapel Hill.

Warner, James H. Papers. James W. Woodruff, Jr., Confederate Naval Museum, Columbus, Ga.

White, Pleasant W. Papers. Collection of the Florida Historical Society, Tampa, Fla.

Yonge, Chandler C. Papers. P. K. Yonge Library of Florida History, University of Florida, Gainesville, Fla.

Yulee, David Levy. Papers. P. K. Yonge Library of Florida History, University of Florida, Gainesville, Fla.

Printed Sources and Memoirs

Abbey, Kathryn T. "Documents Relating to El Destino and Chemonie Plantations, Middle Florida, 1828–1868, Part III." *Florida Historical Quarterly* 8 (July 1929): 1–46.

———. "Documents Relating to El Destino and Chemonie Plantations, Middle Florida, 1828-1868, Part I." *Florida Historical Quarterly* 7 (January 1929): 179–213.

Boggess, Francis C. M. *A Veteran of Four Wars*. Arcadia, Fla.: Champion Press, 1900.

Bornet, Vaughn D. "A Connecticut Yankee Fights at Olustee: Letters from the Front." *Florida Historical Quarterly* 27 (January 1949): 237–59.

Candler, Allen D., ed. *The Confederate Records of the State of Georgia*. 6 vols. Atlanta: Charles P. Byrd, State Printer, 1910.

Chesnut, Mary B. *A Diary from Dixie*. Ed. Ben Ames Williams. Boston: Houghton Mifflin, 1950.

———. *A Diary from Dixie*. Ed. Isabella D. Martin and Myrta L. Avery. New York: D. Appleton, 1905.

Crist, Lynda L., ed. *The Papers of Jefferson Davis: Volume 7, 1861*. Baton Rouge: Louisiana State University Press, 1992.

Dancy, James M. "Reminiscences of the Civil War." *Florida Historical Quarterly* 37 (July 1958): 66–89.

Dickison, J. J. "Florida." In *Confederate Military History*, ed. Clement A. Evans. 13 vols. Atlanta: Blue and Grey Press, 1899.

Dotz, Franklin A. "The Civil War Letters of Augustus Henry Mathers, Assistant

Surgeon, 4th Florida Regiment, C.S.A." *Florida Historical Quarterly* 36 (October 1957): 94–124.

Dowdey, Clifford, and Louis H. Manarian, eds. *The Wartime Papers of R. E. Lee.* New York: Bramball House, 1961.

Eppes, Susan Bradford. *Through Some Eventful Years.* Chicago: Joseph S. Branch, 1926; reprint, Gainesville: University of Florida Press, 1968.

———. *The Negro of the Old South.* Chicago: Joseph S. Branch, 1925.

Gordon, James H. *A War Diary in the War of the Great Rebellion 1863–1865.* Boston: James R. Osgood, 1882.

Gorgas, Josiah. *The Civil War Diary of General Josiah Gorgas.* Ed. Frank E. Vandiver. University: University of Alabama Press, 1947.

Higginson, Thomas Wentworth. *Army Life in a Black Regiment.* Boston: James R. Osgood, 1870; reprint, Boston: Beacon, 1962.

Hodges, Ellen E., and Stephen Kerber, eds. " 'Rogues and Black Hearted Scamps': Civil War Letters of Winston and Octavia Stephens, 1862–1863." *Florida Historical Quarterly* 57 (July 1978): 54–82.

Hopley, Catherine C. *Life in the South: From the Commencement of the War by a Blockaded British Subject.* 2 vols. London: Chapman and Hall, 1863.

Johnston, Joseph E. *Narrative of Military Operations During the Late War Between the States.* New York: D. Appleton, 1874; reprint, Bloomington: Indiana University Press, 1959.

Jones, John B. *A Rebel War Clerk's Diary at the Confederate States Capital.* Ed. Earl Schenck Miers. New York: A. S. Barnes, 1961.

Kean, Robert G. H. *Inside the Confederate Government: The Diary of Robert Garlick Hill Kean, Head of the Bureau of War.* Ed. Edward Younger. New York: Oxford University Press, 1957.

Moore, Frank P., ed. *The Rebellion Record.* 12 vols. New York: G. P. Putnam, 1861–1868; reprint, New York: Arno, 1977.

Pollard, Edward A. *The Lost Cause.* New York: J. S. Morrow, 1868.

Roe, Alfred S. *The Twenty-Fourth Regiment, Massachusetts Volunteers 1861–1865.* Worcester, Mass.: Twenty-Fourth Veteran Association, 1907.

Rowland, Dunbar, ed. *Jefferson Davis, Constitutionalist: His Letters, Papers, and Speeches.* 9 vols. Jackson: Mississippi Department of Archives and History, 1923.

Silliman, Justus M. *A New Canaan Private in the Civil War: Letters of Justus M. Silliman, 17th Connecticut Volunteers.* Ed. Edward Marcus. New Canaan, Conn.: New Canaan Historical Society, 1984.

Southern Historical Society. *Southern Historical Society Papers.* 52 vols. Richmond: Southern Historical Society, 1876–1959.

Tenney, John F. *Slavery, Secession, and Success: Memoirs of a Florida Pioneer.* New York: Peter Smith, 1934.

Ulmer, Herman, Jr., ed. "The Correspondence of Will and Ju Stockton, 1845–1869." Florida Collection, Florida State Archives, Tallahassee, Fla.

Wright, Willard E., ed. "Some Letters of Lucius Bellinger Northrop, 1860–1865." *Virginia Magazine of History and Biography* 68 (October 1960): 456–77.

Bibliography   *Florida:*

Cedar Keys *Telegraph*
Fernandina *East Floridian*
Fernandina *Peninsula*
Gainesville *Cotton States*
Jacksonville *Florida News*
Lake City *Columbian*
Newport *Wakulla Times*
Ocala *Florida Home Companion*
Quincy *Semi-Weekly Dispatch*
Saint Augustine *Ancient City*
Saint Augustine *Examiner*
Tallahassee *Floridian and Journal*
Tallahassee *Florida Sentinel*
Tampa *Florida Peninsular*

Others:

Albany *Patriot*
American Agriculturalist
Atlanta *Southern Confederacy*
Augusta *Daily Chronicle and Sentinel*
Charleston *Daily Courier*
Columbus *Daily Enquirer*
De Bow's Review
Macon *Daily Telegraph*
Mobile *Daily Advertiser and Register*
Montgomery *Weekly Post*
New Orleans *Picayune*
New York Herald
New York Times
New York Tribune
Southern Cultivator

Secondary Sources

Books

Akerman, Joe A., Jr., *Florida Cowman: A History of Florida Cattle Raising*. Kissimmee, Fla.: Florida Cattlemen's Association, 1976.

Anderson, Bern. *By Sea and by River: The Naval History of the Civil War.* New York: Knopf, 1962.

Avant, David A., Jr., ed. *J. Randall Stanley's History of Gadsden County.* Tallahassee: L'Avant Studios, 1985.

Ball, Douglas B. *Financial Failure and Confederate Defeat.* Urbana: University of Illinois Press, 1991.

Ballagh, James C., ed. *The South in the Building of the Nation.* 12 vols. Richmond: Southern Historical Publishing Society, 1909.

Barney, William L. *The Secessionist Impulse: Alabama and Mississippi in 1860.* Princeton, N.J.: Princeton University Press, 1974.

Beringer, Richard E., Herman Hattaway, Archer Jones, and William N. Still, Jr. *Why the South Lost the Civil War.* Athens: University of Georgia Press, 1986.

Black, Robert C., III. *The Railroads of the Confederacy.* Chapel Hill: University of North Carolina Press, 1952.

Bradlee, Francis B. C. *Blockade Running During the Civil War and the Effect of Land and Water Transportation on the Confederacy.* Salem, Mass.: Essex Institute, 1925.

Bryan, Thomas C. *Confederate Georgia.* Athens: University of Georgia Press, 1953.

Cabell, Branch, and A. J. Hanna. *The St. Johns: A Parade of Diversities.* New York: Farrar and Rinehart, 1943.

Cappon, Lester J. "Government and Private Industry in the Southern Confederacy." *Humanistic Studies in Honor of John Calvin Metcalf.* Charlottesville: University of Virginia Press, 1941.

Catton, Bruce. *The Coming Fury.* New York: Doubleday, 1961; reprint, New York: Pocket Books, 1974.

Cauthen, Charles E. *South Carolina Goes to War 1860–1865.* Chapel Hill: University of North Carolina Press, 1950.

Clark, Victor S. *History of Manufacturing in the United States.* 2 vols. New York: McGraw, 1929.

Cochran, Hamilton. *Blockade Runners of the Confederacy.* Indianapolis: Bobbs-Merrill, 1958.

Cole, Arthur C. *The Irrepressible Conflict 1850–1865.* New York: Macmillan, 1934; reprint, Chicago: Quadrangle, 1971.

Connelly, Thomas L. *Autumn of Glory: The Army of Tennessee, 1862–1865.* Baton Rouge: Louisiana State University Press, 1971.

Coulter, E. Merton. *The Confederate States of America 1861–1865.* Baton Rouge: Louisiana State University Press, 1950.

Dacy, George H. *Four Centuries of Florida Ranching.* Saint Louis: Britt Printing, 1940.

Davis, William C. *Jefferson Davis: The Man and His Hour.* New York: Harper-Collins, 1991.

Davis, William W. *The Civil War and Reconstruction in Florida.* New York: Columbia University Press, 1913.

DeCredico, Mary A. *Patriotism for Profit: Georgia's Urban Entrepreneurs and the Confederate War Effort.* Chapel Hill: University of North Carolina Press, 1990.

Dickison, Mary E. *Dickison and His Men*. Louisville, Ky., 1890; reprint, Gainesville: University of Florida Press, 1962.

Dodd, Dorothy. "Florida in the Civil War, 1861–1865." In *Florida Handbook 1961–1962*, ed. Allen Morris. Tallahassee: Peninsular Publishing, 1961.

Doherty, Herbert J., Jr. *Richard Keith Call: Southern Unionist*. Gainesville: University of Florida Press, 1961.

Eaton, Clement. *A History of the Southern Confederacy*. New York: Macmillan, 1954.

Escott, Paul D. *After Secession: Jefferson Davis and the Failure of Confederate Nationalism*. Baton Rouge: Louisiana State University Press, 1978.

Faust, Drew G. *The Creation of Confederate Nationalism: Ideology and Identity in the Civil War South*. Baton Rouge: Louisiana State University Press, 1988.

Foote, Shelby. *The Civil War: A Narrative*. 3 vols. New York: Random House, 1958–1974.

Freeman, Douglas S. *Lee's Lieutenants*. 3 vols. New York: Scribner's, 1942–1944.

Futch, Ovid L. *History of Andersonville Prison*. Gainesville: University of Florida Press, 1968.

Gates, Paul W. *Agriculture and the Civil War*. New York: Knopf, 1965.

———. *The Farmer's Age: Agriculture 1815–1860*. New York: Holt, 1960.

Genovese, Eugene D. *The Political Economy of Slavery: Studies in the Economy and Society of the Slave South*. New York: Knopf, 1965; reprint, New York: Vintage, 1967.

Glatthaar, Joseph T. *Forged in Battle: The Civil War Alliance of Black Soldiers and White Officers*. New York: Free Press, 1990.

Goff, Richard D. *Confederate Supply*. Durham, N.C.: Duke University Press, 1969.

Graham, Thomas. *The Awakening of St. Augustine: The Anderson Family and the Oldest City 1821–1924*. St. Augustine, Fla.: St. Augustine Historical Society, 1978.

Hagerman, Edward. *The American Civil War and the Origins of Modern Warfare*. Bloomington: Indiana University Press, 1988.

Hattaway, Herman, and Archer Jones. *How the North Won: A Military History of the Civil War*. Urbana: University of Illinois Press, 1983.

Hebel, Ianthe B. *Southern Country Folks at War: Volusia County, Florida During the Civil War 1861–1865*. Daytona Beach, Fla.: n.p., 1960. Copy in Florida Collection, R. N. Strozier Library, Florida State University, Tallahassee, Fla.

Henry, Robert Selph. *The Story of the Confederacy*. Indianapolis: Bobbs-Merrill, 1931.

Hesseltine, William B., ed. *The Tragic Conflict: The Civil War and Reconstruction*. New York: Braziller, 1962.

Hilliard, Sam B. *Hog Meat and Hoecake: Food Supply in the Old South 1840–1860*. Carbondale: Southern Illinois University Press, 1972.

Horn, Stanley F. *The Army of Tennessee: A Military History*. Indianapolis: Bobbs-Merrill, 1941; reprint, Norman: University of Oklahoma Press, 1953.

Johns, John E. *Florida During the Civil War*. Gainesville: University of Florida Press, 1963.

Jomini, Antoine Henri. *The Art of War.* 1834; Philadelphia: Lippincott, 1862.

Jordan, Weymouth T. *Rebels in the Making: Planter's Conventions and Southern Propaganda.* Tuscaloosa, Ala.: Confederate, 1958.

Kaufmann, Dale W. *Sodium Chloride.* London: Chapman and Hall, 1960.

Keuchel, Edward F. *A History of Columbia County, Florida.* Tallahassee: Sentry, 1981.

Lash, Jeffrey N. *Destroyer of the Iron Horse: General Joseph E. Johnston and Confederate Rail Transport, 1861–1865.* Kent, Ohio: Kent State University Press, 1991.

Long, E. B. *The Civil War Day by Day: An Almanac 1861–1865.* Garden City, N.Y.: Doubleday, 1971.

Lonn, Ella. *Salt as a Factor in the Confederacy.* University: University of Alabama Press, 1965.

——. *Desertion During the Civil War.* New York: Century, 1928.

Luraghi, Raimondo. *The Rise and Fall of the Plantation South.* New York: New Viewpoints, 1978.

McMillan, Malcolm C. *The Disintegration of a Confederate State: Three Governors and Alabama's Wartime Home Front 1861–1865.* Macon, Ga.: Mercer University Press, 1986.

McMurry, Richard M. *Two Great Rebel Armies: An Essay in Confederate Military History.* Chapel Hill: University of North Carolina Press, 1989.

McPherson, James M. *The Battle Cry of Freedom: The Civil War Era.* New York: Oxford University Press, 1988.

——. *Ordeal by Fire: The Civil War and Reconstruction.* New York: Knopf, 1982.

Massey, Mary E. *Refugee Life in the Confederacy.* Baton Rouge: Louisiana State University Press, 1964.

——. *Ersatz in the Confederacy.* Columbia: University of South Carolina Press, 1952.

Mitchell, Reid. *Civil War Soldiers: Their Expectations and Their Experiences.* New York: Viking, 1988.

Moore, Albert B. *Conscription and Conflict in the Confederacy.* New York: Macmillan, 1924.

Nulty, William H. *Confederate Florida: The Road To Olustee.* Tuscaloosa: University of Alabama Press, 1990.

Oakes, James. *The Ruling Race: A History of American Slaveholders.* New York: Random House, 1982.

Owsley, Frank L. *State Rights in the Confederacy.* Chicago: University of Chicago Press, 1925.

Patrick, Rembert W. *Florida Under Five Flags.* Gainesville: University of Florida Press, 1945.

Phillips, Ulrich B. *Life and Labor in the Old South.* Boston: Little, Brown, 1929.

Potter, David M. *The Impending Crisis 1848–1861.* Completed and edited by Don E. Fehrenbacher. New York: Harper and Row, 1976.

Proctor, Samuel, ed. *Florida a Hundred Years Ago.* Tallahassee: Florida State Library, 1960–1965.

Ramsdell, Charles W. *Behind the Lines in the Southern Confederacy.* Baton Rouge: Louisiana State University Press, 1944.

Ringold, Mary S. *The Role of State Legislatures in the Confederacy.* Athens: University of Georgia Press, 1966.

Roark, James L. *Masters Without Slaves: Southern Planters in the Civil War and Reconstruction.* New York: Norton, 1977.

Robertson, James I., Jr. *Soldiers Blue and Gray.* Columbia: University of South Carolina Press, 1988.

Robinson, William M., Jr. *Justice in Gray: A History of the Judicial System of the Confederate States of America.* Cambridge: Harvard University Press, 1941.

Rogers, William Warren. *Outposts on the Gulf: Saint George Island and Apalachicola from Early Exploration to World War II.* Pensacola: University of West Florida Press, 1986.

Roland, Charles P. *The Confederacy.* Chicago: University of Chicago Press, 1960.

Schwab, John C. *The Confederate States of America 1861–1865: A Financial and Industrial History of the South During the Civil War.* New York: Scribner's, 1901.

Schweikart, Larry. *Banking in the American South from the Age of Jackson to Reconstruction.* Baton Rouge: Louisiana State University Press, 1987.

Shofner, Jerrell H. *Jackson County, Florida—A History.* Marianna, Fla.: Jackson County Heritage Association, 1985.

———. *History of Jefferson County.* Tallahassee: Sentry, 1976.

Sitterson, J. Carlyle. *Sugar Country: The Cane Sugar Industry in the South, 1753–1950.* Lexington: University of Kentucky Press, 1953.

Smith, Julia F. *Slavery and Plantation Growth in Antebellum Florida.* Gainesville: University of Florida Press, 1973.

Stampp, Kenneth M. *The Peculiar Institution: Slavery in the Antebellum South.* New York: Knopf, 1956; reprint, New York: Vintage, 1985.

Strickland, Alice. *Ormond on the Halifax: A Centennial History of Ormond Beach, Florida.* Holly Hill, Fla.: Southwest, 1980.

Sword, Wiley. *Embrace an Angry Wind: The Confederacy's Last Hurrah: Spring Hill, Franklin, and Nashville.* New York: HarperCollins, 1992.

Taylor, Robert A. "A Problem of Supply: Pleasant White and Florida's Cow Cavalry." In *Divided We Fall: Essays on Confederate Nation-Building,* ed. John M. Belohlavek and Lewis N. Wynne. Saint Leo, Fla.: St. Leo College Press, 1991.

Tebeau, Charlton W. *A History of Florida.* Coral Gables, Fla.: University of Miami Press, 1980.

Thayer, William R. *The Life and Letters of John Hay.* 2 vols. Boston: Houghton Mifflin, 1915.

Thomas, Emory M. *The Confederate Nation 1861–1865.* New York: Harper and Row, 1979.

Todd, Richard C. *Confederate Finance.* Athens: University of Georgia Press, 1954.

Turner, Maxine. *Navy Gray: A Story of the Confederate Navy on the Chattahoochee and Apalachicola Rivers.* Tuscaloosa: University of Alabama Press, 1988.

Vandiver, Frank E. *Their Tattered Flags: The Epic of the Confederacy.* New York: Harper's Magazine Press, 1970.

———. *Rebel Brass: The Confederate Command System.* Baton Rouge: Louisiana State University Press, 1956.

———. *Ploughshares into Swords: Josiah Gorgas and Confederate Ordnance.* Austin: University of Texas Press, 1952.

Wakelyn, Jon L. *Biographical Dictionary of the Confederacy.* Westport, Conn.: Greenwood, 1977.

Warner, Joe G. *Biscuits and 'Taters: A History of Cattle Ranching in Manatee County.* Bradenton, Fla.: Great American, 1980.

Wesley, Charles H. *The Collapse of the Confederacy.* Washington, D.C.: Associated Publishers, 1937.

West, G. M. *St. Andrews, Florida* . . . Panama City, Fla.: Panama City Publishing, 1922.

Wiley, Bell I. *The Life of Billy Yank: The Common Soldier in the Civil War.* Baton Rouge: Louisiana State University Press, 1952.

————. *The Plain People of the Confederacy.* Baton Rouge: Louisiana State University Press, 1943.

Wise, Stephen R. *Lifeline of the Confederacy: Blockade Running During the Civil War.* Columbia: University of South Carolina Press, 1988.

Wright, Gavin. *The Political Economy of the Cotton South.* New York: Norton, 1978.

Yearns, Wilfred B. *The Confederate Congress.* Athens: University of Georgia Press, 1960.

Articles

Boyd, Mark F. "The Battle of Marianna." *Florida Historical Quarterly* 29 (April 1951): 225–42.

Brown, Canter, Jr. "Tampa's James McKay and the Frustration of Confederate Cattle-Supply Operations in South Florida." *Florida Historical Quarterly* 70 (April 1992): 409–33.

Cash, William T. "Taylor County History and Civil War Deserters." *Florida Historical Quarterly* 27 (July 1948): 28–58.

Clarke, Robert L. "The Florida Railroad Company in the Civil War." *Journal of Southern History* 19 (May 1953): 180–92.

————. "Northern Plans for the Economic Invasion of Florida 1862–1865." *Florida Historical Quarterly* 28 (April 1950): 262–70.

Coddington, Edwin B. "The Activities of a Confederate Business Man: Gazaway B. Lamar." *Journal of Southern History* 9 (February–November 1943): 3–36.

Coles, David J. "Unpretending Service: The *James L. Davis,* the *Tahoma,* and the East Gulf Blockading Squadron." *Florida Historical Quarterly* 71 (July 1992): 41–62.

Connelly, Thomas L. "The Cycle of Military and Economic Interests: A Theory of Confederate Defeat." *Alabama Historical Review* 30 (Fall/Winter 1968): 111–25.

Cortada, James W. "Florida's Relations with Cuba During the Civil War." *Florida Historical Quarterly* 59 (July 1980): 42–52.

Coulter, E. Merton. "The Movement for Agricultural Reorganization in the Cotton South During the Civil War." *North Carolina Historical Review* 4 (January 1927): 22–34.

Dickinson, M. F., and G. W. Edwardson. "The Salt Works of Salt Island, Florida:

A Site Survey and Historical Perspective." *Florida Anthropologist* 37 (June 1984): 63–74.

Dillon, Rodney E., Jr. "South Florida in 1860." *Florida Historical Quarterly* 60 (April 1982): 440–49.

Dodd, Dorothy. "The Manufacture of Cotton in Florida Before and During the Civil War." *Florida Historical Quarterly* 13 (July 1934): 1–15.

———. "The Secession Movement in Florida, 1850–1861, Part II." *Florida Historical Quarterly* 12 (October 1933): 45–66.

Eisterhold, John A. "Lumber and Trade in Pensacola and West Florida 1800–1860." *Florida Historical Quarterly* 51 (January 1973): 267–80.

Franke, Norman H. "Official and Industrial Aspects of Pharmacy in the Confederacy." *Georgia Historical Quarterly* 37 (September 1953): 175–87.

Frisbie, Louise. "The First Summerlin." *Pioneers* (n.d.). Collection of the Polk County Historical Society, Bartow, Fla.

Hanna, Kathryn A. "Incidents of the Confederate Blockade." *Journal of Southern History* 11 (May 1945): 214–29.

Hay, Thomas R. "Lucius B. Northrop: Commissary-General of the Confederacy." *Civil War History* 9 (March 1963): 5–23.

Jones, Allen W. "Military Events in Florida During the Civil War, 1861–1865." *Florida Historical Quarterly* 39 (July 1960): 42–45.

Kemmerer, Donald L. "The Pre-Civil War South's Leading Crop, Corn." *Agricultural History* 23 (October 1949): 236–39.

Lamson, Harold. "Comments on Florida in the Confederacy." Swisher Library, Jacksonville University, Jacksonville, Fla. (1957).

Lerner, Eugene M. "The Monetary and Fiscal Programs of the Confederate Government." *Journal of Political Economy* 62 (October 1954): 506–22.

Lindstrom, Diane. "Southern Dependence upon Interregional Grain Supplies: A Review of the Trade Flows." *Agricultural History* 44 (January 1970): 101–13.

Lonn, Ella. "The Extent and Importance of Federal Naval Raids on Salt-Making in Florida, 1862–1865." *Florida Historical Quarterly* 10 (April 1932): 167–84.

Lucas, Marion B. "Civil War Career of Colonel George Washington Scott." *Florida Historical Quarterly* 58 (October 1972): 129–49.

McDonald, Forrest, and Grady McWhiney. "The South from Self-Sufficiency to Peonage: An Interpretation." *American Historical Review* 85 (December 1980): 1095–118.

———. "The Antebellum Southern Herdsman: A Reinterpretation." *Journal of Southern History* 51 (May 1975): 147–66.

McMurry, Richard M. "The President's Tenth and the Battle of Olustee." *Civil War Times Illustrated* 16 (January 1978): 12–24.

Markwalder, Donald. "The Ante-bellum South as a Market for Food—Myth or Reality?" *Georgia Historical Quarterly* 54 (Fall 1970): 408–18.

Mealor, W. Theodore, Jr., and Merle C. Prunty. "Open-Range Cattle Ranching in South Florida." *Annals of the Association of American Geographers* 66 (September 1976): 360–72.

Mueller, Edward A. "Suwannee River Steamboating." *Florida Historical Quarterly* 45 (January 1967): 269–88.

————. "East Coast Florida Steamboating 1831–1861." *Florida Historical Quarterly 40* (January 1962): 241–60.

Nulty, William H. "The Seymour Decision: An Appraisal of the Olustee Campaign." *Florida Historical Quarterly 65* (January 1987): 298–316.

Otto, John S. "Open Range Cattle-Herding in Southern Florida." *Florida Historical Quarterly 65* (January 1987): 317–34.

————. "Florida's Cattle-Raising Frontier: Manatee and Brevard Counties (1860)." *Florida Historical Quarterly 64* (July 1985): 48–61.

————. "The Migration of the Southern Plain Folk: An Interdisciplinary Synthesis." *Journal of Southern History 51* (May 1985): 183–200.

————. "Florida's Cattle-Ranching Frontier: Hillsborough County (1860)." *Florida Historical Quarterly 63* (July 1984): 71–83.

————. "Hillsborough County (1850): A Community in the South Florida Flatwoods." *Florida Historical Quarterly 62* (October 1983): 180–93.

Parker, Daisy. "John Milton, Governor of Florida, A Loyal Confederate." *Florida Historical Quarterly 20* (April 1942): 346–61.

Perry, Percival. "The Naval Stores Industry in the Old South 1790–1860." *Journal of Southern History 34* (November 1968): 509–26.

Price, Marcus W. "Ships That Tested the Blockade of the Georgia and East Florida Ports, 1861–1865." *American Neptune 15* (April 1955): 97–132.

Prichard, Walter. "The Effects of the Civil War on the Louisiana Sugar Industry." *Journal of Southern History 5* (August 1939): 315–32.

Rhodes, F. A. "Salt Making on the Apalachee Bay." *Tallahassee Historical Society Annual 12* (1935): 17–20.

Rivers, Larry. "Dignity and Importance: Slavery in Jefferson County Florida 1827–1860." *Florida Historical Quarterly 61* (April 1983): 404–30.

Rothstein, Morton. "The Antebellum South as a Dual Economy: A Tentative Hypothesis." *Agricultural History 41* (October 1967): 373–82.

Schene, Michael S. "Sugar Along the Manatee: Major Robert Gamble Jr. and the Development of Gamble Plantation." *Tequesta 51* (1981): 69–81.

Sellew, A. Robert. "High Prices in the Confederacy." *South Atlantic Quarterly 24* (April 1925): 154–63.

Shofner, Jerrell H., and William Warren Rogers. "Confederate Railroad Construction: The Live Oak to Lawton Connection." *Florida Historical Quarterly 43* (January 1965): 217–28.

————. "Sea Island Cotton in Antebellum Florida." *Florida Historical Quarterly 40* (April 1962): 373–80.

Simpson, James R., and Aubry Bordelon. "The Production-Marketing Connection in Florida's Beef Industry: A Historical Perspective." *Florida Cattleman and Livestock Journal 48* (February 1984): 50–53.

Sitterson, J. Carlyle. "Ante-bellum Sugar Culture in the South Atlantic States." *Journal of Southern History 3* (May 1937): 175–87.

Sloan, Varnie. "Daniel Sloan 1811–1888." *South Florida Pioneers,* no. 3 (January 1975): 1–3.

Smith, Julia F. "Slavetrading in Antebellum Florida." *Florida Historical Quarterly 50* (January 1972): 252–61.

Stearns, R.E.C. "Rambles in Florida." *American Naturalist* 3 (November 1869): 455–58.

Still, William N., Jr. "A Naval Sieve: The Union Blockade in the Civil War." *Naval War College Review* 36 (May/June 1982): 38–45.

Taylor, Robert A. "Unforgotten Threat: Florida Seminoles in the Civil War." *Florida Historical Quarterly* 69 (January 1991): 300–14.

———. "Rebel Beef: Florida Cattle and the Confederate Army, 1862–1864." *Florida Historical Quarterly* 67 (July 1988): 15–31.

———. "Cow Cavalry: Munnerlyn's Battalion in Florida." *Florida Historical Quarterly* 64 (October 1986): 196–214.

Thomas, David Y. "Florida Finance in the Civil War." *Yale Review* 16 (November 1907): 311–18.

Thompson, Arthur W. "Confederate Finance: A Documentary Study of a Proposal of David L. Yulee." *Florida Historical Quarterly* 30 (October 1951): 193–202.

Vandiver, Frank E. "The Confederacy and the American Tradition." *Journal of Southern History* 28 (August 1962): 277–86.

———. "Confederate Plans for Procuring Subsistence Stores." *Tyler's Quarterly Historical and Genealogical Magazine* 27 (April 1946): 273–77.

———. "The Food Supply of the Confederate Armies, 1865." *Tyler's Quarterly Historical and Genealogical Magazine* 26 (October 1944): 77–89.

VanLandingham, Kyle S. "John L. Skipper 1826–1907." *South Florida Pioneers*, no. 12 (April 1977): 24–25.

Williams, Edwin L., Jr. "Negro Slavery in Florida, Part II." *Florida Historical Quarterly* 28 (January 1950): 182–204.

Willoughby, Lynn. "Apalachicola Aweigh: Shipping and Seamen at Florida's Premier Cotton Port." *Florida Historical Quarterly* 69 (October 1990): 178–94.

Theses and Dissertations

Appleyard, Lula D. K. "Plantation Life in Middle Florida 1821–1845." M.A. thesis, Florida State College for Women, 1940.

Brittle, George C. "In Defense of Florida: The Organized Florida Militia from 1820–1920." Ph.D. diss., Florida State University, 1965.

Coddington, Edwin B. "A Social and Economic History of the Seaboard States of the Southern Confederacy." Ph.D. diss., Clark University, 1939.

Coles, David J. "'A Fight, A Licking, and a Footrace': The 1864 Florida Campaign and the Battle of Olustee." M.A. thesis, Florida State University, 1985.

Dillon, Rodney E., Jr. "The Civil War in South Florida." M.A. thesis, University of Florida, 1980.

Gammon, William L. "Governor John Milton of Florida, Confederate States of America." M.A. thesis, University of Florida, 1948.

Guinn, Gilbert S. "Coastal Defense of the Confederate Atlantic Seaboard States, 1861–1862." Ph.D. diss., University of South Carolina, 1973.

Hadd, Donald R. "The Secession Movement in Florida 1850–1861." M.A. thesis, Florida State University, 1960.

Itkin, Stanley L. "Operations of the East Gulf Blockade Squadron in the Blockade of Florida 1862–1865." M.A. thesis, Florida State University, 1962.

Owens, Harry P. "Apalachicola Before 1861." Ph.D. diss., Florida State University, 1966.

Perry, Percival. "The Naval Stores Industry in the Antebellum South, 1789–1861." Ph.D. diss., Duke University, 1947.

Schene, Michael G. "A History of Volusia County, Florida." Ph.D. diss., Florida State University, 1976.

Urbach, Jon L. "An Appraisal of the Florida Secession Movement, 1859–1861." M.A. thesis, Florida State University, 1972.

Williams, Edwin L., Jr. "Florida in the Union, 1845–1861." Ph.D. diss., University of North Carolina, 1951.

Index

Titusville, 33

Tobacco: prewar cultivation in Florida, 2, 6–7, 16; exported through the blockade, 33; wartime demand for, 69, 70; speculation in, 70

Trapier, General James H., 33

Trent affair, 96

Tupelo, Mississippi, 94

Turks Islands, 19

Turpentine, 14, 31, 33, 36, 39, 141

Unionists: in Florida, 22, 88, 112, 117, 133, 137–38, 151

Union prisoners of war, 117, 119, 124, 132. *See also* Andersonville

United States Navy: blockade of Florida by, 30–31, 32, 35, 40, 69, 96–97, 156–58; raids on salt works by, 51, 52, 54, 56, 57, 58, 59, 60, 65; rivalry with Union army, 138, 141; raids on Florida coast by, 142–43, 144

United States Treasury Department, 145

United States War Department, 134, 145, 152

Valdosta, Georgia, 105

Vicksburg, Mississippi, 100, 131, 154

Virginia, 41, 71, 79, 86, 90, 95, 97, 100, 107, 113

Volusia County, 118

Waccahootee, 5

Waldo, 32, 78

Walton County, 88, 124, 128, 135, 138

Warrior River, 58

Washington County, 51

Westcott, Captain J. D., 101, 105

West Point (military academy), 90, 146

White, Major Pleasant W., 100, 101, 102, 103, 104, 106, 107, 108, 109, 110, 111, 112, 114–15, 116, 117, 118, 119, 121, 122, 123, 124–25, 126, 127, 128, 130, 131, 147, 148

White Circular, 147, 148, 150, 152, 159

Williams, J. W., 65

Wilmington, North Carolina, 35, 37, 40, 85

Woodbury, General Daniel P., 139

Woodhull, Commander Maxwell, 95

Wright, John S., 82

Yulee, David L.: and Florida Railroad rails, 43; sugar of impressed, 78–79; plantation of damaged by Union forces, 145

Yulee v. *Canova*, 78–79

About the Author

Robert A. Taylor is Instructor of History at Florida Atlantic University. He received his bachelor's and master's from the University of South Florida and his doctorate from Florida State University. He is co-editor (with Lewis N. Wynne) of *This War So Horrible: The Civil War Diary of Hiram Smith Williams* (1993).